# A+
# Certification
# Success Guide
# for Computer
# Technicians

## Sarah Parks

## Bob Kalman

**McGraw-Hill**
New York • San Francisco • Washington, D.C. • Auckland
Bogotá • Caracas • Lisbon • London • Madrid • Mexico City
Milan • Montreal • New Delhi • San Juan • Singapore
Sydney • Tokyo • Toronto

## McGraw-Hill

*A Division of The McGraw·Hill Companies*

1 2 3 4 5 6 7 8 9 0   DOC/DOC   9 0 3 2 1 0 9 8

ISBN 0-07-048618-2

*The sponsoring editor for this book was Scott Grillo, and the production
supervisor was Clare Stanley. It was set in Century Schoolbook by D & G
Limited, LLC.*

*Printed and bound by R. R. Donnelley & Sons Company.*

McGraw-Hill books are available at special quantity discounts to use as
premiums and sales promotions, or for use in corporate training programs.
For more information, please write to Director of Special Sales, McGraw-Hill,
11 West 19th Street, New York, NY 10011. Or contact your local bookstore.

 This book is printed on recycled, acid-free paper containing a minimum of 50%
recycled de-inked fiber.

# ACKNOWLEDGMENTS

Barb Beelen—Editing

Bob Kalman, Jr.—Photography

Jim Boris—Technical Editing

# CONTENTS

# Contents

Contents

# Contents

# INTRODUCTION

When we wrote the first edition of the *A+ Certification Success Guide for Computer Technicians*, we had no idea how much the exam would affect the computer industry. Since its inception in 1993, A+ Certification has become an industry standard. We are pleased that we have been able to help so many service technicians successfully study and pass the A+ exam.

CompUSA, a major microcomputer reseller, requires all of its service employees to be A+ certified within 90 days of employment. Packard Bell, a manufacturer, demands the same of its new service employees, and Microsoft Corporation hires no computer technicians who are not A+ certified. The A+ certification program is included in many high school, vocational school, and community college curricula. By ensuring that their students are A+ certified, many schools are helping them find jobs and be workforce prepared.

Support for the A+ program comes from all corners of the industry and is steadily growing. Original supporters in 1993 included, among others, Apple, Compaq, Hewlett-Packard, Toshiba, and Digital Equipment Corporation, along with the industry's major service organization, the Association for Field Service Management International. Many others have joined that group, including AST Research, Aerotek-Data Service Group, and Lotus Development.

The ranks of the A+ certified continue to grow since our first edition. In 1993, computer service professionals took 1,949 A+ exams. Since then, more than 50,000 have taken the exam, with projections of 75,000 by the end of 1998.

Why so much interest in the A+ program? As David Mauldin, MicroAge Training Manager says, "We want people to learn skills, not learn how to pass a test." The A+ test criteria require more than reading a book. The criteria are geared to a technician with approximately six months of hands-on experience. The credential is the first available to computer service technicians that allows them to prove they have the basic skills needed to succeed in their profession, and this pleases many employers. It documents competence on a range of fundamental service skills, such as configuring, installing, upgrading, diagnosing, and repairing computer equipment and peripherals. Further, the fundamental skills certified by A+ are valid and useful, regardless of the brand name on the machinery—they apply equally well to the products of any vendor.

As a result, computer service technicians find they are more valuable to their employers after becoming A+ certified, whether their employer is a vendor, reseller, or end-user organization. For many technicians, new avenues to employment, promotions, and improved earning open once they've earned the credential.

This book is an important resource for you, the computer service professional who is aiming for A+ certification. It will help you understand the process of becoming A+ certified, learn important technical knowledge that could be helpful in passing the A+ exams, and then use your new credential to greatest benefit in your career. We also explain why the computer industry uses certification. Why do you care? The industry is changing, becoming more competitive. Job roles are more sophisticated than they once were. Simply repairing computers is not enough. Employers expect a level of business savvy and customer satisfaction experience from their employees. We encourage you to read Chapters 2 and 3 as part of your career development.

Chapter 1 gives you all the information you need to get started. It explains the A+ certification program: what it is, why it was created, and the organization that sponsors it. Then it gives you the detailed, action-oriented information you need to get going: how to register, how to prepare, and hints on how to take your A+ exams.

Chapter 2 steps back to give you the bigger picture. It explains trends in certification, and toward A+ certification in particular, by examining the benefits of the A+ certification to every player in the IT industry. Once you know who benefits and why, you'll be in a better position to use your new certification with greater leverage in your career.

Chapter 3 examines the changing marketplace for IT skills, identifies the major employers of computer service technicians, and shows how A+ certification helps address the need for top-quality service.

Chapter 4 helps prepare you to take the A+ core exam. Its study materials are organized by the major technologies tested on the exam, including desktop and portable systems, basic networking concepts, printers, safety, and common preventive maintenance procedures. Also, the major duty areas of the technician that are covered on the core exam are discussed in Chapter 4, as they relate to these technologies. Chapter 4 concludes with sample exam questions that give you valuable exam practice and important feedback on your skill level.

Chapter 5 helps prepare you to take the Microsoft Windows/DOS exam (candidates for A+ certification must pass both the Core exam and this exam). This chapter is organized by the five major categories of skill tested on the Microsoft Windows/DOS exam. Subsections of the material correspond with each of the individual skills or abilities that the examiners have determined are needed for success in working with Microsoft

Windows or DOS technologies. The chapter concludes with sample test questions.

This book's appendices have been designed to be particularly useful as supplements to the book. Appendix A lists the A+ Cornerstone Funding Partners and Sponsors. Appendix B presents the job profile of a service technician, developed by the A+ sponsors. This important unit identifies the major skills and tasks needed for success in every area of activity undertaken by service technicians today. Some of the skills identified in this profile are not easily tested, and therefore do not appear on the A+ exams. The appendix presents the job task analysis and discusses the areas not tested on the current version of the A+ exam.

No other single resource offers so much information about the A+ program and its exams. For many, this resource will be the only one they need in order to pass the A+ exams and begin to enjoy the many benefits that go with A+ certification. Others, who need to go beyond this book for further reading and instruction, will find in this book significant help to identify their current strengths and weaknesses, and direction to the most useful supplementary resources. Either way, this book will help you to earn and use your A+ certification. And earning that certification may be one of the most important things you can do for your career.

We wish you every success.

# Becoming A+ Certified

This chapter gives you an overview of everything you need to know and do to become A+ certified. It explains what A+ certification is, who it's for, and the purposes it serves. It also gives you the information you need in order to register and pay for your exam, use the study materials in this book, and select other resources that can help you get ready. Finally, it prepares you to study effectively for the exam, take it, and know what to expect afterwards.

# What Is A+ Certification?

A+ certification is a way for microcomputer service technicians to prove their competence by earning a nationally recognized credential. A+ certification is awarded on the basis of successfully completing the A+ certification exams sponsored by the Computing Technology Industry Association. The program is backed by major vendors, distributors, re-sellers, and publications; as well as by a leading industry service organization, the Association for Field Service Management International (AFSMI).

The exams test the basic knowledge, technical skills, and customer-interaction skills needed by a successful computer service technician, as defined by over 45 organizations in the information technology industry. The exams cover a broad range of hardware and software technologies, but do not test knowledge of vendor-specific products.

There are no specific requirements for A+ candidates before they sit for the exams, which are geared to those with at least six months' experience. Although many candidates have several years of experience, others may need training programs in order to pass the A+ exams.

To become A+ certified, candidates must pass two tests: the Core exam and the Microsoft Windows/DOS Exam. When candidates pass the Core exam and the Microsoft Windows/DOS exam, they receive a certificate.

Those who were already A+ certified when the Specialty exams were introduced in April 1995, need not retake the tests to remain A+ certified.

## Who Sponsors the Exam?

The sponsor of the exam—the Computing Technology Industry Association (CompTIA), based in Lombard, Illinois—is a not-for-profit international trade association with over 6,000 members. CompTIA can be reached at:

450 East 22nd Street, Suite 230
Lombard, Illinois 60148-6158
(630) 268-1818

Fax (630) 268-1384

Web: www.comptia.org

Members of the Association, located in all 50 states and Canada, represent every major company that manufactures, distributes, publishes, or resells computer-related products and services. CompTIA's role as an industry-wide umbrella organization is to promote professional competence, sound business practices; and fair and honest treatment of customers, resellers, and vendors. CompTIA committees and task forces address issues affecting the entire computer industry.

One of the most important of CompTIA's several special interest groups —its service section—first developed the industry-wide, standard warranty reimbursement claim form. It went on to create the A+ certification program to certify technicians on a set of fundamental service and support skills. The A+ certification program is the first program to set industry-wide standards without a vendor-specific product focus.

CompTIA was named to the "Associations Advance America" Honor Roll by the American Society of Association Executives. Among the programs that CompTIA was honored for is the A+ certification program.

# Why the A+ Certification Program?

The A+ certification program began in April 1993, in a time of declining customer confidence in the distribution channels for information technology (IT) products and services. Research indicated that customers increasingly hesitated to seek out technical support because service providers were unable to consistently meet their expectations for quality service.

The actual cost of losing customers far exceeds the revenue gained from obtaining new customers. The cost of securing a new customer is at least five times that of keeping a current one; the cost to regain lost customers is approximately 25 times that of keeping current ones.

The entire industry bears the cost of losing customer confidence because the industry is built on customer acceptance and use of new technologies. If the industry cannot adequately service those technologies, industry growth suffers.

Customer confidence is critical to industry health, and that confidence is closely related to the skill of IT technicians, as a study conducted by CompTIA demonstrated. The original survey of over 500 end users indicated that the greatest factor influencing customer satisfaction is the technical skills of the reseller.

The A+ certification program seeks to restore customer confidence by certifying the base skill level of computer technicians, and thereby helping the channel to hold on to current customers and more easily secure new ones. In effect, a respected outside agency is verifying through exam results that a vendor or reseller has the technical skills to back up its marketing promises with action. A+ exam content also goes beyond technical skills into areas of customer interaction, ethics, industry understanding, and professionalism—areas that are crucial to building customer confidence.

The A+ certification helps customers, vendors, and resellers; but it also helps technicians by building confidence in their own skills. It gives them a chance to compare their skills with those of professional peers. Sometimes, without an exam, it can be difficult to gauge one's abilities. Bill Naj, Director of Education and Operations for AFSMI, says of the benefit to employers: "A+ provides a workforce better prepared for in-house training. They know what level an individual is at. It saves problems in hiring and sets a base for their training programs. A+ is a tool that is already passed."

The A+ exams not only point out one's weaknesses, but also give a sense of the range and depth of skills needed to be successful as a computer service technician. The A+ exam content areas, and the related Job Task Analysis for Service Technicians, give an overview of needed skills. With such an overview, one can more easily assess what skills one has; and what skills one needs to develop through education, training, or experience.

The A+ exam content areas are explained in Chapters 4 and 5; the Job Task Analysis for Service Technicians is presented in Appendix F.

A+ certification meets three fundamental goals of CompTIA for improving the professionalism of the IT industry to

- Ensure industry-wide, nationally recognized, basic competency levels in the computer service field
- Provide support and baseline expectations in recruiting, hiring, training, and promoting of employees
- Help the industry fill through identifying individuals with skills needed in the IT industry
- Ensure that job seekers have identifiable career paths, transferable skills, and credentials that are industry-recognized
- Establish education standards that prepare individuals to meet the needed IT job skills

For further discussion about the value of A+ certification to all players in the IT industry, see Chapter 2.

# How the A+ Program Was Developed

To answer the need for industry-wide service technician certification, CompTIA's Service & Support Section invited support from a broad base of participants. Those participants included manufacturers, distributors, resellers, third-party maintenance companies, value-added resellers, industry associations, and others. Industry supporters contributed knowledge to help develop the exam, financial resources to fund the program, and commitments to promote the program in the marketplace.

Cornerstone Funding Partners—the main participants to develop and administer the program—were required to commit a minimum investment of time, expertise, and financial resources. Other companies acted as sponsors, having a lesser commitment than the Cornerstone Funding Partners, and endorsed the program. Both Cornerstone Funding Partners and sponsors contributed their expertise to help define the baseline skills and standards to be tested by the A+ exam. A list of Cornerstone Funding Partners and current sponsors is given in Appendix A.

CompTIA asked both Cornerstone Funding Partners and sponsors for written commitments to help promote A+ certification among their employees and channel partners. In response, Digital Equipment Corporation now requires all employees who service microcomputers and related hardware, as well as all computer service technicians who work for authorized service providers, to become A+ certified.

COMPAQ Computer vigorously promotes A+ certification to its own workforce. Today, the great majority of its phone-support and case-management personnel, along with technical trainers and selected system engineers, are A+ certified. The company also requires A+ certification of its service-authorized partners.

IBM uses A+ as a prerequisite for certain hardware requirements for service providers. IBM, Digital Equipment Corporation, and many others accept the A+ certification as a way for service providers to "test-out" of some or all requirements for basic training on their products. Beyond the original Cornerstone Funding Partners and sponsors, many other companies have established an A+ requirement, often in response to the demand of the marketplace.

In addition, hundreds of resellers have taken advantage of the opportunity to be designated as A+ Authorized Service Centers by having 50% or more of their staff earn the credential. (For more information on A+ Authorized Service Centers, see Appendix B.)

The A+ Advisory Team, made up of senior managers from the Cornerstone Funding Partners, determines the program's overall direction. They establish the specific requirements of the certification program and examination. The A+ Advisory Team also includes technology-oriented subject matter experts who have experience as service technicians or as service trainers.

In creating the A+ certification exam, test developers make every effort to adhere to the Standards for Educational and Psychological Tests established by the American Psychological Association, the American Educational Research Association, and the National Council on Measurement in Education. The creation of test requirements and the writing of test items follow a series of steps to ensure that the exam measures the right skills in the right way.

Originally, a great variety of jobs held by IT service technicians were examined, and the skills actually used in those jobs were defined. Then the skills were weighted to determine how much of the exam should be devoted to each. Test questions were written to measure those skills, and sample tryouts were made of the questions. Finally the exam's pass/fail standards, or the "cut score," was established.

The development of the A+ certification exam is ongoing. Most recently, CompTIA members completed a comprehensive job-task analysis to assess the skills and tasks required of technicians. This analysis included a survey, sent to 5,000 A+ certification holders, which asked them what was important to doing their job successfully. There were 1,300 surveys received, which resulted in a complete test rewrite for the two A+ exams.

The new test was effective July 31, 1998. Prior to July 1998, test candidates had to successfully pass both the Core exam and one of two test modules. Those two modules were the A+ Certification Exam, with a specialty in Microsoft Windows/DOS Environments; and the A+ Certification Exam, with a specialty in Macintosh OS-based Computers. There is no longer a Macintosh specialty module, based on a joint decision between Apple Computer, Inc. and CompTIA.

New exam questions are continually being written, and old ones are removed. The exam is continually re-evaluated for its effectiveness in measuring who has the desired skills and who doesn't. At the same time, the skills that the exam measures are reviewed for appropriateness. The work of computer service technicians is constantly changing, and the A+ certification exam changes to keep pace.

The popularity of the program has exceeded expectations. The A+ certification program was originally projected to certify 5,000 technicians by June 1, 1994. By July 1994, however, there were more than 6,785 A+ certified technicians. By May 1998, over 50,000 computer service technicians became A+ certified. CompTIA projects 75,0000 tests will be completed by December 1998. This has ensured that the A+ certification program is one the most successful programs in the information technology industry.

# International Test Availability

The test is now available in Europe, South America, and Asia. International testing is handled by AFSMI. With 52 chapters in 49 countries, AFSMI represents international companies and strongly supports A+ Certification. AFSMI started international testing in January 1997, and almost 1,000 international (excluding Canada and America) technicians took the A+ exam in 1997. The rate increased in the first quarter of 1998, with almost 750 exams taken in that quarter. Bill Naj, Director of Education and Operations for AFSMI, says, "A+ Certification has become a standard and will be a worldwide standard. It will benefit technicians, stay with them, and give them distinction." The A+ Examination is available in six languages. More information regarding AFSMI is in Chapter 2.

# Test Content and Format

The content of the A+ exams has been selected to represent the kinds of activities typically undertaken by an IT service technician. The A+ exam was designed to represent demonstrable knowledge that technicians with approximately 6 months of experience should have. The CompTIA service members agreed they wanted a test that represented skills and knowledge, not just book learning. The skills and knowledge are to properly install, configure, troubleshoot, and repair. The test is divided into two sections: Core and Microsoft Windows/DOS. Examinees are required to pass both tests to be A+ certified.

## Core Exam

The Core exam content covers procedures and information about technologies that are not related to vendor-specific products. The specific skills tested for each category of activity on the Core exam are explained in

Chapter 4. Within the eight areas of responsibility, the Core exam also tests knowledge of the following technologies, again without reference to vendor-specific products, except in the area of basic operating systems:

- Desktop and portable systems
- Basic networking concepts
- Printers
- Safety
- Common preventive maintenance procedures

Each of the following eight sections corresponds with one of the major areas of job responsibility for technicians. These sections are:

| Section | % of Examination |
|---|---|
| Installation, Configuration, and Upgrading | 30% |
| Diagnosing and Troubleshooting | 20% |
| Safety and Preventive Maintenance | 10% |
| Motherboard/Processors/Memory | 10% |
| Printers | 10% |
| Portable Systems | 5% |
| Basic Networking | 5% |
| Customer Satisfaction 1 | 10% |
| Total | 100% |

**NOTE:**  *The Customer Satisfaction domain is scored, but does not impact your final pass/fail score on the A+ Core exam. However, it is noted on the examinee's score report.*

## Microsoft Windows/DOS Exam:

The Microsoft Windows/DOS exam represents demonstrable knowledge in basic DOS, Windows 3.x, and Windows 95. The five sections representing the major job responsibilities in this exam are:

- ▓ Installing
- ▓ Configuring
- ▓ Upgrading
- ▓ Diagnosing/Troubleshooting
- ▓ Repairing

The Microsoft Windows/DOS exam focuses on service tasks related to the Microsoft Windows/DOS operating system environment. The Microsoft Windows/DOS exam is divided into five sections, with groups of related questions. Each section corresponds to one of the major areas of job responsibility for technicians. These sections are:

| Section | % of Examination |
|---|---|
| Function, Structure, Operation, and File Management | 30% |
| Memory Management | 10% |
| Installation, Configuration, and Upgrading | 30% |
| Diagnosing and Troubleshooting | 20% |
| Networks | 10% |
| Total | 100% |

For the latest information about the A+ exams, contact the official exam registrar, Sylvan Prometric, at 1-800-77-MICRO (1-800-776-4276), or check the CompTIA Web site.

The specific skills tested for each category on the Microsoft Windows/DOS exam are explained in Chapter 5.

The exams are administered via computer at a Sylvan Prometric-authorized testing center in an easy-to-use format. (The testing centers and their use of computers are explained further in separate sections that follow.)

The format of the tests on the computer looks very much like other multiple-choice exams you have taken before. The difference is that you take this exam on a desktop computer connected to a testing network, where all the data is stored centrally and securely.

Directions for using the testing software are displayed on the screen. A tutorial is provided, and a proctor also assists with questions. On-screen "help" is also available, including information at the bottom of the screen that lets you know how to enter your answer, move forward in the test, or mark a question for answering later.

The A+ Core exam includes 69 questions, all multiple choice. The exact set of questions on both exams is different for every person who is tested. Candidates have 1 hour to complete the Core exam. The pass rate for the Core exam is 65%.

The Microsoft Windows/DOS exam also includes 70 questions, all multiple choice. Candidates have 1 hour and 15 minutes to complete this exam. The exam length and number of questions may change over time. Contact Sylvan Prometric for the most up-to-date information about the exam structure. The pass rate for the Windows/DOS exam is 66%.

Although all questions on both exams are multiple choice, some questions have only one correct answer and others have more than one correct answer. Each question has either a circle or a square next to it. Those questions with circles have only one correct answer; those with squares have more than one correct answer. Also, when there are multiple correct answers, a message at the bottom of the screen tells you to "choose all that apply." When questions have more than one correct answer, you must select all correct answers in order to have that question be scored "correct."

Questions on the A+ exams take one of three formats:

- Situational
- Traditional
- Identification

Situational questions describe a situation or scenario commonly encountered by service technicians while on the job. Your choice of answers will list different ways to resolve the problem or situation.

---

**EXAMPLE:** *When you power up the system, the attached display remains blank. You're not sure whether it is a system unit or a display problem, but you can quickly decide which it is by*

**a.** Turning the contrast control all the way up to the test position.

**b.** Installing a wrap connector onto the end of the display cable.

**c.** Unplugging the signal cable from the system unit, then powering the display.

**d.** Running the video tests on the diagnostic diskette.

*The correct answer is "c."*

Traditional multiple-choice questions appear most commonly on the test. These questions ask you to pick the correct answer to a short question from a list of choices.

---

**EXAMPLE:** *What component determines the type of monitor to be used?*

**a.** Parallel controller.

**b.** Memory board.

**c.** Serial controller.

**d.** Video controller.

*The correct answer is "d."*

Identification questions may include a diagram, flowchart, or illustration; with several items called out with arrows, numbers or letters. You are asked to choose the answer that correctly identifies what is being shown or described in the question.

---

**EXAMPLE:** *The item pointed out is a _____?*

**a.** Battery

**b.** Central processing unit

**c.** Floppy disk drive

**d.** Mass storage

*The correct answer is "a."*

Practice exam questions for each of the A+ exams is provided at the end of Chapters 4 and 5.

# Tips for Test-taking

Here are six points to remember when taking multiple-choice tests such as A+:

▪ Answer all questions. An unanswered question is scored as an incorrect answer.

■ Guess if you have to. There is no penalty for guessing.

■ Answer the easy questions first. The testing software lets you move forward and backward through the exam. Go through all the questions on the test once, first answering those you are sure of; and then go back and spend time on the harder questions.

■ Don't try to "psych-out" the questions. There are no trick questions. The correct answer will always be among the list of choices.

■ Eliminate the most obvious incorrect answers first. This will make it easier for you to select the answer that seems most right to you.

■ And finally, remember that if you don't pass this time, you can take the exam again for an additional fee.

# Who May Take the Tests?

A+ certification is open to anyone who would like to take the tests. There are no requirements for taking them, other than payment of the test fees. Candidates may retake the test modules as often as they like. To receive the certification, the candidate must pass the Core and Microsoft Windows/DOS exams within 90 days of each other.

If candidates fail to pass both exams within 90 days, they will not be granted certification. Instead, they have to retake the Core exam—even if they had already passed it—as well as the other exam. Both exams may be taken as many times as needed until certification requirements are met. (The only restriction is that the same exam cannot be retaken on the same day.)

Candidates may take the Core and Microsoft Windows/DOS exam in any sequence; however, it is recommended that they take the Core before the second exam. The candidate may take both exams during the same appointment. The test developers, in fact, recommend this, although it is not required.

# How to Pay and Register

The fee for taking the A+ certification tests depends on whether or not the candidate is employed by an organization that is a member of CompTIA. Additionally, taking one or two exam modules in one seating saves money. The current pricing schedule is:

| Exam | For those employed by CompTIA member organizations | For non-members |
|---|---|---|
| Any module alone | $85 | $120 |
| Core + 1 module | $140 | $215 |

Payment for the exam can be made by Visa, Master Card, American Express, or by check. To pay, contact Sylvan Prometric at 1-800-77-MICRO (1-800-776-4276) to talk to a Sylvan Registrar. Remember, both modules must be taken within 90 calendar days or else all fees will be forfeited, even if you've already passed one module.

Have the following information handy when you call:

■ Social Security number (or Sylvan Prometric ID number)

■ Complete mailing address and phone number

■ Employer or organization

■ Date you want to take the test

■ Method of payment

**NOTE:**  *A Social Security number is not required. If a candidate objects to providing a Social Security number for privacy reasons, Sylvan supplies a unique Sylvan ID number instead.*

Often, the candidate's employer will have paid for the exam in advance by purchasing vouchers from Sylvan. In that case, the candidate needs only to supply Sylvan with the voucher number to complete payment.

Once guaranteed payment is made, the test can be scheduled. Those paying with a credit card or voucher can schedule immediately; those paying by check can call back to schedule three days after mailing the check. Note that cancellations are refundable if made by 7:00 p.m. Central Time on the day before the exam.

The Sylvan registrar helps candidates to schedule their tests at the most convenient testing center and time. Sylvan operates approximately 900 testing centers worldwide, and candidates have access to any of them they choose. Many of the testing centers are open during and after normal business hours and on weekends. Those taking their exam more than four days after they register will receive a confirmation of their test location and time in the mail.

When you first contact Sylvan registration, an electronic file of information will be built with your name, address, phone, fax number, and Social Security number. This eliminates the need to gather redundant data with every registration. Over time, the complete record of your testing history will be kept for you as well.

Sylvan Prometric offers discounts if you register a group of 50 or more people.

Once the registrar has you on file, you need only tell them the exam you are registering for.

# Options for Test Preparation

Chapters 4 and 5 of this book present useful information about all of the skills and all of the technologies tested on the two A+ exams. Of course, the range of material covered by the A+ exams is vast, and no one book can capture all of the knowledge that could be tested. For many, this book will be enough to give them the knowledge, familiarity with the test, and confidence they need to pass the A+ exams. Others may need to supplement their study with other reference books, self-study materials, or courses.

If, after using the study materials presented in this book and taking the sample test questions, you feel the need for further study, you might begin with the resources listed in Appendix C. These books and films are recommended by leading consultants, trainers, and IT organizations to those preparing for the A+ exam.

For those wanting more formal training for the A+ exams, several classroom courses are available. A variety of computer-based courses and other self-study materials are available also. A list of CompTIA-approved resources is listed in Appendix D.

# How to Study

The amount of study needed to pass the A+ certification exams varies greatly from one candidate to another, depending primarily on the amount of time one has spent as a practicing computer service technician.

Those with several years of experience may need only a quick review of the materials in this book before passing the A+ exams on the first try. Very experienced technicians, in fact, may want to try the sample questions before even reading Chapters 4 and 5, and then read only the materials on the subject areas they had trouble with on the sample questions. Those new to the field may need to carefully study this entire book, and then turn to supplementary resources.

Most of those preparing for the test will need to spend many hours identifying weaknesses in understanding and skill, and then gaining new knowledge in those areas. For those undertaking such study, we offer the following suggestions:

Honor the way your mind works. Study when you're well-rested and free from distractions, and don't try to study more than 1-1/2 to 2 hours at a time. Too much study at any one sitting is fatiguing, frustrating, and counterproductive. Try to study at the same time each day; regular study time trains the mind to be ready to learn new material.

Make the environment right for learning. Ideally, you'll want to study in an area dedicated especially for it: a private, quiet study or home office. If you can't have that environment at home, try using your company office after normal business hours. If that fails, try the library. In any case, study in an environment where you'll be least likely to feel pulled to do chores, or respond to the needs of family members or coworkers. Choose a comfortable, efficient environment that will make your study time really focused and productive.

Set goals for each study session. Review the kinds of progress you make from one study session to the next; and set ambitious yet realistic goals for each session, based on your past track record. Set goals to inspire yourself, but don't strain to achieve them. Know where you would like to be in the material by the end of the session, but allow yourself the time you realistically need to absorb the information.

Use a variety of study techniques. Talking, listening, writing, reading, and working on the computer use different areas of the brain. Using each of these methods will reinforce your learning and make it stick. Some ways to employ a variety of study techniques: discuss the materials you're studying with your coworkers; have someone quiz you; recite out loud the facts you're trying to memorize; and use your computer as a study tool to illustrate or further investigate topics raised in the materials.

# Taking the Test

After you register, the only thing you must do is show up to take the test. Bring two forms of identification—both with signatures, and one with a photo. For example, you might bring a valid driver's license or passport as a photo ID, and a major credit card as a secondary ID.

Books, calculators, laptop computers, or other reference materials are not allowed during any A+ test. Because the tests are computer-based, you will not need pens, pencils, or paper.

Arrive early at the testing center to have plenty of time to settle down and make yourself comfortable.

To allow candidates to get familiar with the various question types and how to answer them, an on-line tutorial is available to use before the test. All testing appointments include an extra 15 minutes to sign-in and use the tutorial.

The tutorial is connected to the test to be taken and teaches specifically how to answer the kinds of questions that will appear in that test. The A+ exams offer question types that include multiple-choice, single-answer and multiple-choice, multiple-answer. On-line graphics and exhibits also sometimes appear within questions. Your tutorial explains and gives examples of these question types.

The center administrator is also available to help with the tutorial and ensure that candidates understand how to answer questions. In addition, on-line help is always available during the exam.

Sylvan delivers tests by using a sophisticated, yet easy-to-use Windows-based computerized testing system. Directions for using the testing software are displayed on the screen.

Figure 1-1 shows a typical format for questions.

In addition to on-line help, these features have been built into the testing system for ease of use:

- Answers can be selected with keyboard or mouse.

- Candidates can mark questions for later review.

- The software keeps a record of questions that are not fully answered and prompts the candidate to review them.

- Candidates can review any question before the test is complete.

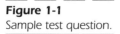

**Figure 1-1**
Sample test question.

| Item 3 of 14 |
|---|
| ☐ Mark                    Current Time: 10:50:27 AM |

What is the official language of Ivory Coast?

- ○ a. Akan
- ◉ b. French
- ○ c. Kiswahili
- ○ d. Kikuyu

**Select the best answer.**

| Next | Previous | Help |

■ An on-screen clock reminds candidate of time remaining.

■ Every answer is immediately and automatically backed up by the system, in case power is lost or the system is interrupted.

The test may be completed without answering all questions; however, any unanswered question will be scored as incorrect. If you finish the exam before the time limit, you may leave. If time runs out, the exam automatically ends.

## After the Test

As soon as you complete the test, your exam results are shown to you on-screen. In addition, a hard copy of the score report is printed for you at the test center and embossed to indicate that it is an official score report.

The score report has two pages. The first page is the Testing Fee Reimbursement Form, which you can use if your employer is reimbursing you for your test fee. The second page is the report showing the score needed to pass your exam and your score. You will also see the percentage of questions that you answered correctly in each section, but you will not see the specific questions that you missed.

No other printed report of exam results is made; CompTIA receives results electronically from Sylvan. No one else will see the report except the testing center Administrator.

The score report will look like what's shown in Figures 1-2 and 1-3.

After you pass the Core exam and one Microsoft Windows/DOS exam, an A+ certificate will be mailed to you within two to three weeks. You will also receive a credit card-sized credential that shows you are A+ certified.

You will also be able to add the A+ logo to your business cards, although guidelines apply to the logo's size and location. And your employer will

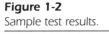

**Figure 1-2**
Sample test results.

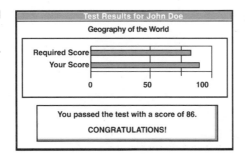

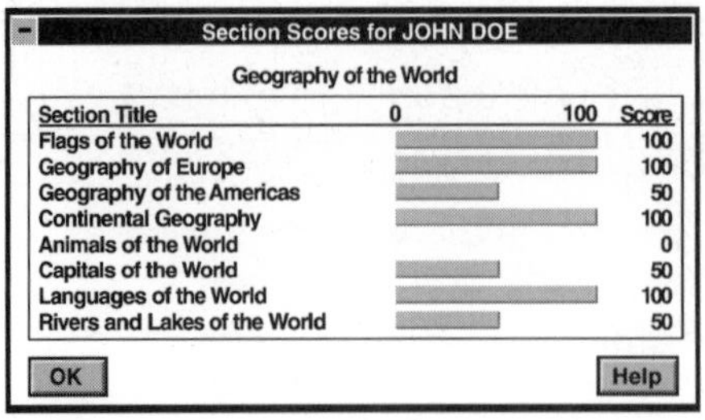

**Figure 1-3**
Sample test results by sections.

```
┌──────────────────────────────────────────────┐
│ ▬      Section Scores for JOHN DOE            │
│            Geography of the World             │
│ ┌──────────────────────────────────────────┐ │
│ │ Section Title          0        100  Score│ │
│ │ Flags of the World     ▓▓▓▓▓▓▓▓▓▓▓  100   │ │
│ │ Geography of Europe    ▓▓▓▓▓▓▓▓▓▓▓  100   │ │
│ │ Geography of the Americas ▓▓▓▓▓      50   │ │
│ │ Continental Geography  ▓▓▓▓▓▓▓▓▓▓▓  100   │ │
│ │ Animals of the World                  0   │ │
│ │ Capitals of the World  ▓▓▓▓▓         50   │ │
│ │ Languages of the World ▓▓▓▓▓▓▓▓▓▓▓  100   │ │
│ │ Rivers and Lakes of the World ▓▓▓▓▓  50   │ │
│ └──────────────────────────────────────────┘ │
│ ┌────┐                           ┌──────┐     │
│ │ OK │                           │ Help │     │
│ └────┘                           └──────┘     │
└──────────────────────────────────────────────┘
```

receive additional details about using the A+ certification name and logo as a marketing feature. The rules for doing so are presented in Appendix E.

If you do not pass the exam, you can register to take the exam again. But remember that the two exams must be taken within 90 days of each other. If you wait more than 90 days you must take both tests.

Once you earn your A+ certification, your status in the IT skills marketplace increases. A+ carries important proof of skills to you, the certificate holder; and to your customers, employer, and potential future employers. Understanding the value of your certification will help you use it to the greatest advantage in your career. Chapter 2 explains why, as a certified professional, you are of distinctly greater value to employers and to the IT industry as a whole.

CHAPTER 2

# The Value of Your Certification

Certification benefits everyone in the information technology industry. Understanding its worth to those who employ IT technicians will help you use your certification to its greatest advantage wherever you work. This chapter looks at the benefits of certification in and then looks at the particular benefits of A+ certification from the perspectives of the technician, the vendor, the reseller, end-user organizations, and key industry associations. This chapter emphasizes the value of the A+ certification program to you.

# Certification from the IT Professional Perspective

Certification programs validate your knowledge or skill. They show the marketplace that you have the skill and knowledge to perform a particular job. Typically, service technicians and their employers choose a certification "path" after completing their A+ certification. This path may be to become a Certified Novell Engineer, a Microsoft Support Engineer, or an other networking or O/S specialist. Passing the A+ certification is the first step in enhancing your resume and showing your commitment to the IT field. Some companies require A+ certification as a prerequisite for other training courses. MicroAge feels strongly that the successful service technician must have the base level A+ certification before moving along one of the following specialty tracks:Novell, Microsoft, or SCO/Unix.

The IT industry has been among the most enthusiastic in embracing certification. This fast-growing, constantly changing industry needs the basic guidelines and standards that certification provides. Increasingly, the value of certification is recognized by IT employers, and the credential can be a passport to better jobs or promotions with your current employer. Certified IT professionals are also often rewarded with higher salaries.

But employers aren't the only ones who believe in the value of certification. As customers increasingly recognize the value of certified IT professionals, they prefer those professionals to uncertified competitors. After all, in a world of rapidly changing technology, certification may be among the best reasons to believe that a computer professional really can get the job done.

And certification provides a variety of benefits to professionals, beyond just landing a job or bringing in new business. For example, the certification process seems to provide professionals with enhanced self-esteem. Some believe that the sense of accomplishment is the greatest reward of attaining a certification. Objective testing and measurement also build confidence by giving a powerful feedback on skills. Those who have been certified have a greater appreciation for their own skills and how those skills make them a valuable part of the information technology industry.

Certification is often said to give IT professionals more confidence in the interviewing process and more weight in the review process. When cutback or reorganization time comes around, some also find that certification is the lifejacket keeping them afloat.

Driven, in part, by the interest of IT professionals in certification, the number of certification-testing programs has grown rapidly in the information technology industry within the past six years. Today, all leading industry vendors and their customers use certification results to help manage their businesses. Vendors and many industry associations offer a wide range of exams that test fundamental technical skills as well as product-specific knowledge. The exams test skills in networking technologies, operating systems, client/server, databases, developmental tools, and many applications. The IT certifications in the marketplace represent eleven professions common to the industry, including network administrator, network engineer, service technician, instructor, sales representative, office worker, applications specialist, applications developer, systems administrator, systems operator, and systems engineer.

The growth figures of Sylvan Prometric, the largest provider of certification examinations for the information technology industry, show well the rapid growth of interest in certification. Figure 2-1 illustrates the growing number of programs administered by IT Suppliers since 1993. In 1989, there were fewer than five tests; now there are 76 certification programs, most administered by manufacturers.

Figure 2-2 shows the number of certification tests administered since 1993.

**Figure 2-1**
Programs administered by IT Suppliers.

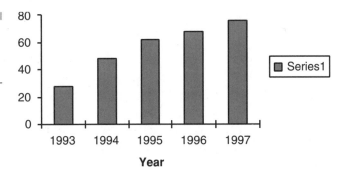

**Figure 2-2**
Certification tests administered.

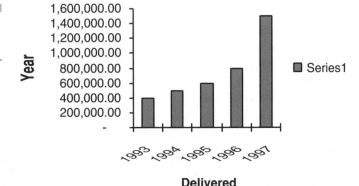

# Certification from the Perspective of Industry Associations

Several organizations address the issues of accountability and professionalism. These organizations are bringing together vendors, resellers, and end users to pool their knowledge and collectively develop standards, courses, and—in some cases—certification programs that advance the interests of the profession as a whole. Although vendor-driven certification has led the way over the past five years, industry-driven certification, represented by these programs, is playing an increasingly important role in the certification of IT professionals. We encourage you to review vendor-specific programs. A Web search will help you find programs for Microsoft, Apple Computer, and others. Following are two key industry specific programs.

## The Certified Network Expert Certification Program

Network General Corporation and Hewlett-Packard Company joined with other companies in the network protocols analyzer marketplace to address the needs of managers in dealing with the broad spectrum of networking technologies.

In 1993, the group announced a certification program called Certified Network Expert (CNX). The CNX program identifies individuals who are experienced and knowledgeable in managing, designing, troubleshooting, and maintaining sophisticated multi-vendor networks. Certification is available in four technology areas: Ethernet, Token Ring, FDDI data link topologies, and LAN cabling. The program does not test for product-specific expertise. Individuals must understand organization and interpretation of elements in a layered, interprocess communications system. To become a CNX, you must pass a Core test plus two specialty exams. CNX testing is available worldwide. The Ethernet and Token Ring exams are also available in German and Japanese.

Sponsoring vendors currently include Azure Technologies, Bay Networks, Cisco Systems, Hewlett-Packard, Microtest, Network Associates, Optimized Engineering, Pine Mountain Group, The AG Group, TOYO Corporation, and Wandel & Golterman. The CNX is affiliated with the Novell and Network Professional Association testing programs. The test is administered by Sylvan Prometric.

For more information about the program, call 1-800-CNX-EXAM or 1-612-820-5000 in North America. Their Web site is www.cnx.org.

## The Institute for Certification of Computer Professionals

Founded in 1973, the ICCP was the original organization to certify computing knowledge and skills. Together with over 20 constituent and affiliate societies, the ICCP represents more than 250,000 IT practitioners; nearly 50,000 have been awarded the certification.

To earn the Certified Computing Professional (CCP) designation today, an applicant needs to satisfy professional experience requirements and pass an exam. Four years of professional computing experience are normally required before sitting for the exam, although educational achievements can account for two of the four years.

The ICCP Core exam consists of sections on human and organization framework, systems concepts, data and information, system development, technology, and associated disciplines. Candidates also must pass two additional exams chosen from seventeen specialty areas. The ICCP believes that its exams go beyond vendor-specific tests because they assess technical, management, and interpersonal skills.

In addition to the professional designation of CCP, the Institute also offers an Associate Computing Professional designation, or ACP. To earn the ACP, candidates need to pass a Core examination and one computing language exam.

ICCP also believes in the value of keeping skills up-to-date, and requires certificate holders to re-certify by completing a minimum of 120 hours of continuing education requirements every three years. The Institute offers self-assessment exams to help certificate holders identify developmental needs and design continuing education plans. (Proficiency certificates can also be earned in any of the specialty or language exams offered.) Re-certification can be earned through university courses, vendor courses, authorship, self-study, and other means.

The ICCP is also interested in ensuring the ethical practices of IT professionals, so it requires its certificate holders to commit themselves to the ICCP Code of Ethics and Standard of Conduct. Along with product vendors, the ICCP believes that IT industry self-regulation is preferable to state-enforced licensing. Its programs strive to protect both the public interest and the interest of IT professionals in a way that makes licensing unnecessary.

The ICCP can be reached at 847-299-4227 or 800-U GET CCP. Their Web site is www.iccp.org.

# The Value of A+ Certification

## A+ from the Perspective of Industry Supporters

Support for the A+ program comes from all corners of the industry and is growing steadily. Original Cornerstone Funding Partners included industry giants like Apple, Compaq, Hewlett-Packard, Toshiba, and Packard Bell, among others; along with the industry's major service organization, the Association for Field Service Management International. That group has been joined by 27 other financial contributors since January 1994. (See Appendix A for a complete list of program sponsors.)

Because sponsoring companies found that the program would give them an important competitive advantage, they contributed not only knowledge and cash, but also jump-started the program by requiring their own employees to be A+ certified. For example, as of October 1995, Digital Equipment Corporation had 2,022 A+ certified technicians, Bull Information Systems employed 692, Entex had 592, Ingram Micro had 550, Packard Bell had 967, and Technology Service Solutions had 1,169. This year, CompUSA has approximately 900 A+ certified technicians. Several other companies count hundreds of A+ certified technicians on their payrolls.

Packard Bell makes A+ certification a condition of employment for all new service employees, giving them 90 days to become certified after employment. MicroAge gives new employees six months to become certified after employment.

Ernie Raymond, President of the Permond Solutions Group, Inc., says that for them, "the key selling point for A+ certification is that the first sponsors should have a tremendous edge. They can challenge their competitors on the breadth and depth of their capability to service customers effectively."

Permond considers itself an important A+ supporter. The company was working on its own plan for cross-platform training in a joint venture with vendors when it became aware of CompTIA's plans for A+. Permond joined its program with A+ and began designing its training programs to meet A+ certification requirements.

Many organizations employing A+ certified technicians are also taking advantage of the program designation: the A+ Authorized Service Center (AASC), by ensuring that at least half their service professionals are certified. Of the 80 MicroAge service centers, 64 are A+ Authorized. The program is changing, so check the CompTIA Web site. As of May 1998, more than 1,000 service centers were A+ Authorized Service Centers.

## A+ from the Perspective of the Technician

While A+ growth has been promoted by the IT industry's leading companies, it owes just as much to the enthusiasm of individual technicians. There are many reasons for their enthusiasm.

Don Hurd, a senior field engineer for VanStar, says that A+ material gives "a broad view of what's out there." For Hurd, much of the Macintosh OS-based material was new. Learning it gave him a broader background, which he has found useful in his work. The exam, he believes, really covers the bases of the knowledge needed to be successful as a technician today. "If you pass it," he says, "you're thoroughly prepared."

Kenneth Conn, a service technician for Data Source/Connecting Point, says the preparation is especially important for new technicians. " A+ is a base starting point. Preparing for it helps new technicians cement the basics in their minds and helps them feel confident to go out to the customer's site."

Greg Dodge, a senior system engineer for Dataflex, believes that technicians today need to have some knowledge of many things, as well as in-depth knowledge of a few. Like Don Hurd, he believes the A+ exam helps technicians learn a great range of general knowledge, including skills in troubleshooting and customer interaction. He says, "With A+, you don't just get people who know a few things and can talk the rest of it. People who've passed the A+ exam have a broad range of knowledge and skill."

Dodge believes that A+ is becoming a kind of requirement to do the job of the technician, or "a ticket to show up for the game." When Dodge goes for hardware training these days, he often encounters one question from the vendor: "Are you A+ certified?" The training requirements, he finds, are often fewer for him as an A+ technician.

Dodge has seen the program's growth in influence first-hand. As one of the early A+ test-takers, Dodge says he intended to give his career a boost by adding a credential to his business card. Within months, though, he found that the area competitors were all doing the same. A+ certification was getting attention from area resellers, and soon also from customers who came asking for certified technicians. Today, Dodge's employer, Dataflex, requires their technicians to be A+ certified within 90 days of hire, and one of the chief competitors in their geographic area does also. Dodge believes that A+ is becoming to computer technicians what the CPA is to accountants.

Like accountants facing the CPA exam, technicians often find the A+ exam challenging. For example, Mark Romanowski of U.S. Computer Group is surprised that many people who consider themselves experts are really challenged by A+. Romanowksi praises the real-world quality of the test, especially its testing of customer-interaction skills which, he says, "are 70-80% of what technicians do."

David Duanne, a senior engineer for VanStar, agrees. He says the A+ exam is a competency exam, not just a test of book learning or theoretical knowledge. He believes it's difficult to do well on the exam without some field experience to your credit.

Kenneth Conn of Data Source/Connecting Point says, " A+ is not just a paper certification; it reflects a working knowledge of computers. Other certifications are more theoretical, but A+ is a real-world test of skill. You need some experience on the job to pass it."

On the other hand, those technicians who do pass the exam coming right out of school often find that the certification is viewed by some employers as a substitute for experience. Mike Beach, an operations manager at Datasource/Connecting Point, says, "People with strong skills, as shown by exams like the A+ exam, and who have a very healthy work ethic are in demand, even if they don't yet have job experience."

Because of the effectiveness of A+ in measuring the skills needed in the market, having the certification is a great advantage when job-hunting. Peter Sizemore, a systems engineer for Micro Star Co., Inc., says, "During most of the interviews I had—and I had quite a number—they offered me a job because of my A+ certification. A+ is increasingly becoming a necessity."

Ben Eckart, an instructor at the Manhattan-area technical center in Kansas, says that A+ certification has opened new doors for his students, even after they have landed a job. For example, one of his students applied to a company that had no interest in the A+ certification program. They hired him, but for other reasons. Within a few months, however, the company was so sold on the A+ program that they stopped providing training to any of their employees who weren't A+ certified.

Eckart has always encouraged his students to pursue A+ certification, even before they find work. He says his students were not all convinced of the value of A+ certification, but they are finding with A+ that they are getting better jobs and advancing more quickly. Eckart says, "Whether you personally believe in the value of certification or not, you'll find that you need to be certified today to get ahead."

Because of the recognition given the credential, being A+ certified often increases a technician's level of self-assurance. Kenneth Conn says, "Anyone in any line of work needs to feel value, needs to understand how they fit into the group that is their peers. A+ gives you that sense of value. When you have it, you feel more confident of your abilities." John Hlavac of Packard-Bell says, "By being A+ certified, there is an extra level of job satisfaction and personal satisfaction; of confidence in abilities and skills—and recognition for it."

Bill York, a past co-chair of the A+ Advisory Committee, says that the A+ program "is a step higher than certification on particular products because it is recognized throughout the industry." York reports that his own technicians at SolutioNetics embrace the program enthusiastically. "All of my technicians are standing in line," he says, "so they can prove their value to me and to their peers and clients."

## A+ from the Vendor Perspective

Among the chief benefits of A+ certification for vendors is that it provides a way to ensure quality of their product resellers. Gary Turner, Director of North American Service Operations at Exide Electronics in Raleigh, NC, says that A+ certification is part of a strategic decision Exide made to become partners with its value-added resellers rather than just with suppliers. "With A+ certification, we can help them grow their business, which of course strengthens the channel by taking our products to our customers."

At the same time, A+ helps vendors to reduce training costs. Many hardware vendors are saving time and money by relying on A+ certification training to cover "the basics." The vendor no longer has to teach the fundamentals of laser printers or color displays when their classes consist of A+ certified technicians. This allows vendors to spend training time on the features that differentiate their products.

Some hardware vendors are shortening their training programs as a result. Bill York, former co-chair of the A+ Advisory Committee, reported shortening of at least some training classes at Packard Bell, IBM, Toshiba, Hewlett-Packard, and Epson. "This means a technician spends less time in class and gets back on the job sooner," York said.

Dennis O'Leary, PSG Training Group Manager of IBM, says that A+ certification reduces redundancy in training programs. Before their business partners can take an IBM course they must be A+ authorized. Thus, IBM can maintain a stronger, more consistent training level.

A+ certification also helps vendors prepare their own in-house technicians to be successful. For example, Tom Brooks, Manager of Technical Training for AST Research, says that while AST doesn't require A+ certification of its resellers, it does strongly encourage it for all of its phone and field technicians. A+ certification minimizes the training needed once a technician is hired, and lets the technician focus on learning AST's own technologies.

A+ requirements strengthen the level of confidence that vendors have in their technicians. Don Jones, technologist for Microsoft North America, says that with A+, "We can put a new person in front of a customer without being terrified. We won't hire technicians without it."

With the certification as a hiring guideline, the hiring process can be much shorter. Don Jones says, "With A+ certification, there is a lot less screening needed. We no longer have to conduct three interviews for each potential new hire. We now can get by with just one."

A+ is also helpful with planning for internal training and promotions. As Don Jones says, "because of the way A+ certification test results are reported back to us, I can see the areas where my people need further training."

Packard Bell is one manufacturer that has chosen to require A+, both for the field technicians supporting its products and for its in-house technical support staff. David McWilliams, Training Manager of Packard Bell's service and support group, says that requiring A+ of outside service providers guarantees a higher skill set for them as well as a more positive response by the end user.

At the same time, requiring A+ of its internal technical support staff means that Packard Bell has a standard against which to compare the skills of those technicians, and therefore a way to keep their quality high. McWilliams also values the way the exam focuses the attention of those preparing for it. For test candidates from Packard Bell, it means passing the Microsoft Windows/DOS specialty exam, which includes knowledge that is fundamental to working with Packard Bell systems.

## A+ from the Reseller Perspective

Many resellers report that certification allows them to promote themselves on quality of service, and thereby build solid relationships, which are the basis of their success.

For winning new business, the certification may well continue to grow in importance as customers, including government, increasingly appreciate its importance. Some believe that the certification will soon be required in government requests for proposals (RFPs).

The A+ program is listed in the Guide to National Professional Certification Programs, a book used by government agencies, their contractors, and private sector human resource departments.

In addition to bolstering consumer confidence, A+ certification strengthens the channel in another important way: it significantly reduces costs. Costs for service at all levels—end user, reseller, and manufacturer—have been skyrocketing in recent years. An important component of those costs has been the training expense to bring sales and service representatives up to speed on the variety of new products entering the marketplace. Through A+ certification, training costs are significantly lowered.

A manager at a major reseller praises A+ for helping avoid redundant costs. "I have to be authorized on all of the different manufacturers' products," he says. "To do that, I have to spend a lot of time and money to go to all of the different training events across the country. The cost of training and travel and time away from the job is very critical to us. The A+ program allows us to eliminate the base level of training. Then we can concentrate on learning the specific technology required by the different manufacturers."

Tracy Ligon agrees. While Senior Director of Service Operations for Tandy, Ligon wrestled with training requirements imposed by approximately 50 of the 90 manufacturers with whom Tandy did business. When those 50 manufacturers each required service technicians to take basic training, the total training cost to Tandy was "outrageous," Ligon says. But today, when those same manufacturers accept the A+ certification as satisfying their basic training requirements, the training burden has fallen by about one day per technician per manufacturer. This saves Tandy approximately one week of training per year for each of its 1,600 technicians.

Now an independent consultant, Ligon advises his clients, both resellers and end-user organizations, to have their technical staffs A+ certified.

Lex Darr, a service manager at VanStar, says that A+ is helpful to him as a hiring manager. Without A+ certification as a guide in hiring, he says, hiring good service people is sometimes a matter of luck. But, he says, certification results, "don't lie like resumes sometimes do." Darr also believes that A+ certification is much more useful information to a manager than a certificate from a vendor-sponsored training program. Technicians may receive the course certificate, he says, whether they learned anything or not. The A+ certificate, in contrast, shows that technicians have the knowledge to produce results.

Tim Fell, a service manager for InaCom Information, says that InaCom requires A+ certification for all of its technicians. He says that it satisfies the base-level training requirements of many of its manufacturers and also serves as a steppingstone in the natural career progress of technicians. Technicians, he says, progress from the A+ certified basics into more product-specific knowledge as they develop. He likes to have his technicians A+ certified before they branch out into the product lines of several manufacturers or into the networking field.

## A+ from the Customer and End-User Organization Perspective

A+ Certification has become visible to the customer, specifically large companies and government agencies. Many resellers report that bids from the government state that technicians must be A+ certified. Janet Nash of CompUSA says that A+ is a requirement for bidding on the contract for most government agencies. As to the program's effects on customer confidence, David Bossi of IBM says that A+ has helped IBM to deliver better service, both internally and through their reseller organizations. Service, he says, is a logistics problem. "It's the right personnel with the right part at the right time with the proper professionalism." Professionalism, he believes, can make up for lateness of parts and other logistical problems. And A+, he says, has improved its rating on professionalism.

Bill York says that A+ has improved the satisfaction of customers at SolutioNetics. He says that with the wide product mix they service, A+ helps them to prove they have invested the needed time and effort to give quality service.

Galen Davis, Intel Service Program Manager, says, "At Intel Corporation, we look at A+ certification as a basic competency test; something that is of primary benefit to our customers rather than to us directly."

Some technicians report that A+ is not yet well known among smaller clients. But the larger accounts know it and require it. David Duanne of VanStar says that Sprint required A+ certification for technicians working on an on-site project. Many of those slated to be on the project went off to become A+ certified in a hurry.

A+ certification has also been embraced by end-user organizations that use A+ as a requirement for their own technical staff. Increasingly, organizations require their own technicians, and even telephone support and sales people to be A+ certified. Many also structure internal training programs around A+ certification requirements, and use A+ as a useful reference when hiring.

## A+ and Industry Self-Regulation

The A+ program serves a variety of needs common to the IT industry, not least of which may be strengthening industry self-regulation in a way that avoids government controls. Nathan Morton, former CEO of CompUSA, says that the A+ program has established important "self-policing" mechanisms for the industry.

A CompTIA representative says, "Several states have already proposed legislation that would regulate the information technology industry. A self-regulating industry that certifies its members with a program like A+ can minimize such government-imposed efforts."

# 3

# The Changing Market for Information Technology Skills

This chapter discusses the rapidly changing skill sets required of IT technicians; and the technicians' needs for training and development, and for certification. It will give you a sense of the skills that will be useful for your professional development in a variety of IT work environments.

The chapter also gives an overview of the IT product distribution and service chain, identifying the major employment areas for service technicians. The chapter concludes with career advice from three experts, who know both the market for IT services and the A+ exam.

# A Changing Market for Skills

Typically, employers look for experienced people or for people who have a capacity to learn quickly. They raid other companies, hire people from trade shows, and provide in-house training when needed. Robert Half International reports that "the hiring outlook in the information technology employment area is bright. The need for professionals who can design and implement advanced systems will remain strong as companies of all sizes continue investing more freely in technology."

"Nationally, companies are reporting demands for microcomputer programmers, programmer analysts, and systems administrators" (Robert Half International, Inc.). Robert Half also finds firms investing in network technology in record numbers, resulting in very strong demands for administrators and engineers who specialize in Local Area Network and Wide Area Network environments.

In regions with a shortage of these experts, firms are paying higher salaries and, in many cases, at least a portion of relocation costs for top candidates. The demand for networking skills is predicted to grow.

The U.S. Department of Labor also sees a bright future for information technology skills. It estimates there are over 100,000 current openings for computer technicians. In fact, according to the industry magazine, *Service News*, the average salary in 1997 in the hardware-maintenance area was $48,757 for managers and $35,484 for technicians. Some companies, such as Sun Microsystems and Digital Equipment, gave higher salaries to certified employees. Christianne Moore, of IDC, is seeing people test for multiple certificates. She says, "The more you have, the more valuable you are, and the more money you make." She sees growth in the following IT Skills: software, project management, and work on multi-million dollar engagements. These are all next steps to your career development.

The IT industry as a whole is very healthy, and so is that subset of the IT industry in which computer technicians most commonly work: the microcomputer market. For example, in 1993, United States personal computer industry revenues were $66 billion. According to Dataquest, revenues are projected to be $187 billion in 1998.

In the growing IT and microcomputer industries, service is increasingly becoming a crucial source of profits, more important than hardware sales. Service is important for all phases of activity in which computer technicians will find themselves working in the coming years, including computer maintenance and work with system software and networking.

Customer reliance on service and support for hardware, software, and related areas continue to grow. For example, today's users must determine whether they need a PC or a workstation, which operating system to use, and whether to buy custom programming or off-the-shelf software to fit their needs. They must also determine which network, protocol, and corresponding cables they need for their Local Area Network and Wide Area Network. Customers need quality advice and consulting, as well as quality service and support for increasingly complex products.

With new technologies flooding the market, the IT education and training market is flourishing, and includes both computer professionals and end users among its customers. This has led to a tremendous growth in certification testing and training. In 1997, certification-related testing and training was a $3 billion business worldwide. By the year 2001, certification testing and training will grow to over $4 billion. Testing and training revenues are shown in Figures 3-1 and 3-2.

**Figure 3-1**
Certification testing and training—1997.

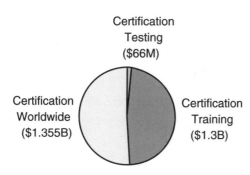

**Figure 3-2**
Certification testing and training—2001.

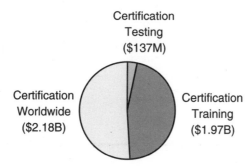

# Data Center Operation

IT departments have changed their skills along with their tools to better exploit advanced technologies. For example, the new corporate environments are both smaller and more "open," in the sense that computing is no longer an isolated function but one that connects every worker in the enterprise. IT professionals within the corporation need to become more responsive and service-oriented, able to deliver the solutions their corporate users require.

At the same time, the importance and complexity of networks force their companies to consolidate data centers with the Local Area Network (LAN) and Wide Area Network (WAN) groups.

Data center managers see themselves as being increasingly responsible for LAN, WAN, and data processing simultaneously. They believe that these services are not provided through traditional mainframe technologies, but more often through server operating systems such as UNIX and Microsoft's Windows NT.

Key skills that data center employees need are knowledge of the following:

- UNIX operating systems and systems programming
- Capacity planning in distributed environments
- Host and server scheduling procedures
- Disaster recovery and backup for PCs
- Graphical user interfaces and artificial intelligence for automated operations

## Applications Development

Programmers must be able to program using object-oriented languages. In essence, the system generates the code. This rise of "computer-aided software engineering" will decrease the programmer's need to code and test, while increasing the needs to understand the business; plan, analyze, and design software; and measure the results in productivity.

## LAN Operations

LAN administrators expect to be increasingly viewed as "mission-critical." The LAN is the first layer of access into the corporate computing hierarchy and will need the same level of integrity, security, recoverability, and scalability that is offered on today's mainframes. To accomplish this, LAN professionals need new technical abilities along with management skills.

LAN professionals spend less time on repetitive, labor-intensive functions such as adds, moves, and changes. They spend more time on strategy, including measuring performance, handling software distribution, managing applications, disaster recovery, and security.

The top skills needed to support the LAN environment are knowledge of the following:

- LAN process/traffic-flow analysis
- Directory-services maintenance
- PC and network operating systems skills

## WAN Operations

Those working with WAN communications need to learn a variety of skills for working with client/server networks, internets, extranets, intranets, and LAN technologies. At the same time, like the LAN professional, the WAN operator must be able to view corporate communications strategically.

For example, technologies such as Asynchronous Transfer Mode (ATM) and Switched Multimegabit Data Service (SMDS) compel WAN managers to rethink the sources of their services, the designs of their networks, and the financial impact of redesigning their WANs. They are less concerned with ordering bandwidth and more concerned with understanding the applications requirements of the business.

The top skills in this area include expertise in the following:

- Negotiation
- Network management tools
- Business project management

# Architecture and Planning

Systems architects need to create "non-technical" systems to better communicate with users. They need to build systems that work easily and promote productivity.

Among the top skills needed in this area are expertise in the following:

- Business modeling
- Technology transfer
- Migration planning

The connection of certification with productivity was documented in an October 1995 study by the International Data Corporation, called "The Financial Benefits of Certification." The study focused exclusively on internal corporate IT departments in client/server environments, and drew input from 253 IT managers and directors.

The study compared the efficiency and effectiveness of organizations that embrace certification with those that do not. Certification supporters were defined as those who pay for or otherwise support employees' becoming professionally certified and/or require professional certification when hiring IT employees. In the study sample, certification-supporting companies had about three times the proportion of certified staff than non-supporting companies did.

The study found the following:

- Certification supporters operate more sophisticated client/server environments than those companies that do not support certification.
- The productivity of IT staff in companies that support certification is greater than that of companies that do not support certification.
- The payback time on investments in certification is typically less than nine months.

Some of their results are shown later.

Certification supporters seemed to accomplish more with technology without employing larger staffs; their staffs were not larger, but were more productive. It is not only the certification supporters who view certified employees as more productive—many of the non-supporters also viewed certified employees as more productive. Figure 3-3 shows that 78% of companies supporting certification feel that certified employees are more productive in at least their area of certification, while only about half of certification non-supporters feel that this is the case.

The top five benefits that the sample group expected to receive from certifying employees included the following capabilities:

- Providing a greater knowledge and increased productivity
- Assuring a certain level of expertise and skill
- Improving support quality
- Reducing training costs
- Providing higher morale and commitment

For the great majority, those benefits of certification were realized. (See Figure 3-4.)

**Figure 3-3**
Are certified employees more productive? (International Data Corporation)

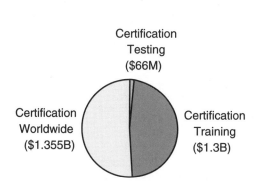

**1997**

Certification Testing ($66M)

Certification Worldwide ($1.355B)

Certification Training ($1.3B)

**Figure 3-4**
Ninety two percent realized expected benefits from certification. (International Data Corporation)

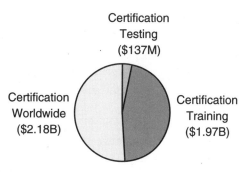

**2001**

Certification Testing ($137M)

Certification Worldwide ($2.18B)

Certification Training ($1.97B)

The technical skills needed to operate productively in the workplace are escalating sharply; pushing demands for training and development, as well as for certification. The value of certification, and of A+ certification in particular, is continually growing.

A+ has proven valuable for reducing redundant training and thereby making training dollars go farther. It has also focused attention on those areas of skill that are truly cross-product and fundamental, and that can be valuable as a base for learning other specific new technologies as they come on-line.

Finally, in a world of rapidly changing demands on the skills of computer technicians, A+ has focused attention on those skills that all technicians need to have, regardless of the environment they work in. In that way, it has become a useful gauge for technicians for evaluating their current skills and planning their future development.

See Appendix F for the Job Profile of a Computer Technician. This profile, developed and updated in 1998 by CompTIA in coordination with dozens of IT industry leaders, identifies the major skills required of service technicians. That profile also identifies some areas of responsibility not currently tested on the A+ exam including business management, administrative skills, and professionalism. Each skill is included in Appendix F because of its importance in the work of technicians today.

# The Information Technology Distribution Channel and its Service Requirements

The distribution system for computer products is constantly changing, and adapting to requirements imposed by technology and by the end-user. A distribution model is shown in Figure. 3-5, and is followed by a discussion of the role played by each link in the distribution chain today and the concerns of each for quality service. Each link in the chain is an employment area for computer technicians, and each area benefits from the A+ certification program.

Understanding the needs of each of these employers for quality service can help you, as an A+ certified technician, to use your professional skills to your greatest advantage, both in finding jobs and in serving well in the jobs you take. For materials on job networking, interviewing, and resumes, see the book list provided in Appendix C.

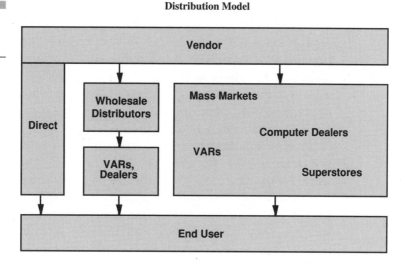

**Figure 3-5**
The data model.
(Dataquest 1995)

A customer may purchase a computer from a variety of sources. The collective group of all sources is called the distribution channel. Examples of purchasing possibilities are direct sales from the manufacturer (also called the vendor); and sales from computer stores, value-added resellers (VARs), and mail order. Value-added resellers and computer dealers, in turn, may receive their products directly from the vendor, or through distributors or aggregators.

## The Manufacturer as a Service Provider

When corporations need to make a large purchase of IT equipment, they may try to negotiate a sale at a discount, directly from the manufacturer. A corporate buyer may also ask the manufacturer to reconfigure personal computers in order to meet custom requirements for hardware or software configuration.

Some corporate buyers prefer direct purchases, not just for the savings and the chance to have products customized, but because they want to receive service and support directly from the manufacturer. In recent years, some vendors have encouraged this by publishing their own catalogs and marketing themselves more aggressively to end users.

The computer manufacturer determines the warranty period and the guidelines for service of its products. The manufacturer may provide all warranty service or authorize other service providers, including dealers, to handle warranty work. Either way, it is important to the manufacturer that the warranty work be done completely and accurately. When the manufacturer provides the service itself, it may either require that the product be sent to the manufacturing site, or it may send service technicians to the customer's site.

A manufacturer's warranty may cover the complete costs for certain kinds of repairs. Other repairs may require the customer to pay for the costs of repair time and materials.

Both manufacturers and resellers are working to reduce costs through better management of parts inventory and other overhead costs. Manufacturers are also designing hardware systems to be more easily serviced.

At the same time, both manufacturers and resellers are abandoning the old view of service as a cost of doing business, and looking at service as a major revenue opportunity. This new view is taking them beyond merely servicing and maintaining hardware into servicing software and providing a range of professional services. These services include software integration (SI), network integration, facilities management, help desk support, and education and training.

Many manufacturers are planning to increase opportunities to earn service revenues by building customer loyalty through extended warranty periods, and bundling of more free warranty support and service into the product purchase.

At the same time, in order to provide the new services, many manufacturers and service providers are investing in training to give employees the skills they need.

Service technicians working for manufacturers will play an increasing number of roles. They will continue to provide board or component repair to end users, as well as troubleshooting support to technicians in reseller organizations. Increasingly, however, they will also serve as help-desk support, trainers and educators, and providers of networking and software-integration support.

## Resellers as Service Providers

The reseller channels are responsible for ensuring ongoing service and support for the products they represent. Most resellers employ their own technicians, although some may contract with a servicing company for them.

Technicians working for resellers are typically responsible for all the product brands sold. They provide warranty service, and may perform all of the key tasks and duties listed in the A+ service technician job profile. Resellers service customers, either through a "depot" or service desk in the reseller's location, or by having the technician travel to the customer location to provide on-site service.

The various components of the reseller distribution network are discussed in the following sections.

**DISTRIBUTORS/AGGREGATORS**   Distributors handle large inventories of products, deal with many different brands, and provide cost-effective distribution help to manufacturers who sell to multiple types of resellers and VARs.

Often, distributors offer service support for their customers and warranty support for manufacturers. They typically handle both small and large-volume sales; some sell through catalogs directly to end users.

Aggregators, in contrast, sell only to large reseller organizations and pass along to them considerable savings, based on large volume purchases. Examples of aggregators are Intelligent Electronics and MicroAge, Inc. Some vendors, such as Compaq and IBM, sell much of their product through aggregators; others, such as Apple Computer, Inc., have tried to bypass aggregators and sell directly to resellers.

**VALUE-ADDED RESELLERS**   Value-added resellers (VARs) buy products from the manufacturer or from wholesale distributors, and then add additional software or hardware that provide the "added value." Often, VARs do not service and support the manufacturers' hardware—just the value-added portion of their sale. Technicians employed by VARs must learn their products in great depth to successfully support customized versions of those products.

**ORIGINAL EQUIPMENT MANUFACTURERS**   An Original Equipment Manufacturer (OEM) is similar to a value-added reseller. The major difference is that the OEM buys products from a manufacturer, integrates a specific application or change into the product, and sells it under a different name. For example, an OEM may buy monitors from several monitor manufacturers; and then make some internal changes, and add its logo and company name. OEMs provide all the same kinds of service support to their products that manufacturers do.

**COMPUTER STORES/DEALERS**   A computer store may be independently owned, a franchise, or part of a national or regional chain. They are often called resellers or "dealers." An individually owned store is a retail business responsible for all aspects of sales, service, and support. Franchised stores are contractually part of a larger computer reseller network. Individual store owners enter into franchise agreements in order to share in larger discount purchases with other stores; and to gain other benefits such as national advertising, name recognition, and a larger service support network.

Some computer resellers are regional chains, in which several stores in a geographic area are under one ownership. These stores are usually required to have service technicians to provide customer support and installation. The service technicians in regional chains may also provide warranty work on behalf of the computer manufacturer.

**MASS MARKETS AS SERVICE PROVIDERS**   Mass marketers, such as Sears and Wal-Mart, purchase IT products in large volume and sell in large volume directly to end users. As computer prices drop, the mass market is increasingly important in the distribution chain. Few of the mass marketers service and support the products they sell, and mass-market customers often seek service from the product manufacturer.

## Mail Order and Service

Mail order can be a simple and effective way to buy computers for customers who already know the equipment and applications they want, and need no help from salespeople in making buying decisions. Generally, mail-order products needing repair within the warranty period are shipped back to the mail-order house. These repairs are usually made by swapping a new component for the defective one.

## Third-Party Maintenance Providers and Service

Third-party maintenance providers (TPMs) are usually part of regional chains, and provide service transactions and warranty repairs as their primary business. TPMs typically service many brands of computers, peripherals, and related products. Some offer depot service, so that customers can mail or drop off computer equipment to them for exchange or repair.

TPMs represent the product manufacturer; usually the TPM's contact with the customer begins when the customer service call is transferred or dispatched from the manufacturer. For example, Apple Computer does not employ servicing technicians for customer support. When customers call Apple Computer's 800-service number, the operator dispatches the call to the servicing agent in the customer's area, who acts as Apple's representative.

For most of the organizations in the distribution chain, and certainly for distributors, VARs, OEMs, computer stores, and TPMs, the success of their businesses comes increasingly from the success of their service. The more maintenance, support, and value-added service they provide, the more successful their businesses will be in the coming years. High-quality service technicians who are well trained in the basics, and ready to take on new roles for service and support will be of great value to these organizations. For this reason, many of them are encouraging, if not requiring, their technicians to be A+ certified.

## Service and the Corporate End-User

Large businesses that use many brands of IT equipment and that need immediate service to avoid downtime, may set up their own internal service and support organizations. Such businesses send their service technician employees to product-training seminars that are sponsored by vendors, and keep key spare parts in their company inventories. In-house service technician jobs can be found in corporations, government, and universities.

Although in-house support makes a company more independent and potentially less subject to downtime, going outside for service helps businesses cut their overhead and provides them the kind of specialized skills needed for their increasingly complex applications. Many companies, of course, use a combination of in-house and external IT support. Dataquest estimates that, overall, the proportion of company IT budgets going to internally provided services will increase slightly in the near-term future, relative to outside services.

As the microcomputer industry continues to grow, the need for quality service technicians grows also. Those with solid technical skills and with an appreciation for the fundamentals of customer satisfaction will add value to their employers, no matter where they are in the distribution chain.

Developing and certifying a broad range of skills, from the A+ fundamentals on up to networking and product-specific expertise, will open new opportunities at every turn. Seeking out employers who value the role of training and the need for excellence in customer satisfaction will also keep your career on the fast track.

# Some Advice from the Experts

Following, three IT-industry experts offer career advice and perspectives on the credential you are about to earn.

## Advice to Beginner Computer Technicians

Aaron Woods, Services and Alliances Program Manager at Tektronix in Wilsonville, Oregon, says, "Most technicians today start their training in a technical school or two-year or community college; sometimes springboarding from there into a four-year college degree. People can get a diploma as a computer technician in nine months to two years.

"There are many options, but people really need to do their homework when choosing where to study. The technical institutes can be very expensive and may not provide the kind of state-of-the-art training that new graduates require. Those programs may be limited by the knowledge of their instructors or by the kinds of equipment they have available to students for hands-on training.

"I often recommend junior colleges over technical schools because they may provide an excellent computer-technician program along with studies in other areas.

" After becoming a technician, one usually opts today for either the networking area or a non-networking-focused technical support area, including telephone support. Networking techs may advance into networking analysis, and then into management positions. Those outside the networking specialty may go on to supervise a service department or telephone support group on their way up to management.

"The networking services area is more a professional services area, geared toward installing and maintaining complex systems. The non-networking services area is more geared toward fixing what is broken, and typically takes place in a reseller environment. Providing sales and support to the reseller's clients is often particularly time-sensitive and requires excellent customer-interaction skills.

"A+ certification is useful for either of the two tracks. It demonstrates a broad general knowledge of computer principles that are helpful, both to networking specialists and to non-networking service specialists. The A+ program is also working now to develop an additional module that will help to bridge the language and skills gap that separates these two groups of professionals.

"That gap today is large and frustrating for many. A technician may go out to the client's site to repair a bad drive. The technician repairs and replaces the drive, and brings the drive back up; and the unit works fine until it is connected back to the network. At that point, the technician may not have enough knowledge to isolate the problem. The A+ program will soon help on-site technicians to ensure they have the skills they need to at least talk intelligently to network engineers and play a constructive role in resolving such problems.

"The A+ program is dynamic; it will always keep up with the changing needs of the industry as they become evident. A+, as well as certifications provided by the product vendors, will play an increasingly important role for computer technicians, who will inevitably be involved in a life-long learning process."

## A+ and a Suggested Skills Progression for Computer Technicians

Mariano Dy-Liacco, Vice-President of Service and Support Operations for Dataflex Corporation of Clearwater, Florida, says, "At Dataflex, we've developed a curriculum of four distinct levels for computer technicians. These steps of progress are useful not only for technicians here; they could be a model for others to follow in developing their careers. The progression is from general knowledge to more specific product-related skills.

"Level One of our curriculum requires technicians to meet the basic training requirements of the manufacturers whose products we work on, including Apple, Compaq, Hewlett-Packard, and IBM. We also require at Level One that all of our technicians earn A+ certification. In fact, they need to earn that credential within 90 days of hire date as a condition of employment. We put together study groups for our A+ people, and encourage them to work together and share study materials.

"The knowledge tested by A+ is the solid basis on which other, more specific components of knowledge and skill can be built. A+ has been essential for our industry in identifying those fundamentals and so helping to chart career progress for computer technicians.

"Level Two of our curriculum has our technicians focus on software, including operating systems and applications programs. In the mid-1980s, 80% of what a technician had to know was hardware-related, while only 20% was software-related. Today, those percentages are reversed. Because hardware systems have become more modular and easier to repair, while software programs have proliferated and become more complex, technicians need to focus most of their energies on learning the software side. At Level Two, our technicians learn such software as Microsoft programs and OS/2, and take electives such as Excel, Word, and others.

"Level Three requires our technicians to develop deeper knowledge about both hardware and software, and to learn some networking skills. The best technicians have all of these skills well developed.

"Our fourth level is a particular product specialization, which technicians choose for themselves.

"I would recommend something like these four steps of progression for every technician. But the exact direction of the specialization will differ from one technician to another, and appropriate directions of specialization will change constantly as the marketplace changes.

"Technicians need to watch the trends. You don't want to specialize in one kind of technology when the trends are all pointing to another. In every case, though, training for technicians at some point needs to include customer-interaction skills. A+, by testing those, helps get technicians off to the right start in this area, too.

"Everyone's career is ultimately his or her own responsibility. Take the initiative to manage your own. Decide where you want to be with your skills, then give yourself the specific training you need to get there."

## Real World Skills and Your A+ Certification

Ben Eckart, Instructor in Computer Repair at Manhattan Area Technical Center of Manhattan, Kansas, says, "I try to give my students what they need to succeed—and not just as an entry-level technician. I believe that we are actually giving students much of what they need to be successful senior technicians right out of school. A+ certification, which I recommend to all my students, plays an important role in this.

"Senior-level technicians differ from entry-level technicians because of their greater breadth of knowledge. Entry-level technicians are sometimes called "board-swappers" because they are basically repairing or replacing individual components, and do not understand the more fundamental issues that are often involved with computer problems.

"Anyone can learn to be a board-swapper in a couple months and go to work for $5-$8 per hour; typically working in a retail store to upgrade and swap parts, or to do repairs. When board-swappers meet a problem, they often can't determine its cause because they don't really know how a computer works. Most technical schools produce this kind of technician.

"But most repair shops have no use for board-swappers. What they need is really the senior-level technician: someone with component-level troubleshooting skills, an in-depth knowledge of the operating system, and an understanding of electronics.

"Without that kind of knowledge, your work is often not cost-effective. You might replace an entire board when a 10-cent piece was the cause of the problem, or tell the client it's time to replace a $400 monitor when it could have been repaired for $30. Without understanding electronics, you may never be able to repair a computer, not even by replacing every board in it.

"You have to be able to troubleshoot computers in the way that a senior-level technician can. The senior-level technician has more of a knowledge base than the board-swapper does and, as a result, produces much better results and earns much more, starting at $12 or more per hour.

"The A+ exam shows if you have many of these kinds of senior-level abilities. It shows if you have a technical knowledge of the hardware and a technical knowledge of DOS and Windows, not just a knowledge of applications.

"To do well on the A+ test, you must also have the attitude of the senior-level tech: the attitude that if you understand fundamental principles, you can solve any computer problems, including ones you've never encountered before.

"For example, the test may ask about installing CD-ROM drives. The candidate may know about installing hard drives, but never have been taught how to install CD-ROM drives. If you're just a board-swapper, you'll be stumped by this or other situations you meet for the first time on the A+ exam.

"But if you have the broader vision of a senior-level technician, you know that the concepts and procedures used when interfacing with the computer are exactly the same, no matter what kind of device you're hooking up. The technician with the senior-level perspective could answer that question, whether it was about hooking up a mouse, a keyboard, a CD-ROM drive, or a sound card. The same considerations are involved in every installation. You'll get the answer right if you understand generic troubleshooting concepts.

"A+ tests you on general knowledge—the kind that's equally relevant in repairing PS/2s, Hyundais, notebooks, or anything else. You can deal with all those questions if you have the basic concepts, and mastering those concepts is equally important to passing the A+ exam and to making money in the real world.

"A+ certification itself is increasingly valued in the marketplace. I see it all the time in the experiences of our graduates. They're finding employers who accept the A+ certification in lieu of one year's work experience, and who allow them quickly to take responsibility for hundreds of computers and for networks. Some companies even tie their pay scales directly to certification and give an automatic pay raise to those who earn A+ certification.

"Today, salary for computer technicians depends less on college education and more on certifications. It only makes sense because certification (and very importantly the A+ certification) proves you have the ability to solve real-world problems."

CHAPTER

# The Core Exam

The study guides for each of the two A+ exam modules (Chapters 4–5) are divided in a way that reflects the structure of the exams themselves. Both the study guide and the A+ exam have sections that reflect the major areas of responsibility for a technician. For the core exam, those areas or domains are

- Installation/configuration/upgrading
- Diagnosing/troubleshooting
- Safety/preventive maintenance
- System Board/processors/memory
- Printers
- Portable systems
- Basic networking
- Customer satisfaction

Refer to Table 4-1 for the extent to which these domains are covered in the A+ Core exam.

**Table 4-1**

Domain
Percentage
Breakdowns

| Domain | % of Examination |
|---|---|
| 1.0 Installation, Configuration, and Upgrading | 30% |
| 2.0 Diagnosing and Troubleshooting | 20% |
| 3.0 Safety and Preventive Maintenance | 10% |
| 4.0 Motherboard/Processors/Memory | 10% |
| 5.0 Printers | 10% |
| 6.0 Portable Systems | 5% |
| 7.0 Basic Networking | 5% |
| 8.0 Customer Satisfaction | 10% |
| Total | 100.00% |

**NOTE:**   *The customer satisfaction portion of this test will be scored, but will not affect the final pass/fail score on the A+ Core examination. However, it will be noted on the examinee's score report.*

The core exam tests major areas of responsibility with reference to a variety of technologies. These technologies include microcomputers, printers, portable systems, storage media, displays, and basic networking.

Chapter 4 is organized principally by these technologies. Under each of the technologies, each of the duty areas is explained as it relates to that technology. We hope this organization will be effective in preparing the reader for the A+ core exam, and may also serve later as a useful quick reference when working on any of the technologies described.

The core exam items cover procedures and information that are not related to vendor-specific products, but instead cover the fundamental knowledge needed to perform the tasks of a computer service technician.

**NOTE:**   *This chapter is not intended as a comprehensive course in microcomputers, operating systems, and peripherals; but as a guide to the knowledge required for passing the A+ core exam. If, upon reviewing a section of this or the other study guide chapters, you feel a need for more information, please refer to Appendices C and D for recommended sources of further reading and training.*

The specific skills and knowledge that the A+ core exam tests are listed as follows. Each skill or knowledge is covered in the preparatory materials that follow. All the skills and knowledge measured by this examination were derived from an industry-wide job task analysis and validated through a survey of 5,000 A+ Certified professionals. The results of the worldwide survey were used in weighting the domains and ensuring that the weighting is representative of the relative importance of that content to the job requirements of a service technician with six months on-the-job experience. We have also presented additional topics where we felt these would be helpful. Be sure to concentrate your preparation in these areas. This chapter concludes with sample test questions and answers.

### SECTION I—OBJECTIVES AT A GLANCE
The A+ certification core exam tests your ability to do the following:

# Domain 1.0 Installation, Configuration, and Upgrading

This domain requires the knowledge and skills to identify, install, configure, and upgrade microcomputer modules and peripherals; following established basic procedures for system assembly and disassembly of field replaceable modules. Elements include the ability to identify and configure IRQs, DMAs, I/O addresses, and set switches and jumpers.

### Content Limits
1.1 Identify basic terms, concepts, and functions of system modules, including how each module should work during normal operation.

Examples of Concepts and Modules:

- System Board
- Power Supply
- Processor/CPU
- Memory
- Storage Devices
- Monitor
- Input Devices
- Output Devices
- BIOS
- CMOS

**1.2** Identify basic procedures for adding and removing field replaceable modules.

Examples of Concepts and Modules:

- System Board
- Power Supply
- Processor/CPU
- Memory
- Storage Devices
- Monitor
- Modem
- Input Devices
- Output Devices

**1.3** Identify available IRQs DMAs, and I/O addresses; and procedures for configuring them for device installation, including identifying switch and jumper settings.

Content may include the following:

- Standard IRQ settings
- Differences between jumpers and switches
- Locating and setting jumpers/switches
- Modems
- Sound Cards
- Network Cards

**1.4** Identify common peripheral ports, associated cabling, and their connectors.

Content may include the following:

- Cable types
- Cable orientation
- Cable and connector location—internal/external
- Serial versus parallel
- Pin connections
- Cable handling/routing

**1.5** Identify proper procedures for installing and configuring IDE/EIDE devices.

Content may include the following:

- Master/Slave
- Devices per channel

**1.6** Identify proper procedures for installing and configuring SCSI devices.

Content may include the following:

- Address/terminator conflicts
- Cabling
- Types (example: regular, wide, ultra-wide)
- Power supply
- Internal versus external
- Switch and jumper settings

**1.7** Identify proper procedures for installing and configuring peripheral devices.

Content may include the following:

- Monitor/Video Card
- Modem
- Storage devices
- Associated drivers
- Configuring, installing, and upgrading displays

**1.8** Recognize the function and effective use of common hand tools.

Content may include the following:

- Chip-puller
- Torx bit
- Regular bit
- Multimeter

**1.9** Identify procedures for upgrading BIOS.

Content may include the following:

- Upgrade system BIOS (flash or replace)
- Upgrade system hardware

**1.10** Identify hardware methods of system optimization and when to use them.

Content may include the following:

- Memory
- Hard Drives
- CPU
- Cache memory

# Domain 2.0 Diagnosing and Troubleshooting

This domain requires the ability to apply knowledge relating to diagnosing and troubleshooting common module problems and system malfunctions. This includes knowledge of the symptoms relating to common problems.

**Content Limits**

**2.1** Identify common symptom and problems associated with each module and how to troubleshoot and isolate the problem.

Content may include the following:

Processor/Memory symptoms

- Keyboards/Mouse/Track Ball/Pen/Microphones/Touch Pad
- Floppy drive failures
- Hard Drives
- Sound Card/Audio
- Modems
- BIOS
- Power Supply
- Device Drivers
- POST audible/visual error codes

**2.2** Identify basic troubleshooting procedures and good practices for eliciting problem symptoms from customers.

Content may include the following:

- Troubleshooting/isolation/problem determination procedures
- Determine whether hardware or software problem

**2.3** Gather information from user regarding:
- Customer environment
- Symptoms/Error Codes
- Situation when problem occurred

# Domain 3.0 Safety and Preventive Maintenance

This domain requires the knowledge of safety and preventive maintenance. With regard to safety, it includes the potential hazards to personnel and equipment when working with lasers, high voltage equipment, ESD, and items that require special disposal procedures that comply with environmental guidelines. With regard to preventive maintenance, this includes knowledge of preventive maintenance products, procedures, environmental hazards, and precautions when working on microcomputer systems.

**3.1** Identify the purpose of various types of preventive maintenance products and procedures, and where to use/perform them.

**3.2** Identify procedures and devices for protecting against environmental hazards.

**3.3** Identify the potential hazards and proper safety procedures relating to lasers and high voltage equipment.

**3.4** Identify items that require special disposal procedures to comply with environmental guidelines.

**3.5** Identify ESD (Electrostatic Discharge) precautions and procedures, including the use of ESD protection devices.

# Domain 4.0 Motherboard/ Processors/Memory

This domain requires knowledge of specific terminology, facts, and ways and means of dealing with the classifications, categories, and principles of motherboards, processors, and memory in microcomputer systems.

Distinguish between the popular CPU chips in terms of their basic characteristics.

**4.1** Identify the categories of RAM (Random Access Memory) terminology, their locations, and physical characteristics.

**4.2** Identify the most popular type of motherboards, their components, and their architecture (e.g., bus structures and power supplies).

**4.3** Identify the purpose of CMOS (Complimentary Metal-Oxide Semi-conductor) what it contains, and how to change its basic parameters.

# Domain 5.0 Printers

This domain requires knowledge of basic types or printers, basic concepts, printer components, how they work, how they print to a page, paper path, care and service techniques, and common problems.

### Content Limits

**5.1** Identify basic concepts, printer operations, printer components, and field replaceable units in primary printer types.

**5.2** Identify care and service techniques, and common problems with primary printer types.

**5.3** Identify types of printers and configurations.

# Domain 6.0 Portable Systems

This domain requires knowledge of portable computers and their unique components and problems.

**6.1** Identify the unique components of the portable system and their unique problems.

# Domain 7.0 Basic Networking

This domain requires knowledge of basic network concepts and terminology, ability to determine whether a computer is networked, knowledge of procedures for swapping and configuring network interface cards, and knowledge of the ramifications of repairs when a computer is networked.

**7.1** Identify basic networking concepts, including how a network works.

**7.2** Identify procedures for swapping and configuring network interface cards.

**7.3** Identify ramifications of repairs on the network.

# Domain 8.0 Customer Satisfaction

This domain requires knowledge of, and sensitivity to those behaviors that contribute to satisfying customers. More specifically, these behaviors may include the following:

■ Quality of technician-customer personal interactions

■ Professional conduct at the customer site

■ Credibility and confidence

■ Resilience, friendliness, and efficiency

**8.1** Differentiate effective from ineffective behaviors as they contribute to the maintenance or achievement of customer satisfaction.

**SECTION II**   With those objectives in mind, let's begin.

In the early 1980s, a number of new architectures emerged, as illustrated in Figure 4-1.

Although these systems did not have the speeds and capabilities that we see in today's microcomputers, for their time, they were "state of the art." Each system had its supported microprocessor families, communication bus structures, and software operating environments. The evolution to today's architecture has been incredibly fast, but much has remained unchanged. The technology has grown faster and more capable, but the basic building blocks are still quite similar. Many field-replaceable modules make up the typical microcomputer. These include:

■ System Board

■ Power supply

■ Hard disk drives and floppy drives

■ Cabling

■ Backup batteries

■ Input/output ports

■ Keyboard and mouse devices or other input/output devices

**Figure 4-1**
New architectures emerging in the early 80s, including the (a) Apple Macintosh, (b) IBM PC/XT, (c) IBM AT, and (d) IBM compatibles.

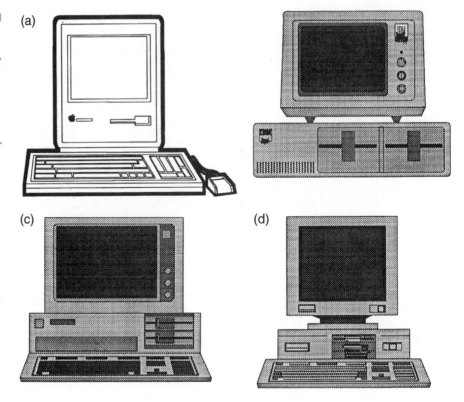

(a)

(c)

(d)

## System Board

The system board, also referred to as the motherboard or planar, is considered to be the main circuit board in the microcomputer and contains a majority of the main circuits needed for operation. Some of these circuits are the microprocessors, memory (RAM, ROM, Cache), BIOS, and Bus interface connectors. Even though most motherboards contain similar circuitry, this does not mean that they are fully compatible. Besides electrical compatibility, we must concern ourselves with physical compatibility, the system board's form factor.

Form factor refers to the physical dimensions and size of the system board. It is this characteristic, or specification, which dictates what type of case the system board will fit into. In simpler terms, this means that a system board from one manufacturer will not always fit into another manufacturer's case. There are several variations when speaking of form factor. They are:

**Backplane Systems**—Instead of all circuits or components being mounted on a single circuit card, they are broken down into various modules and plug into a common backplane. This means you could have a CPU/Memory card, a video board, peripheral controller, etc. The common backplane can be either active or passive. If the backplane contains active circuitry, it is considered active. If it is comprised of just the connectors to interconnect the other modules, it is considered passive.

**Full-size AT**—This board matches the original IBM AT motherboard design, hence its name. This motherboard will fit only in full-size AT or tower cases.

**Baby AT**—The Baby AT is the original IBM XT motherboard design, with modifications to fit an AT style case.

**LPX**—The LPX was originally developed by Western Digital and has been duplicated by other manufacturers. LPX boards contain several distinct features. The most noticeable is that the expansion slots are mounted on a bus riser card that plugs into the motherboard. One other distinguishing feature is the standard placement of connectors on the back of the board.

**ATX**—This form factor combines the best of the Baby-AT with that of the LPX design. The official ATX specification was released by Intel in 1995. There are several major areas where this form factor has improved on the others. These include a built-in double high I/O connector panel, a single-keyed internal power supply connector, relocated CPU and memory so as not to interfere with expansion, improved cooling, and lower cost to manufacture.

**NLX**—The NLX is the latest in motherboard technology. It is a low profile board, and similar in appearance to the LPX with some improvements. One of the limitations of the LPX design was its inability to handle the physical size of newer processor technologies, and their higher thermal characteristics. The NLX has been designed specifically to address these issues.

# The Microprocessor

The microprocessor is usually considered to be the primary component of the system board and is capable of accepting coded instructions (software) for execution. From 16-bit internal CPU registers in the 8088 series to

300-bit internal CPU registers in the Pentium II microprocessors, the basic concept remains the same. Although there are many terms used when describing microprocessors, most often we are referring to bus width and clock speed. Refer to Table 4-2 for a list of the various Intel microprocessors used in microcomputers. Several companies, including AMD and Cyrix, have also developed processors that are compatible with the Intel processors. They are fully Intel-compatible, thus they can emulate the processor instructions in the Intel chips. These processors are both hardware and software compatible with those that work on Intel systems.

Even though the microprocessor is the central component in microcomputers, we must always consider the other areas of a computer, as well, when we refer to throughput, or overall system performance. You could have the fastest microprocessor available; however, if other circuitry acts to slow it down, total system performance is effected. For example, if you have state-of-the-art processors, but not enough memory, you have greatly limited the capabilities of that microprocessor. So often we look at clock speed as the sole determining factor in a system's performance. Keep in mind that different instruction execution times from processor to processor make it difficult to base our judgment purely on clock speed because one processor may operate more efficiently than another.

## Buses

System boards in IBM and compatible systems are available with a variety of expansion slot designs that are further divided into two families: those based on Industry Standard Architecture (ISA), including Extended Industry Standard Architecture (EISA); and those based on Micro Channel Architecture (MCA). In addition, many specialty buses and interfaces have evolved. These include VESA (Video Electronics Standards Association), PCI (Peripheral Component Interface), PCMCIA (Personal Computer Memory Card International Association), Universal Serial Bus (USB), and Accelerated Graphics Port (AGP).

ISA expansion slots are illustrated in Figure 4-2.

Each bus design has a primary connector, and one or more extension connectors for additional capabilities. MCA also adds a video extension connector exclusively for video on one of the slots. Neither MCA nor EISA requires the use of any switches or jumpers for configuring. Configuration for MCA and EISA is accomplished through the use of software. For example, the EISA configuration utility allows you to configure serial or parallel

**Table 4-2**  Microprocessor Specifications

| Processor | Register Size | Data Bus | Address Bus | Maximum Memory | Internal Co-Processor | Internal Cache |
|---|---|---|---|---|---|---|
| 8088 | 16-bit | 8-bit | 20-bit | 1M | No | No |
| 8086 | 16-bit | 16-bit | 20-bit | 1M | No | No |
| 286 | 16-bit | 16-bit | 24-bit | 16M | No | No |
| 86SX | 32-bit | 16-bit | 24-bit | 16M | No | No |
| 386SL | 32-bit | 16-bit | 24-bit | 16M | No | * |
| 386DX | 32-bit | 32-bit | 32-bit | 4G | No | No |
| 486SX | 32-bit | 32-bit | 32-bit | 4G | No | 8K |
| 486SX2 | 32-bit | 32-bit | 32-bit | 4G | No | 8K |
| 487SX | 32-bit | 32-bit | 32-bit | 4G | Yes | 8K |
| 486DX | 32-bit | 32-bit | 32-bit | 4G | Yes | 8K |
| 486SL | 32-bit | 32-bit | 32-bit | 4G | Optional | 8K |
| 486DX2 | 32-bit | 32-bit | 32-bit | 4G | Yes | 8K |
| 486DX4 | 32-bi | 32-bit | 32-bit | 4G | Yes | 16K |
| Pentium OD | 32-bit | 32-bit | 32-bit | 4G | Yes | 2 x 16K |
| Pentium 60/66 | 32-bit | 64-bit | 32-bit | 4G | Yes | 2 x 8K |
| Pentium 75+ | 32-bit | 64-bit | 32-bit | 4G | Yes | 2 x 8K |
| Pentium Pro | 32-bit | 64-bit | 36-bit | 64G | Yes | 2 x 8K |
| Pentium II | 300-bit | 64-bit | 36-bit | 64G | Yes | 16K code 16K data |

**Figure 4-2**
ISA expansion slots.

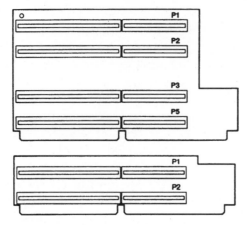

ports; enable or disable the mouse; or define the LAN module video settings, memory, boot device, system board speed, and type of hard drive or floppy drive system. Regardless of type, all communication buses have the same purpose, distributing important signals. These signals can be grouped into the following categories:

Address

Data

Control

Power & Ground

Clock and/or Timing

In the original IBM PC, the ISA PC bus ran at the same speed as the microprocessor—an astonishing slow 4.77 MHz compared to today's systems. The 16-bit version, which was used in the AT (Advanced Technology) systems, ran at 6MHz or 8MHz. Later on, the industry settled on an 8.33-MHz maximum speed for the ISA bus. This met with backward compatibility requirements, which allowed older-type boards to be used in this bus. Please keep in mind that ISA is still used in some systems today, and still runs faster than most peripherals that attach to it.

The MCA (Micro Channel Architecture) bus was introduced by IBM in order to meet the demand of 32-bit data transfers. MCA was first used in the PS2 line of microcomputers. (Not only did IBM want to replace the ISA standard, they also wanted to receive royalties on MCA, along with retroactive royalties on the previous ISA architecture.) This led other manufacturers in the industry to develop the EISA (Extended Industry Standard Architecture) standard.

MCA ran asynchronously with the main CPU, eliminating the possibility of timing problems among adapter cards. In addition, MCA did away with the old switches and jumpers for configuration. One of the key features of MCA was its capability to support bus mastering. In a bus-mastering scenario, any device capable of acting as a bus master can request unobstructed use of the bus when communicating with another device. This environment was controlled by a Central Arbitration Control Point that arbitrates all requests for the bus from masters to ensure that all devices have access, and no one monopolizes the bus.

We mentioned earlier that when IBM introduced MCA, other manufacturers got together and developed EISA. EISA provided 32-bit slots at an 8.33-MHz cycle rate for use with 386DX or higher systems. EISA also offered downward compatibility in that it allowed the use of older 16-bit adapter cards, a feature that MCA did not have. Both EISA and MCA allowed configuration to be performed via software utilities, rather than switches and jumpers.

Even with all these improvements, there was still a barrier. All these buses, ISA, EISA, and MCA, were relatively slow. With the advent of Graphical User Interfaces (GUI, pronounced "gooey") such as Windows, there were bottlenecks on the I/O bus due to the amount of video data and/or information that had to be processed. The solution to this was the local bus, allowing devices to communicate directly with the CPU on its local processor bus at greater speeds. Please keep in mind that a system board does not have to have a specific connector to incorporate local bus technology. It can be built into the system board. Also, these local buses are considered extensions to the earlier standards and did not replace them.

## Video Electronics Standards Association (VESA) Local Bus

The VESA local bus or VL-Bus, as it came to be known, offered direct access to system memory at the speed of the processor, and was able to move 32 bits of data at a time. Its main purpose was to improve video performance, although other manufacturers of adapters, such as hard drive companies, were attempting to utilize this new bus performance. Originally founded by NEC, the VESA committee came up with the first VL-Bus Standard.

Although it did a lot to improve system performance, there were some deficiencies in this design. It was dependent on the 486 processor, which did little with the arrival of the Pentium processors. There were speed limitations of 33 MHz, even though the specification provided for speeds up to 66MHz. Load limitations on the processor bus were being exceeded, causing electrical limitations and this also limited the number of cards that could be added.

## Peripheral Component Interconnect (PCI) Bus

The PCI Bus is unique in that it does not directly interface with the system processor, or CPU. It communicates with the processor through a circuit of bridges that act as a buffer. Rather than tap into the processor bus directly, a new set of controller chips are used to extend the bus. This made it processor-independent. With processor independence, PCI became the first 64-bit bus appropriate for the Pentium architectures. Also, we are now seeing speeds of 66 MHz.

PCI also became the model for the Intel PnP (Plug and Play) specification. PCI Plug and Play capability and updated BIOSs allow the automatic configuration of adapters. Whenever you add or remove a card in your system, you will usually get a message during boot-up that indicates the system has detected the addition or removal.

## Personal Computer Memory Card International Association (PCMCIA)

The laptop-computing environment is responsible for many new technological advances, one of them being the PCMCIA interface. Some companies have as much as 80 percent of their work force using laptop computers, so there is a constant need to build them smaller, yet with more capabilities and power.

PCMCIA was originally developed as a standard for add-on circuit boards to support the laptop, or portable-computing environment. Two typical add-ons most often asked for in laptops is more memory and modem/network cards. However, we have seen more than that with the use of removable hard drives, and in some cases complete software applications on a card, a PCMCIA card of course.

Refer to Figure 4-3 to view a PCMCIA modem card.

PCMCIA cards occupy one of three type card slots. A type 1 card is a memory card, either a RAM or "flash" memory card with software loaded on it. These cards occupy a slot whose thickness is 3.3 mm with a 68-pin connector. Type 2 slots are usually modem cards, and occupy a slot whose

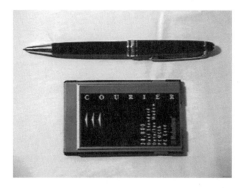

**Figure 4-3**
PCMIA modem card

thickness is 5.0 mm. Please note that a type 1 PCMCIA card will work in a type 2 slot. The most recent addition is the type 3, whose thickness can be 10.5 mm. These type 3 slots are used to support removable hard drives. Be cautious when buying a type 3 card because some can be 13 mm thick and would not fit in a standard 10.5 slot.

Some of the features of the PCMCIA card are its capabilities to support up to 64MB of memory, to support PnP (Plug and Play), and theoretically to support up to 4,080 card slots on a PC. So much for the laptop environment!

One final note is that because of the low power consumption by the PCMCIA cards, they are not only ideal for the laptop environment, but are also used in some "green" PC's today.

## Universal Serial Bus (USB)

The Universal Serial Bus (USB) was developed by a consortium of computer manufacturers. Compaq, Digital, IBM, Intel, Microsoft, NEC, and Northern Telecom were all involved. This system can connect up to 127 different peripherals to a computer using a single type connector. USB will allow "hot" insertion of peripherals without powering down the system. It also makes things easier for the user by doing away with the technicalities of IRQ and DMA settings. This benefit of self-identifying peripherals definitely makes installations less complicated.

USB is fully compatible with PnP type systems and provides the industry for future connectivity. Although many system boards are incorporating this technology, it is important to make sure that your current operating system environment supports this.

## Accelerated Graphics Port (AGP)

The Accelerated Graphics Port (AGP) is a bus that gives the PC's graphics controller fast access to the system memory circuits. This is important when complex video (such as 3D scenes, which occupy large amounts of memory) need to be updated without causing bottlenecks in the existing system. AGP improves system performance by providing a high-speed pathway between the graphics controller and the system memory, thus enabling the graphics controller to execute texture maps directly from system memory rather than caching them in its limited local video memory. A texture map is a bitmap that describes the surfaces of three-dimensional objects in detail.

True AGP-compliant hardware can actually make applications more simple. But PC hardware with AGP will come in three flavors, and software will be necessary for all three:

**Type 1**: This hardware has an AGP interface, but does not exploit its AGP-texturing features. It just transfers data faster than a PCI device could.

**Type 2**: This hardware renders textures from AGP memory, thus the application does not need to swap textures into local memory. The hardware may or may not be able to texture from local memory also.

**Type 3**: This hardware runs best when concurrently exploiting both local memory and AGP memory for texturing. Frequently used textures or smaller textures would best reside in local memory, while larger, less-frequently used textures should reside in system memory. Thus the bandwidth drain on main memory is minimized, reducing conflicts between the CPU and graphics controller.

# Memory

When reviewing the subject of memory in Personal Computers, we have to look at it in two respects. One, we need to understand the physical organization of memory, and secondly we also need to understand the system logical memory layout. The physical part deals with the actual physical components, types of packaging, and hardware limitations of the processors and/or system boards. When speaking of the logical memory layout, we are looking at the mapping of memory, how it is logically divided, and how the BIOS (ROM), RAM, and other components fit into the large memory management picture.

# Logical Memory

Oh how easy it would be if when we referred to memory, it only meant one area with one definitive explanation. Anyone who has been around the microcomputer industry knows that memory has provided us some of the greatest challenges. The logical layout of memory forces us to look at memory in a number of different ways or areas. These are:

- Conventional Memory or Base Memory
- Upper Memory Area (UMA)
- High Memory Area (HMA)
  Video Ram
  Adapter ROM
  System Board ROM BIOS
- Extended Memory
- Expanded Memory

  Refer to Figure 4-4 during the following discussions.

# Base Memory

The 8088 microprocessor in the original personal computers had a 20-bit addressing capability, which gave it the capability to access up to 1M of directly addressable memory. It was determined that the top 384K of this 1M area was needed for reserved system uses. System uses could include system BIOS use, adapter cards, etc. The lower 640K became the area that DOS could use to run its programs/applications. This 640K area also became known as conventional memory.

# Upper Memory Area (UMA)

The Upper Memory Area (UMA) refers to the reserved 384K at the top of the first megabyte of memory on a PC/XT and AT systems. This area is broken down as follows:

- 128K For Video Ram
- 128K For Adapter BIOS
- 128K For System BIOS

**Figure 4-4**
Standard PC memory map.

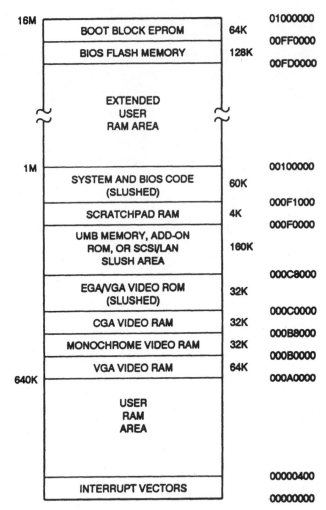

The amount of free UMA space varies from system to system, and this is dependent on the type of adapter cards used. For example, many network cards and SCSI adapters require some of UMA for built-in ROMS or special purpose RAM.

## Extended Memory versus Expanded Memory

It is important to note that the early PCs could only access up to 1M because they had 20-bit addressing capabilities, while the AT technologies broke that barrier by utilizing 24-bit addressing. So we can see that the memory limitations are based on the processor address bus width. Early Pentium processors had a 4G extended memory limit, while the Pentium two extends that to 64G. Basically speaking, extended memory refers to all directly addressable memory above the first one-megabyte boundary. It is important to keep in mind that the processor must be in the protected mode in order to access memory above the 1M boundary. The real mode used in AT system processors allows the processor to be fully compatible with early DOS or PC-type application programs.

Expanded memory was a specification originally developed that allowed a PC/XT system to address memory above the 1M boundary. Expanded memory is a segment or bank-switching scheme in which a custom memory adapter has a large number of 64K segments onboard, combined with special switching and mapping hardware. Simply speaking, a 64K area in the UMA was reserved and this was where the processor could access or work directly with any information. Then this information was switched, or transferred, to another physical memory card for storage. So every time more information was needed it would be moved from the special memory card to the reserved area of UMA where the system could work with it directly. Extended memory was originally designed for the PC/XT systems and is obsolete today.

## Power Supply

All systems require power supplies; however, not all power supplies are created equal. Early PCs were rated 65 watts to 150 watts. When users upgraded and added options, many had to replace the power supply also. This was most frequently necessary for IBMs and compatibles.

In most microcomputer applications, the output voltages available from the power supply are ±5 Vdc (voltage direct current), ±12 Vdc, and +3.3 Vdc on some systems. In addition, many power supplies have a digital output that indicates that all output voltages are within the specified tolerance of that particular supply.

The positive voltages, +5 and +12, are used for logic and motors; and the negative voltage, -12, is used by the serial port circuits. The -5 voltage was used by early floppy controllers, and is only provided today because it is a required part of the ISA bus standard.

When adding components to a system, it is important to know the limitations of the power supply in the unit. These are usually clearly printed on the labels that are often affixed to the power supply. Most power supplies today are switch-mode supplies and should never be opened unless you are familiar with their internal workings. Severe shock could occur because these supplies typically switch a very high voltage at a very high frequency prior to its conversion to DC (Direct Current) low voltage.

A computer interior is shown in Figure 4-5.

**Figure 4.5**
The general interior of the standard computer.

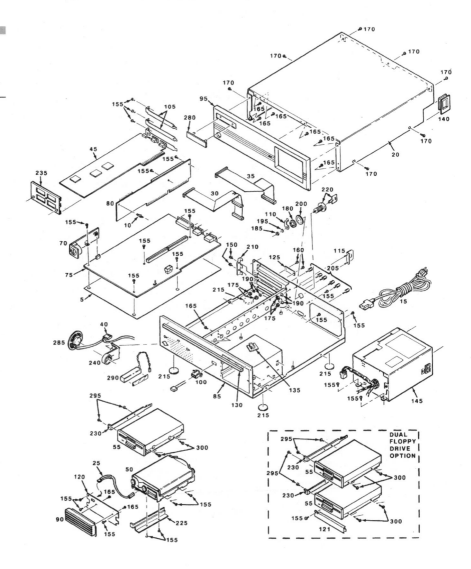

## Storage Devices

The hard drive in any computer system is the primary storage device for all operating system environments, applications programs, and data. It is an important item to consider when purchasing new software because many of today's applications require up to 15–20 megabytes or more of space just for installation.

Unlike the hard drives of the early PCs, which were in the 10 megabyte to 100 megabyte range, most computers today have drives in excess of 1 Gigabyte, with 4G–10G being common. In many business environments today, it is not uncommon for applications programs to occupy one to two gigabytes of drive space. This includes word processors, spreadsheets, databases, email, presentation, and project-planning software, to name a few.

Refer to Figure 4-6.

Today's hard drives have faster data transfer rates, quicker seek times, and lower purchase costs. In addition, the size of the drive has gone from full-height 5 1/4 inch to small 3 1/2-inch drives; necessary for laptops, drives as small as 2 1/2 inch.

Although many hard drives are considered to be fixed disk drives because the platters are non-removable, there are removable drives, like the Iomega Jaz drive, which also uses rigid platters (except that they are in a cartridge). These Jaz cartridges can store up to 1G of information. Many companies that have large mobile or laptop environments use the Jaz drive as a standard for backing-up data. One thing to keep in mind here is that all hard drives will eventually fail. This is something to consider when you put off backing up the data on your hard drive.

The basic components that comprise a hard drive consist of the following:

- Disk platters
- Logic board

**Figure 4-6**
Small, laptop style hard drive.

- Read/write heads
- Head actuator mechanism
- Spindle motor
- Cables and connectors
- Configuration components (switches and/or jumpers)
- Hard drive controllers

The platters, spindle motor, heads, and head actuator mechanisms are usually contained in a sealed chamber that is rarely opened (and are opened only in a "clean room" environment). Other parts external to that chamber, such as the logic boards and configuration hardware, can be disassembled and removed and/or replaced on the drive.

Hard disk platters are traditionally made from an aluminum alloy, for their characteristic light weight and strength. With the desire for higher and higher densities, many drives now use platters made of glass, more specifically, a glass-ceramic composite-type material. Glass platters offer greater rigidity and can be up to the thickness of the conventional aluminum platter. In addition, glass platters are more thermally stable, which means they will not expand or contract with changes in temperature.

Regardless of the substrate of the platters, they need to be coated with a layer of magnetically retentive material, in which the magnetic information can be stored. Two types of media used today are Oxide and Thin-film media. The primary ingredient in an Oxide film is iron oxide. These oxide coatings on the platters are normally about 30-millionths of an inch thick. Thin-film media is thinner, harder, and more efficiently formed than the oxide coating. One of the original design enhancements offered by Thin-film was lower head floating heights, which allowed for greater drive densities. The application of a Thin-film coating is accomplished through electroplating, which can be compared to the way chrome is placed on a car bumper.

Most hard drives originally spun at 3,600 RPM, which is approximately 10 times faster than a floppy drive. Today's drive manufacturers have increased the speed from 4,852 RPM to 10,000 RPM.

The hard drive's logic board contains the electronics that control the drive's mechanical functions—such as drive spindle speed and head actuator movement. Additionally, the logic board handles the signal flow of information from the PC to the drive, or vice versa. Logic boards can be removed and/or replaced quite easily because they simply plug into the drive and are mounted by standard hardware screws.

Read/write heads are the components of the hard disk drive that float over each surface of each platter. These components write information to the magnetic surface or read previously written information from the disk surface. Four types of read/write heads have been utilized in hard disk drives:

- Ferrite
- Metal-in-gap
- Thin-film
- Magneto-resistive

Ferrite heads have an iron-oxide core wrapped with electromagnetic coils. A magnetic field can be produced by energizing the coils or by passing another magnetic field near the coils. Thus, the capability to write and read magnetic data stored on the drive surface.

Metal-in-gap heads are enhanced versions of the ferrite heads. A metal substance is used in the recording gap on the trailing edge of the head. These heads offered increased resistance to magnetic saturation, allowing for higher density recording.

Thin film heads are produced in a process that allows many thousands to be created on a single circular wafer, similar to the method used in the semiconductor industry. Thin film heads offer an extremely narrow head gap, and its head core is a combination of iron and nickel alloy. This alloy makes it two to four times more powerful than a ferrite head core. Thin film heads are used in most high-capacity drives, especially those with a smaller form factor.

Magneto-resistive heads, invented by IBM, offer the highest performance available. These are widely used in smaller drives that offer greater than 1G-capacities. One important item to keep in mind here is that the magneto-resistive head is a "read only" head, and is usually used in conjunction with a thin film head for writing. These heads rely on the fact that the resistance of a conductor changes slightly when an external magnetic field is present. Rather than put out a voltage by passing through a magnetic field, the magneto-resistive head senses the flux reversal and changes resistance. A small current flows through the heads, and the change in resistance is measured by sense current. Basically, these heads are powerful read heads that act more like sensors than generators.

Regardless of the type of read/write head, all drives require a head actuator assembly. This is the mechanism that moves the heads across the disk surface and positions them accurately above the desired cylinder or track. The two basic types of actuators are:

- Stepper motor actuators
- Voice coil actuators

In more ways than you may realize, the actuator plays a very important role in the performance of a hard disk drive. We are not just discussing speed here. Included are accuracy, sensitivity to temperature, vibration, and reliability. Considering all these factors, the voice coil actuator will outperform the stepper motor. The voice coil is faster, less temperature-sensitive, does not require preventive maintenance, and has proven to be more reliable.

A stepper motor is an electrical motor that can "step" from position to position as it is electrically pulsed. Stepper motors cannot position themselves between step positions, but must stop only at the predetermined intervals.

A voice coil actuator works by pure electromagnetic force. It has no predetermined intervals, like a stepper, and has a special guidance system. This guidance system uses a feedback signal from the drive to accurately determine the head position or adjust as necessary. Voice coils are extremely quick and efficient, and also much quieter than systems driven by stepper motors.

The spindle motor is the motor that actually spins the disk-drive platters. These are direct connect motors, meaning that they are connected directly to the spindle and do not use any belts to drive the spindle. A spindle motor must be precisely controlled for speeds ranging from 3,600 RPM to 7,100 RPM, or more. In order to maintain precise control of the speed, the motor has a control circuit with a feedback loop to monitor and control this speed.

## Cables and Connectors

There are several connectors on hard disk drives where you can attach the interface and power connectors. Please refer to Figure 4-7. The interface cable carries the data and control (command) signal to the hard drive from the computer system. There are many different interfaces that can be used, depending on the hard drive. We will discuss these in more detail in the Configuration section of this book.

Power is supplied to the hard disk drives using the same type of Molex connector as utilized by the other storage devices in the systems, such as floppy and CD-ROM drives. This connector supplies both + 5 Vdc and +12 Vdc to the drive. The +5 is for the logic circuitry and the +12 is for the motors, both stepper (if applicable) and spindle.

**Figure 4-7**
Connectors on a
typical hard drive.

## Configuration Components (Switches and/or Jumpers)

To configure a hard disk drive for installation, several jumpers and a terminating resistor must be set or configured properly. We will cover hard disk drive configuration in more detail later in this book.

## Hard Drive Controllers

The main function of any hard disk controller is to transmit and receive data to and from a hard disk drive. There are many different interface types, and they all offer different levels of performance. It is crucial to know the type of interface you are working with at any given time because, in many cases, you cannot mix and match and you must replace like for like when repairing a system.

When judging performance factors of a hard disk drive setup, you must consider the drive's average seek time, and the data-transfer rate between the drive and controller circuitry. Although you may have the fastest hard drive around, your performance can be negatively affected if the controller's data transfer rate is slow, or vice versa. As we discussed in the processor section, we must consider total system throughput and involve all factors in any equation.

The following are several hard disk drive interfaces that have been used over the years, and some of which are still being used today:

- ST-506/412

- ESDI (Enhanced Small Device Interface)

■ IDE (Integrated Drive Electronics)

■ SCSI (Small Computer System Interface)

**ST-506/412**  This interface was developed by Seagate Technologies around 1980 and used for their ST-506 5M drive. In today's software market, this drive would serve very little useful purpose. However, in its day, it was new technology. What made this interface popular was that many manufacturers adopted this standard in their XT- and AT-compatible machines. No custom cables or modifications were needed for the drives, which meant that almost any ST-506/412 drive would work with any like controller. The only compatibility concern had to do with the system ROM BIOS and its level of support for this interface.

Originally, BIOS support for this interface was on the controller card itself. It wasn't until the AT systems came out that this BIOS support was moved to the ROM on the system board. This did not do away with the adapter BIOS altogether, and many manufacturers still included BIOS support on their controllers. When it came to configuration, you would use both BIOSs together, or disable one or the other.

For the most part, this interface is considered obsolete and is not in use today.

**ESDI (ENHANCED SMALL DEVICE INTERFACE)**  ESDI, like ST-506/412, was popular back in the late 1980s, but it is considered to be obsolete today. It offered greater speeds and increased reliability over the ST-506/412, with data-transfer rates as high as 24Mbit/set, although many drives limited it to 10 or 15Mbit/sec.

**IDE (INTEGRATED DRIVE ELECTRONICS)**  IDE refers to drives that have an integrated, or built-in, drive controller. Many of you may remember the hard cards that were used extensively many years ago. These were expansion cards that plugged into the standard ISA bus, and contained both drive and controller electronics. Hard cards were considered to be the first IDE devices.

Reliability was definitely increased because of the IDE technology. Whenever you do anything to reduce the number of logic boards, cable, and/or connections, your reliability factor will increase because you are providing a more compact, noise-free environment. A primary advantage of IDE drives is their cost. Because the separate controller or adapter is not needed, and the cable connections are simplified, IDE drives cost less than a controller-and-drive combination.

Also, because the controller is embedded on the drive, a variety of performance statistics from various manufacturers is possible. When purchasing any IDE drive, please refer closely to the specifications. Because the manufacturer does not have to adhere to any controller standards, it is free to do anything with its product. In other words, some IDE drives are great performers, and others that are just plain "dogs." Advances in IDE technology have spun off more performance-oriented drives such as EIDE (Enhanced IDE) and Ultra IDE.

**SCSI (SMALL COMPUTER SYSTEMS INTERFACE)** The first thing to keep in mind is that SCSI (pronounced "scuzzy") is not a disk drive interface; it is a systems level interface. It is not a type of controller, but a bus that supports as many as eight devices, one being the host adapter. This host adapter acts as the gateway between the SCSI devices and the system bus. The SCSI bus does not communicate directly with the devices, but to the controller that is built into the device or drive.

Some of the many devices that are supported by the SCSI interface include hard disks, tape drives, CD-ROMS, and graphic scanners. Many systems will support up to four SCSI adapters, each with seven devices attached, for a total of twenty-eight devices. Even newer SCSI designs will allow as many as fifteen devices on each adapter bus.

## Floppy Disk Drives

Most applications use the floppy drive to load new software, back up small applications, and load or run diagnostics. Floppy drives have evolved from the 8" disk drives of the late 1970s, to the 5.25" drives of the early 1980s, to the 3.5" drives in use today. Floppy drives are an integral part of the system, although they are slow compared to their hard drive counterparts. Data is written to both sides of the floppy diskette, with each side divided into tracks. Each track is subdivided into sectors.

The early 5.25-inch floppy disk drives were available in the following formats:

**5.25-inch DSDD (double-sided, double density),** which is found either in a 320K or 360K arrangement. The 320K has eight sectors per track, and the 360K has nine sectors per track. These disks are formatted on both sides at 48 TPI (tracks per inch), using only 40 of those tracks per side.

**5.25-inch DSHD (double sided-high density)**, which can store 1.2MB of information. This format consists of a track density of 96 TPI, using 80 tracks per side. Each track is subdivided into 15 sectors per track.

The 3.5-inch floppy disk drives consist of the following formats:

**3.5-inch DSDD**, which can store 720K of information. These disks are formatted at 135 TPI, using 80 tracks per side, and nine sectors per track.

**3.5-inch DSHD**, which can store 1.44MB of information. These disks are formatted at 135 TPI format, using 80 tracks per side, and 18 sectors per track.

In 1987, Toshiba announced a 3.5-inch floppy disk drive capable of storing 2.88MB of information. This drive went into production in 1989. DOS versions 5.0 and higher support this configuration.

The primary components of the floppy drive are similar to that of a hard drive:

■ Read/write heads

■ Head actuator

■ Spindle motor

■ Logic boards

■ Connector and cables

■ Floppy disk controller

A floppy drive typically has two heads, making it a double-sided drive. There is a head for each read/write surface on the disk, and both heads are used for reading and writing. These heads are made of soft ferrous (iron) materials with electromagnetic coils. Each head is a composite design, with a read/write head centered within two tunnel-erase heads in the same assembly. Unlike a hard disk drive environment, the floppy read/write heads actually clamp the diskette from either side when placed in the drive, and there are no sealed chambers. The diskette, heads, and other mechanisms are in the environment, so to speak, and do require periodic cleaning. More on this in the preventive maintenance section.

The head actuator is the device that moves the read/write heads back and forth along the disk surface. This actuator is simply a stepper motor, as we discussed in the hard disk drive section.

A spindle motor spins the diskette in the floppy drive at either 300 RPM or 360 RPM, depending on the type of drive, so it is not as fast as the hard drive. Refer to Table 4-3 for a breakdown of the various floppy drives and their spin speeds.

**Table 4-3**

Floppy Disk Drive
Spin Speeds

| Floppy Drive Size | Formatted Capacity | Spin Speed (RPM) |
| --- | --- | --- |
| 5 1/2" | 360K | 300 |
| 5 1/2" | 1.2M | 360 |
| 3.5" | 720K | 300 |
| 3.5" | 1.44M | 300 |
| 3.5" | 2.88 | 360 |

A floppy disk drive incorporates one or more logic boards that contain the circuitry to control the read/write head movement, the actual reading and writing of information to the drive, the spindle motor, and the disk sensors. Included among the disk sensors are the write-protect sensor and the speed sensor.

All floppy drives have at least two connectors. One for power is a four-pin, in-line connector called Mate-N-Lock (by AMP), which comes in both large and small styles. 5.25" drives typically use the large style, while 3.5" drives use the smaller version. Data and control signals utilize a 34-pin ribbon cable in both edge and pin header designs. 5.0" drives usually use the edge connector, while the 3.5" drives use the pin header configuration. Refer to Tables 4-4 and 4-5 for pin-out and signal information of the 34-pin data/control cable on both PC/XT and AT systems.

**Table 4-4**

PC/XT Internal
Floppy Disk Drive
Interface Pinout

| Floppy Disk Drive Adapter Pin No. | Internal Floppy Disk Drive |
| --- | --- |
| 1-33 | Ground to all odd number pins |
| 2,4,6 | Unused |
| 8** | Index |
| 10* | Motor Enable A |
| 12* | Drive Select B |
| 14* | Drive Select A |
| 16* | Motor Enable B |
| 18* | Direction (Head Stepper Motor) |
| 20* | Step Pulse |
| 22* | Write Data |

*continues*

**Table 4-4**

Continued.

| Floppy Disk Drive Adapter Pin No. | Internal Floppy Disk Drive |
|---|---|
| 24* | Write Enable |
| 26** | Track 0 Sensor |
| 28** | Write Protect Sensor |
| 30** | Read Data |
| 32* | Head Select 1 |
| 34 | Ground |

\* signal originates on the Floppy Adapter

\*\* signal originates on the Floppy Disk Drive

**Table 4-5**

AT Floppy Disk
Drive Interface
Pinout

| Floppy Disk Drive Adapter Pin No. | Floppy Disk Drive |
|---|---|
| 1–33 | Ground on all odd numbers |
| 2* | Reduced Write |
| 4 | Unused |
| 6 | Unused |
| 8** | Index Sensor |
| 10* | Motor Enable 1 |
| 12* | Drive Select 2 |
| 14* | Drive Select 1 |
| 16* | Motor Enable 2 |
| 18* | Direction Select |
| 20* | Step Pulse |
| 22* | Write Data |
| 24* | Write Enable |
| 26** | Track 0 Sensor |
| 28** | Write Protect Sensor |
| 30** | Read Data |
| 32* | Side 1 Select |
| 34** | Diskette Change |

\* signal originates on the Floppy Adapter

\*\* signal originates on the Floppy Disk Drive

The floppy disk controller contains the circuitry that acts as an interface between the floppy disk drives and the system. In the earlier PC/XT systems, the controller was a separate adapter card; today it is integrated into the motherboard. There were also boards that included both hard and floppy drive controller circuitry. Many signals are provided by the controller. The floppy drive itself provides vital information back to the drive. When accessing a floppy diskette drive there are certain criteria that need to be addressed. Here is the order of events when accessing a floppy drive:

- Drive Select and Motor Enable
- Direction Control of Read/Write Head (Direction Select)
- Positioning of Head (Step Pulse)
- Head Select (Side 1 or Side 2)
- Read or Write the drive

  Vital feedback signals from the drive include:

- Index—Helps controller monitor speed (RPM) of diskette
- Write Protect—Denotes write protection
- Track 00—Lets the drive know when the heads are over track 0 for positioning
- Diskette change—Lets the controller know when the media has been changed

## CD-ROMs

CD-ROM is an acronym for Compact Disk Read-Only Memory. CD-ROMs offer two important qualities: extensive storage capacity and fast data retrieval. CD-ROM disks can store approximately 600MB of information with access times up to 380 milliseconds, and data transfer rates of 1.2 megabits per second.

New data-compression techniques, which can filter out massive quantities of unneeded data, have given the CD-ROM the capacity to include sound and image, as well as text storage. CDs are ideal for storing waveform and MIDI (Musical Instrument Digital Interface) sound files, pictures, and video files. Today you can even get full-length motion pictures for viewing on your computer.

The CD-ROM stores information in a digital format. To read or play back information from a CD-ROM, a low-powered laser beam reads the digital data through the reflective surface of the disk itself.

Many of today's CDs meet the Multimedia Personal Computer (MPC) requirements for data-transfer rate and seek time:

**Data-Transfer Rate:** The speed at which the CD-ROM drive reads information from the CD into your PC. For multimedia PCs, the MPC-required minimum transfer rate is 150K per second while using no more than 40% of the CPU's processing capacity.

**Seek Time:** The amount of time required to locate the data on the CD. The maximum acceptable time is one (1) second. Seek times under 500 milliseconds are recommended, and times under 300 milliseconds are available. The total time required to transfer data is the sum of the data-transfer rate and the seek time.

As with any device on a SCSI chain, the CD-ROM drive must have a unique hardware address and a software device driver to be used in the microcomputer environment. Once properly installed in a system, the CD-ROM will take on a logical device name, just like any other storage medium. For example, in systems where the hard disk drive is designated C, the CD-ROM usually becomes D.

The CD consists of a plastic disk with data storage on one side. Data storage is accomplished with a series of microscopic pit and no-pit (level) areas. (The level areas are also referred to as "lands.") These areas represent billions of ones and zeros that form the digital code for any type of data.

When installing any CD-ROM drive, always take the time to read the documentation included with the drive. This document will familiarize you with the terminology and give helpful hints for installation. There are many areas to keep in mind during installation, such as mounting hardware, cabling, and software requirements.

Typically, there are mounting rails or runners that attach to the side of the CD-ROM and slide into brackets on either side of an unused drive bay in your PC.

The required cabling consists of the following:

- **Data cable**: The data cable is a 50-pin ribbon cable connecting the CD-ROM and controller.
- **Audio cable:** The audio cable connects the output of the CD-ROM to either the controller or the soundboard.
- **Power cables**. These connections are very similar to those of a hard disk or floppy disk drive. Use any unused drive power cable that is available in the PC.

Most CD installations require some software installation. There is a device driver required to provide the interface between the CD-ROM and the operating system. This driver will specify the drive letter of the CD so it will behave just like any other drive in your system or network. Along with this file, there is usually a .sys file provided that will interface the CD-ROM to its controller board.

Remember that most installations will also modify the AUTOEXEC.BAT and CONFIG.SYS files. Usually the AUTOEXEC.BAT is modified in the PATH statement and is modified to load any .EXE device drivers. The CONFIG.SYS is modified for FILE and BUFFER size and to load the .SYS device driver.

If everything has gone well, you should be able to put a CD disk in the drive and access it through File Manager.

## Video Displays

There are two primary components of the video subsystem that deserve discussion: the video display and the video adapter located inside the computer.

First, let's explore the video standards that we have seen evolve in this industry, which allows us to understand more clearly the need for all the different video displays, monitors, and the host of adapters that are available. Video adapters are also known as video cards and video graphic adapters.

The following are the standards we have seen evolve in the computer industry:

- MDA: Monochrome Display Adapter
- CGA: Color Graphics Adapter
- EGA: Enhanced Graphics Adapter
- VGA: Video Graphics Array or Virtual Graphics Adapter
- SVGA: Super VGA

These standards supported various monochrome and/or color capabilities, along with different resolutions. Resolution refers to the number of pixels, or picture elements (dots) that a video display can support. When referring to resolution support, the first number indicates horizontal pixels, and the second number refers to vertical pixels. So if we say it had a resolution of 640 × 200, we mean that there are 640 pixels horizontally and 200 pixels vertically. As you may be aware, more dots give higher resolution, and a better or clearer picture.

MDA, CGA, and the EGA standards are old technology and are considered obsolete in today's market.

The Monochrome Display Adapter (MDA) was a character-only type of video with no graphic capabilities. It supported a resolution of 720 × 350 and was fine for the typical word processing and spreadsheet programs of the time. It could never support the graphics required in today's games and business applications, however. Later on, another monochrome standard called Hercules evolved. Hercules provided the same features of the MDA specification with additional support for graphics.

The Color Graphics Adapter (CGA) became the first color standard of the personal computer. It was a digital output and initially was capable of supporting eight colors. Later, sixteen colors were supported. It is important to understand how we obtain the number of colors we do from a video adapter. Because the CGA was a digital output and its outputs for color selection were called Red, Green, and Blue (RGB); all signals could be off or they could be on. If we represent these as binary numbers this means that all colors could be off (000), or all colors could be on (111). Again, looking at these as a binary-number equivalent, our color combinations go from 000 to 111. In binary, that is the equivalent from zero (0) to seven, or eight distinct combinations. Eventually, the CGA standard added a fourth bit, called intensity, which changed our signals from RGB to RGBI. This fourth bit changed the scheme of things from 0000 (all off) to 1111 (all on). This increased the number of supported colors to 16. 0000 to 1111 is the binary equivalent of 0–15 decimal, or sixteen distinct combinations. Intensity, as its name implies, added intensity to the RGB signals simultaneously. Although CGA also supported both text and graphics applications, its resolution was limited to 320 × 200, and 640 × 200. This was only a limitation when comparing it to the standards of today.

The Enhanced Graphics Adapter (EGA) increased both color and resolution capabilities. EGA had the capability to support 64 colors, and resolutions of 640 × 350 and 720 × 350. It is interesting to note how the color capability increased. As we mentioned earlier, the RGBI outputs of the CGA standard gave us 16-color capability. With EGA, the color outputs became RrGgBb: primary red (R), secondary red (r), primary green (G), secondary green (g), primary blue (B), and secondary blue (b). The secondary colors were individual intensity bits for each of the primary colors. Unlike CGA, which applied intensity simultaneously to the RGB, EGA had the capability to supply intensity individually to each primary RGB color. This equates to $2^6$ or 64 available colors.

Up until this point, most color adapters were providing digital outputs to the video monitors. This changes with the VGA standard. VGA utilized an analog output and it was this characteristic that allowed it to take the number of supported colors and increase it dramatically. To help understand this, we use the following example.

If you were to represent a digital signal with the light in a room, that light is either on or off; either 1 or 0. Now, take that same light and add a dimmer switch. Instead of that room light being fully on or fully off, you can adjust it to any level between those two extremes. That is the same principle behind the VGA color support. By making the RGB signals an analog output, you can now have all the colors fully on, fully off, or at any level in-between (like a dimmer switch on each of the RGB outputs). This analog output increased the color capability of VGA to 256 distinct colors. Resolution with the VGA standards also increased to 640 × 480.

It is important to bring up another topic of concern with respect to video. Even though many of these standards improved color capabilities and resolutions, there were some initial limitations. For example, if you wanted to support 256 colors in VGA, you were limited to a resolution of 320 × 300. If you wanted a resolution of 640 × 480, that dropped the color capability to 16. This limitation was imposed because of memory requirements (refer to Table 4-6).

As you can see, any increase of color or resolution will alter the video memory requirements. For this reason you see video boards with increased memory of 8MB or more these days.

SVGA or super VGA provides capabilities that surpass those offered by the VGA adapter. However, one thing to keep in mind is that SVGA encompasses a large number of different capabilities and does not necessarily meet a particular specification. For example, one SVGA card may offer several resolutions, while another may offer the same resolutions with increased color capabilities. Even though they are different, they are both considered SVGA. Because the specifications vary so much, it is difficult to provide a complete technical overview in this text.

Because these differences obviously created some problems, the Video Electronics Standards Association (VESA) developed a standard called the VESA BIOS Extension. If a video card incorporates this standard, a program can easily determine the capabilities of the video card and access it. Today, most SVGA cards support the VESA BIOS Extension.

**Table 4-6**

Video Memory Requirements

| Video Resolution | Number of Colors | Memory Required |
| --- | --- | --- |
| 640 x 480 | 16 | 256K |
| 640 x 480 | 256 | 512K |
| 800 x 600 | 16 | 256K |
| 800 x 600 | 256 | 512K |
| 1024 x 768 | 16 | 512K |

The current VESA SVGA standard covers just about every resolution and color capability, up to 1280 × 1024 with 16MB, 24-bit colors. You still have to be aware that all standard drivers will not work with all video adapters, however, most manufacturers will include their driver with the video adapter they sell.

## Video Monitors

Because of all the standards that have evolved, there have been just as many video monitors (because all monitors will not work with all video adapters). The monitor must be able to perform as the video adapter directs it. If it does not, you may have poor picture quality or no picture at all.

Besides the video colors and resolution, we need to understand horizontal and vertical scan frequencies. Probably the most popular technology with monitors is the Cathode Ray Tube (CRT). (We will discuss some of the other technologies in the portable computer section of this book.) A monitor displays information by projecting an electron beam inside the CRT onto a phosphor-covered glass panel (your monitor screen). When this beam strikes the phosphor, it glows and will fade out unless it is struck again. This means that the electron beam must retrace its steps and keep striking a particular area of the phosphor if it is to remain lit, or "excited." Electron beams continually sweep horizontally from left to right, and then down, line by line, until they have covered the entire screen. The beam is then brought back to the upper left corner of the monitor (retrace), where it then repeats the process. Keep in mind as you view your monitor that this occurs over and over again at an extremely rapid rate. As we mentioned earlier, the phosphor glow will begin to fade in intensity unless it is stuck again.

The process of doing this over and over is called refreshing the screen. Most monitors have an ideal refresh rate, also referred to as vertical scan frequency, of about 70Hz, or 70 times per second. It is extremely important that the scan rates expected by your monitor match those produced by your video card. If they are mismatched, you may not see the image or damage could result. Some monitors have a fixed refresh rate, while others will support many. Those that support many are usually referred to as multi-sync monitors.

So, besides providing color signals to your monitor, the video adapter must also provide horizontal and vertical scan frequencies to drive the direction and movement of the electron beams within your CRT.

**Figure 4-8**
Typical internal view
of video monitor.

Consider the number of horizontal lines that a monitor must draw per second. In basic VGA, each screen has 480 lines and there are 60 screens per second. Thus, 480 times 60 is 28,800 lines per second. That is called the horizontal scan frequency because as it is the number of times that the electron beam sweeps horizontally per second. This would equate to a horizontal scan frequency of 28.8kHz. However, most VGA monitors have a slightly higher horizontal scan rate because the monitor has extra lines that you cannot see, called overscan. So the typical VGA monitor has a horizontal scan frequency of 31.5kHz. For comparison, a CGA monitor has a horizontal scan rate of 15.8kHz, and EGA has 21.*kHz.

Refer to Figure 4-8.

As with most devices, the monitor must have a power supply to power the internal circuits, which it does by converting the incoming AC voltage to whatever design requirements that the monitor has. Other circuits include the interface, vertical, and horizontal circuits. There is also a high-voltage power supply driven by the horizontal oscillator circuits.

Unless you are properly trained in the troubleshooting and repair of monitors, it is recommended that you "farm out" these repairs to a qualified service company or to the original manufacturer. Most color monitors today produce high voltages, in the area of 25,000 volts. This is definitely an attention-getter, should you come in contact with it.

## Backup batteries

Backup batteries were introduced with the advent of the AT-compatible systems. These systems introduced setup menus that stored configuration information required by the system. The settings were stored in a Complementary Metal-Oxide Semiconductor (CMOS) memory component that required power to maintain data integrity. Most systems used lithium batteries to accomplish this task. As long as the battery was good, the needed information was available to the system at boot-up.

The batteries in today's systems are mounted by a variety of methods. Some systems use a socket and battery, similar to a standard AA-type battery; others use batteries with longer leads that are actually soldered to the main board. Other battery styles include the round packaging that we see in a typical watch battery (although much larger).

Note that the batteries that require soldering to be removed also require a special knowledge of soldering. Because many of today's circuit boards are thinner and multi-layered, we need to be careful with the appropriate soldering material as well as the heat used in soldering.

# Adding and Removing Components

In this section, we will discuss adding and removing field-replaceable modules in the personal computer system. One important aspect of adding and removing any component, besides having the correct tools, is to observe how everything fits together before you take it apart. A keen "sense of the obvious" will save you much time and energy. As much as we would like to have all the documentation for the systems we work on, that is not always the case. Observation is key to many areas of microcomputer maintenance.

Before tearing into any computer there are some steps that you might want to keep in mind. These steps will protect you from any accusations that you may have caused more problems to the machine. Please examine the following steps pertaining to installation and setup:

1. Initial examination of systems and preliminary diagnostics

2. Cover disassembly and module identification

3. Identification of main system components and any add-on options

4. Physical installation of upgrade

5. Verification of all configurations and connections

6. System power-up verification

7. Software installations or ROM setup, if necessary

8. Final diagnostic tests (all system areas)

Before any upgrade or installation, run system diagnostics. This will uncover any resident bugs in the system before you perform any other work. You do not want to take responsibility for a problem that was present before you got there. It is important to report to the customer any errors found—before disassembling.

Once you are assured that the system is error-free from a hardware standpoint, move on to the next step. Keep in mind that errors may occur due to previous customer configuration or configuration of the disk-based diagnostics. Also, depending on the installation and/or upgrade being performed, you may want to be sure that the customer has a current backup of all information, including the hard drive and CMOS setup information. Finally, it is usually a good idea to inspect the environment, such as external power cords, cables, etc. These observations may provide you with some insight into how to avoid problems as you go about your work.

Before removing the machine cover, be sure you have followed proper anti-static (ESD) procedures to avoid damage to the machine. No integrated circuit(s) or field replaceable units should be handled outside of their protective wrapping without following these procedures.

Many companies today have made anti-static procedures a requirement of employment, and some educate their customers on ESD procedures. This is so that they are aware of what service personnel should be doing, and can report problems to the technician's company if proper steps are not taken. Although we will discuss ESD practices in more detail later, please refer to the following basic ESD procedures.

Be sure to have with you an anti-static kit, including:

- Wrist strap and attachment cord
- Anti-static mat
- Anti-static bags to transport electronic circuit boards and/or components

The whole purpose of this kit is to allow you to neutralize any difference of potential between you and the equipment you are working on.

Lay out the anti-static mat, and place the computer on it. Put on your wrist strap and connect it to the computer, and then connect the computer to the mat.

By doing this, any charge that has built up between you and the computer will be dissipated through the connection, and you will be at equal potential with the machine.

Besides the static prevention, if you are working on a customer's desk, the anti-static mat will protect the desk from any scratches caused by moving the machine around.

After following the static-prevention steps, remove the machine cover, following any instructions offered by the service documentation, if available, and identify the major assemblies that are installed. What expansion slots are available? Is there any cable routing to be concerned with? Do you have to remove anything to perform the task at hand?

Attention to detail, no matter how insignificant, is important. Refer to Figure 4-9 Damaged PCMCIA Card.

This figure shows the considerable damage done to this PCMCIA modem card. If you look closely, you will see that there is a strip of adhesive on the case of this modem. This modem, when it was installed, had a company asset tag attached to it. However, due to the thickness of this tag, it would not fit properly in the laptop system it was being installed in. So the obvious answer was to remove the tag but not the adhesive. There was no problem until this modem had to be removed and the adhesive prevented it from sliding out of its slot. In fact, even when the machine was disassembled, the PCMCIA card had to be pried out with a pair of pliers. Had the offending installer taken a couple of minutes with some solvent (even nail polish remover), this adhesive could have been removed, thus avoiding wasted time and damage. I must add that it took close to an hour to remove this card and prevent damage to other areas of the system.

After the cover is removed, always take note of any physical configuration information. This includes information about jumpers, switches, and placement of cables and connectors. The most important factor to consider with cabling is what the cabling connects to and how it is routed through the computer system. When removing any cabling, make special note of which connectors the cabling fits into and which end of the cabling fits into the connector. Drawing a diagram may help you to remember.

In some early systems, connectors were not "keyed," and could accidentally be reversed. This caused the system not to work or, worse, could cause physical damage. Especially in all-in-one-type systems (computer and monitor as one piece), cabling must be routed away from any high-voltage display circuits. This is because of the natural tendency of any wire to act like

**Figure 4-9**
Damaged PCMCIA card.

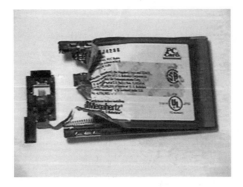

an antenna and pick up noise from display circuits, thus causing communication errors. Also, make a diagram of where the different adapter cards are installed. It is always best to put the cards back in their original slots.

When reviewing any installation, know what type of connectors need to be used, where the board must be placed, the distance needed for cabling, and any software that must be installed in order to make use of all the features that module offers.

## Cover Removal

There are basically two types of covers in the PC environment: the desktop PC and the tower configuration. Refer to Figures 4-10 and 4-11 for an example of each. Ideally, if you have the service documentation for the system you are working on, a few minutes of research can save you a lot of time and trouble. If you do not have the service literature, examine the PC case to determine what screws are actually securing the cover, and what screws are holding an internal component mounted to the frame or

**Figure 4-10**
Typical desktop PC.

**Figure 4-11**
Typical tower PC.

base of the computer. A few minutes of careful examination will usually make this very clear. Do not worry if you remove the wrong screws; there will be an indication to will alert you, such as some component falling inside the computer. On desktop-style cabinets, covers will usually slide forward, slide to the rear, or lift straight up. In any event, please make sure that as you remove the cover, your are careful not to snag any wiring of cables along the way. Even a slight scratch on a disk drive ribbon cable can cause you problems later on, especially if you do not have another cable with you. Always observe how a cover comes off when removing it, since they never seem to go back on as easy.

The tower cabinets come apart in a variety of ways. Again, as we mentioned earlier observe closely how the cover comes off. In some towers covers come off as one piece, others in two, with a side panel having to be removed first. Also, some tower cover panels fit together with a typical tongue-n-groove arrangement that must be fitted first when doing the reassembly.

Once you are inside the unit, there are a number of other components that you need to be aware of, even though they may seem insignificant, including:

- Power-supply connections
- Speaker connections
- Key-lock connections
- Turbo switch or other front panel connections
- Brackets and braces

Drawing a diagram or keeping notes may seem like a major chore, but it can save you lots of time and aggravation later.

In order to get to the system board, and sometimes to remove the disk drives, it may be necessary to remove many or all of the installed adapter boards. Refer to Figures 4-12 and 4-13. First, remove any cabling that may be attached to the board, making sure to keep notes or a diagram. Next, remove the board's mounting screws, grasp the board firmly along its top edge, and rock it back and forth while exerting upward pressure. Once the board is removed, avoid touching the edge connectors and put it safely off to the side.

When you get more than one adapter out, it may appear that each of them looks alike. If you look closely, though, you will always find some distinguishable characteristics to will set each adapter apart: manufacturing stickers, IC chips with distinctive stickers or markings, unusual connectors, etc. There will always be something on one board that sets it apart from another. If all else fails, make your own label from a piece of paper and stick it on the board.

**Figure 4-12**
Internal view of
typical desktop PC.

**Figure 4-13**
Internal view of
typical tower PC.

# Storage Device Removal

Storage devices include hard drives, floppies, CD-ROMs, tape backups, and more. All storage devices are removed in very similar ways, regardless of the type of device you are dealing with. Most drives are also mounted in a cradle, which allows the drives to slide in and out when the mounting hardware is removed. Typically, there are four screws holding a device in its cradle—two on each side. When these screws are removed, the drive will slide out either one way or the other. Keep in mind that all cables (power and interface) must be removed prior to sliding the drive out of its cradle.

Most drives have one or two types of power connectors attached to them. The most common are the large Molex-type connector and the smaller Berg connector. Refer to Figure 4-14. As with cover removal, when you are removing the drive, be careful not to rip out any components, which may be sitting high, that could catch on the cradle or another drive. If you are replacing this drive with another, please be sure to check each device when it is removed for any mounting hardware or rails. The mounting hardware or rails must be reinstalled with the new drive in order for it to mount correctly.

**Figure 4-14**
Molex power
connector.

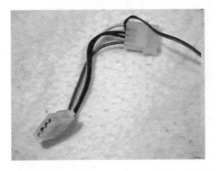

**Figure 4-15**
Desktop power
supply.

## Power Supply Removal

Now that the adapter cards and the drives are removed, let's examine the process of extracting the power supply. Refer to Figure 4-15. The only connections that you should have to remove at this point are the power supply cable connections to the system board. All drive power connections were removed when the drives were taken out. There are usually four screws that secure it to the rear panel of the machine, and possibly one or two that secure it to the bottom of the machine. If there are no screws securing it to the bottom, the supply is typically latched into a bracket. The power supply can be removed from this bracket by sliding it toward the front of the case until it clears that bracket. It can then be lifted out.

## System Board Removal

As with all board removals and/or replacements, there is a fair amount of configuration that is required. When removing the system board, pay attention to all configuration devices, including jumpers and switches. If any of these are moved or tampered with while the board is out of the system, you may have to refer to the manufacturer's documentation to set it up again so it will work properly. Prior to taking the system board out of the case, it is necessary to remove any expansion cards and disconnect any cabling, such as power, drive interfaces, and front panel devices. Please make sure that all ESD precautions are followed.

The system board usually attaches to the case with one or more screws and many plastic standoffs. These standoffs will typically come out when you remove the system board, and will have to be transferred to the new system board if you are putting one in. Please be aware that there also may be some insulating spacers used under the system board. If these are used, it is extremely critical that they be replaced or you are at risk of causing an electrical short to the case.

**NOTE:** *If you have to insert a brand-new system board, make sure the board is ready to accept a microprocessor because many system boards do not come with a microprocessor. Many system boards have jumpers that control CPU clock speed, as well as the voltage supplied to the chip. If these are not set properly for the microprocessor, the system will not work or may possibly be damaged.*

You must also know how to uninstall or reinstall memory on the system board. Most system boards have either SIMM- or DIMM-type socket arrangements. Pay particular attention to the way the memory is installed because most memory is installed in the lower numbered bank, or socket, first. If you are not sure, consult the documentation that accompanied the system board. Memory modules are normally keyed to the socket by a notch on the side or on the bottom, so that they will only fit in one way. Do not force them in.

## Running the Setup Configuration Program

The final step in any system board replacement is to run the setup configuration program. You will have the opportunity to do this after the POST (Power on self-test) has successfully completed, and prior to boot-up. Refer to Figure 4-16.

Many systems have the setup program built into the ROM BIOS. There are certain key sequences to access it, such as CTRL-ALT-ESC, or you may be prompted to hit the DELETE key after the POST test. This information is critical to the proper operation of the computer.

**Figure 4-16**
The hardware setup
configuration
program.

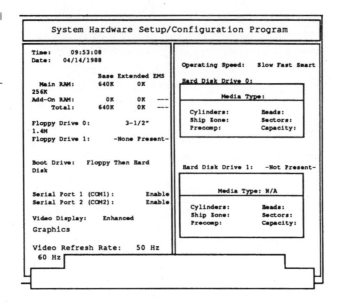

**Figure 4-16**
The hardware setup
configuration
program.

Any module added to a computer system must work without conflicting with any previously installed option. This requires a good working knowledge of the I/O mapping, interrupt usage, and DMA channel assignments. These are referred to as system resources because all components of a computer require their use in order to communicate with the rest of the system. Refer to Tables 4-7 and 4-8 for typical I/O addressing and interrupt usage. Typical documentation with most upgrades will recommend an I/O or memory address, along with a recommended interrupt level setting. Also, there are a many utility software programs that can be run to perform a system audit and show all current I/O and interrupt usage.

In order for devices to work together and not conflict with each other, it is necessary that each have a unique I/O address. This also expands the capabilities of your system because it will be able to add more devices and to distinguish between them. This can be compared to the mailing address of your house: if each house did not have a unique address, getting the mail would be very confusing.

Most systems are configured for two COM (serial) ports and one LPT (parallel) port. The two serial ports are COM1 and COM2; the parallel port is LPT1. There can be up to four COM ports and three LPT ports supported. Besides the I/O address, each port is typically assigned an interrupt request number.

Any device in a system that must request the attention of the system does this through Interrupt requests (IRQ). The computer is always doing something, so it cannot be paying any attention to a specific device.

For instance, let's set the stage for a brief example showing the way a computer handles a keyboard interrupt. For a moment, imagine that your computer is in the midst of recalculating some spreadsheet data. You hit the ESC key which, according to your particular application, should stop the calculations and return control to the main menu. When you strike that

**Table 4-7**

Typical I/O addressing

| Device | Port address (hex range) |
| --- | --- |
| Serial port (COM1) | 3F8-3FF |
| Serial port (COM2) | 2F8-2FF |
| Floppy controller | 3F0-3F7 |
| Hard drive controller | 320-32F (8-bit ISA)   1F0-1F8 (16-bit ISA) |
| Parallel port (LPT1) | 378-37F |
| Parallel port (LPT2) | 278-27F |
| Color graphics adapter | 3D0-3DF |
| Monochrome adapter | 3B0-3BF |
| Game control | 200-20F |
| Game I/O | 201 |

**Table 4-8**

Interrupt Usage

| IRQ (interrupt request) | Device |
| --- | --- |
| NMI (nonmaskable interrupt) | Memory parity error |
| 0 | System timer |
| 1 | Keyboard |
| 2 | Cascaded interrupts (from second PIC) |
| | PIC = programmable interrupt controller |
| 3 | Serial port (COM2) |
| 4 | Serial port (COM1) |
| 5 | Parallel port (LPT2) |
| 6 | Floppy controller |
| 7 | Parallel port (LPT1) |
| 8 | Real-time clock |
| 9 | Redirected as IRQ2 |

key on the keyboard, the keyboard processor sends an interrupt signal to the system board. This is typically routed to a device called a PIC (Programmable Interrupt Controller), which is the focal receiving point for all interrupts in the system and prioritizes the interrupts by the interrupt number. For example, Interrupt request 0 will have a higher priority than Interrupt request 1. After the PIC prioritizes the interrupt, it will send the interrupt signal (INT) to the CPU. At this point, the CPU knows it is being interrupted, but still does not know by what device. The CPU then jumps into a routine where it will save all the CPU register contents in a stack so it will know where to go back to at the end of servicing the interrupt. After that, the CPU will send a signal back to the PIC acknowledging the interrupt (INTA—Interrupt Acknowledge). The PIC, in turn, will now provide the CPU with an address where it will find the interrupt routine to address the particular interrupt that has occurred. In this case, the CPU will request the information from the keyboard processor, determine that it has received an ESC key, and will perform according to the direction of the application program. The application program, in this case, will halt the recalculation of the spreadsheet we were working on.

Interrupts allow your system to handle device requests in a timely manner. Interrupts of this nature are called maskable interrupts, in that they can be ignored if programmed to do so. Although you can program your PIC to ignore any keyboard interrupt, try pressing CTRL-ALT-DEL to get its attention. The only way around this is a cold boot.

DMA (Direct Memory Access) channels are utilized by high-speed communications devices. Serial and parallel ports do not fit this category; but a sound card, floppy disk, or hard drive does. Refer to Table 4-9 for typical DMA channel usage. The only standard DMA channel used in all systems is DMA2, which is used for the floppy controller. Unlike I/O addresses and interrupts, the DMA channels can sometimes be used by more than one device, as long as the devices are never used simultaneously (a network adapter and a tape backup unit, for example). The tape backup unit should be used when the network is not being used, and vice-versa.

Read through all available documentation when adding or replacing components to ensure that you are not missing any critical steps. When possible, read the documentation before you arrive at the customer site. Configuration of the system resources we discussed earlier could be accomplished through hardware switches and jumpers, or software. Examine every component very carefully and do not rush. Sometimes, a more thorough observation of the board or adapter you are about to install may reveal a jumper or switch you did not see the first time.

**Table 4.9**

Typical DMA
Channel Usage in
8-bit ISA and 16-bit
ISA systems

| DMA Channel | 8-bit ISA | 16-bit ISA |
|---|---|---|
| 0 | Dynamic Ram Refresh | Available |
| 1 | Available | Sound Card/ Available |
| 2 | Floppy Controller | Floppy Controller |
| 3 | Hard Drive Controller | ECP Parallel and/or Available |
| 4 | Not present in 8-bit systems | 1st DMA Controller |
| 5 | Not present in 8-bit systems | Sound Card / Available |
| 6 | Not present in 8-bit systems | SCSI Adapter / Available |
| 7 | Not present in 8-bit systems | Available |

After the installation or upgrade, run diagnostics on the system to ensure that all system components are functioning properly. This will also let you know whether all assemblies were put back properly and whether all associated cables have been reconnected. Often, this step is left out in haste. If possible, also have the customers perform some of their normal tasks as a further confirmation for them and you that the system is operating properly. If an error occurs after the technician has left the premises, customers can be annoyed, and it leaves a poor perception of the service performed.

Installing and configuring microcomputers requires knowledge of the software as well as the hardware. Operating system software is, of course, essential to make the hardware perform. Software operating environments include MS-DOS, Windows 3.1, and Windows 95. These operating environments will be discussed in more detail in Chapter 5.

Proper documentation is not always available. That is why it is important for service personnel to be able to identify the various modules. Can you tell the difference between a serial I/O port and a parallel I/O port? We could easily identify a board type by examining the connector on the printed circuit board. Is it 25-pin or 9-pin; male or female? What components are on the card? We rely on our ability to observe. It is this skill, when properly used, which gives us greater speed and accuracy in microcomputer installation, upgrading, and troubleshooting.

Whenever you have the opportunity to perform an upgrade or installation that is new to you, take the time to look at the components involved —whether they be modules, cables, ICs (integrated circuits), etc. As new technology emerges, these modules may perform functions similar to previous ones, although they may not look like their predecessors.

**Figure 4-17**
General I/O ports.

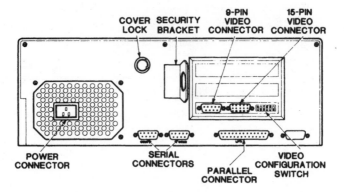

Refer to Figure 4-17. The serial communications port is a D-type, 9-pin male connector. It is important to note that in earlier systems this serial port would have been a D-type, 25-pin male connector. Regardless of the connector configuration, most serial ports that are RS-232C operate between +12 and -12 volts and have the same timing characteristics. There were some serial ports in the laptop environment that operated at the +5- and -5-volt levels.

## Serial Communication

Serial communication is accomplished by sequentially transmitting data over a single conductor, one bit at a time. With only one conductor, crosstalk or interference induced from one wire to another is not a significant factor when transferring data. Serial communication overcomes the distance limitations imposed by parallel communications because of its greater voltage allowance. Thus, it works well in applications over longer distances. The maximum recommended length for serial communications is 50 feet, compared to 15 feet for parallel communications.

There are two forms of serial communication: asynchronous and synchronous. In asynchronous communication, the receiving and transmitting devices have their own clock circuits. Transmitted data is preceded by a start bit and followed by one or two stop bits, which enable the receiving device to synchronize with the transmitting device. Synchronous communications uses a single clock circuit, located in the transmitting device. This clock synchronizes the data transfer within the system by defining the beginning and end of data, making start and stop bits unnecessary. The clock also determines the speed of the transmission. Of these two forms, asynchronous is more common. Although not as fast as synchronous communication, asynchronous communication does not require such complex interfaces.

The best-known and most frequently used standard for serial communications is the RS-232C standard. This standard was developed by the EIA (Electronics Industries Association) so devices from one manufacturer could be plugged directly into products from another manufacturer. The standard defines connector-pin assignments for data signals, control signals, timing signals, and electrical grounds to ensure compatibility.

The primary signal lines typically used in a serial data transfer between a computer and a printer include the following:

- Serial Data Out (TxD), the output line over which data is transmitted from the computer to the printer.
- Serial Data Receive (RxD), the input line to the computer to accept serial data from the serial device.
- Data Terminal Ready (DTR), an output line from the transmitting device that informs the receiving hardware that data is ready to be transferred. This line is usually connected to the Data Set Ready (DSR) input line on the receiving hardware.
- Data Set Ready (DSR), an input line to the receiving hardware from the transmitting device that informs the receiving device that data is ready.
- System Ground, the ground reference voltage between the computer and the printer.

When dealing with serial communication signals, remember whether you are referring to the computer side or the printer side of the connections. For example, TxD (transmit) on the computer side is connected to RxD (receive) on the printer side. So, to verify that the computer is transmitting data to the printer, the technician will monitor the receive pin on the printer. Also, make sure that both devices, transmitting and receiving, are configured identically. All details for serial communications, such as baud rate, number of stop bits, and type of parity, must be addressed before transmission. Typically, this is set up through the software installation. Refer to Table 4-10 for the 25-pin, D-type connector serial port pin connections; and refer to Table 4-11 for the 9-pin, D-type connector for the pinout information.

## Parallel Communication

Refer to Figure 4-17 for a depiction of the parallel connector. Parallel communication signals are separated into two groups: data and control. The data group consists of all signal lines that transfer data, while the con-

**Table 4-10**

9 Pin D-type
Connector Serial
Port Connections

| Pin Number | Signal Name |
| --- | --- |
| 1 | No Connection |
| 2 | Transmit Data |
| 3 | Receive Data |
| 4 | Request to Send |
| 5 | Clear to Send |
| 6 | Data Set Ready |
| 7 | Signal Ground |
| 8 | Received Line Signal Detect |
| 9 | +Transmit Current Loop Data |
| 10 | No Connection |
| 11 | - Transmit Current Loop Data |
| 12 | No Connection |
| 13 | No Connection |
| 14 | No Connection |
| 15 | No Connection |
| 16 | No Connection |
| 17 | No Connection |
| 18 | + Receive Current Loop Data |
| 19 | No Connection |
| 20 | Data Terminal Ready |
| 21 | No Connection |
| 22 | Ring Indicator |
| 23 | No Connection |
| 24 | No Connection |
| 25 | - Receive Current Loop Return |

**Table 4-11**

25 Pin D-type
Connector Serial
Port Pin
Connections

| Pin Number | Signal Name |
|---|---|
| 1 | Carrier Detect |
| 2 | Receive Data |
| 3 | Transmit Data |
| 4 | Data Terminal Ready |
| 5 | Signal Ground |
| 6 | Data Set Ready |
| 7 | Request to Send |
| 8 | Clear to Send |
| 9 | Ring Indicator |

trol group handles all of the control functions or handshaking functions —the signals that devices send to each other to confirm readiness to transmit or receive.

Parallel communication gets its name from the eight parallel conductors used to transfer data at one time. In early parallel communications, the port was unidirectional; today, it is bidirectional, connecting to a host of devices that are both unidirectional and bidirectional.

The primary control signals are as follows:

■ Acknowledge: input from parallel device that it has received data and is ready for more.

■ AutoFeed: the CPU typically sets this line low to tell a printer to generate an automatic line feed.

■ Busy: input from the parallel device that it cannot receive information at the present time.

■ Error: the parallel device can assert this line low to indicate an error.

■ Grounds: electrical ground/chassis ground.

■ Init (Initialize): the CPU uses this line to send an initialization pulse to the parallel device.

■ Slct (Select): the parallel device sets this line high to acknowledge Slctin (see following).

■ Slctin (Select input): the printer is selected when this line is asserted low.

■ Strobe-Asserted: tells the receiving device that valid information is present on the data lines.

■ Paper End: the "paper out" indicator from the printing device.

The remaining lines of the parallel connector are the parallel data lines PD0 to PD7.

Understanding the way signals operate together enables you to examine each signal and determine whether it is functioning properly. For example, the printer (a parallel device) must be initialized by the computer, which is accomplished by the INIT signal. The Slctin (Select Input) is then used to select the printer and the printer acknowledges this by sending a signal back, called Slct (Select).

A strobe signal is used to tell the receiving device that valid information is present on the data lines and, if the BUSY signal does not indicate that the printer is busy, transmission will take place. After the printer has received data and is ready for more, it sends an acknowledge signal back to the computer. Refer to Table 4-12 for the pin-out information on the 25-pin, D-type parallel connector.

It's nice to know about the workings of these ports, but if the cables and connectors are not joined properly, they will not function as they should. Part of this is identification. Even though many connectors are similar in looks and name, they can be quite different.

For example, Figure 4-17 showed the DB-9 and DB-25 type connectors. If the DB-9 is the male type, it is a serial port connector. However, if you make it a DB-9 female connector, it is an older video connector for CGA and EGA systems. Similarly, take the DB-25 female type connector, which is a parallel port connector, make it a male type, and it becomes an older version of the serial port connector. (By the way, DB connectors are referred to as D-type connectors because of their shape, which looks like the letter "D.") Now, take a DB-15 female type connector—physically, it is the same size as a DB-9 connector, but it has 15 pins and is used for the VGA video output. It sounds confusing, but if you take your time and couple it with a "keen sense of the obvious," you will never slip up.

The RJ11 and RJ45 connectors are easy to identify. Most of us would immediately recognize the RJ11 because it is the standard connector from the telephone to the wall jack. It is a 4-pin connector and has a definite snap when you plug it into its mating connector. Because of its construction and shape, it will only fit one way.

The RJ45 connector looks identical to the RJ11, except that it is physically larger and has 8 pins. The RJ45 is typically used as an adapter to tie into LANs (Local Area Networks).

**Table 4-12**

25 Pin D-type
Connector
Parallel Port Pin
Connections

| Pin Number | Signal Name |
| --- | --- |
| 1 | Strobe |
| 2 | Data Bit 0 |
| 3 | Data Bit 1 |
| 4 | Data Bit 2 |
| 5 | Data Bit 3 |
| 6 | Data Bit 4 |
| 7 | Data Bit 5 |
| 8 | Data Bit 6 |
| 9 | Data Bit 7 |
| 10 | Acknowledge |
| 11 | Busy |
| 12 | Paper End |
| 13 | Select |
| 14 | Auto Feed |
| 15 | Error |
| 16 | Initialize Printer |
| 17 | Select Input |
| 18 | Data Bit 0 Return (GND) |
| 19 | Data Bit 1 Return (GND) |
| 20 | Data Bit 2 Return (GND) |
| 21 | Data Bit 3 Return (GND) |
| 22 | Data Bit 4 Return (GND) |
| 23 | Data Bit 5 Return (GND) |
| 24 | Data Bit 6 Return (GND) |
| 25 | Data Bit 7 Return (GND) |

The PS2-mini DIN connector is one that we all should be familiar with. It is the connector most often used with keyboards, mice, and other pointing devices. DIN stands for German Industrial Norm (Deutsche Industrie Norm), which is a committee that sets German dimensional standards. These connectors are round, and come in 5-pin and 6-pin configurations.

As you may have noticed, we have listed two of the content limits from the first domain. This was done because of some overlapping steps when installing an IDE- or SCSI-type device in your system. Many hard-drive manufacturers offer most of their newer drives in both IDE and SCSI versions. Typically, the only difference between these drives is the additional SCSI bus adapter chip on the logic board of the SCSI version.

## Installing SCSI Devices

First, we will look at setting up hard drives from a generic point of view. Then we will highlight some thoughts on the IDE interface and address installation procedures. Finally, we will illustrate some SCSI characteristics and get into the installation process involved with these devices.

Installation of any hard drive, regardless of the controller type, involves eight basic steps. It is important, however, to always consult the documentation that accompanies the components you are working with, so that you may be aware of any peculiarities. Because these are steps generic to both IDE and SCSI, we will discuss both controllers in this section. The eight steps of setting up a hard drive are as follows:

1. Order the necessary hardware (hard drive, interface if needed, and cable).

   Gathering the correct hardware may seem easy, but it can be confusing when you make the purchase or order the parts for your customer. Three key areas to keep in mind are compatibility, size, and speed. Compatibility is key because it is important to know what system board and BIOS are present in your customer's machine. Does it support IDE or SCSI? Most of the newer systems do, but you must make sure.

2. Compile all necessary configuration information (please do not throw anything away).

   We shouldn't have to explain this one. However, when setting up a new purchase, whether it be a new stereo or computer, most people do not look for the owner's manual until something goes wrong. An example many of us may be familiar with is the programming of the common-household VCR. People have set up businesses to do just this. Recently, I heard of a high school student who started a business whose sole purpose was to reprogram his neighbors' electronic devices whenever there was a power failure (from digital clocks to computers). Now there is someone with an entrepreneurial spirit!

**3.** Perform any jumper or switch configuration, if necessary.

This is where that documentation you didn't throw away in step 2 comes in handy. Please follow our directions; we are not making any of this up.

**4.** Install, terminate, and attach cabling to the disk drive.

Please exercise some caution and common sense here. Everything should fit well together without having to be forced, cabling should be routed so that is does not interfere with any other component of the system, and make sure to connect the power cables. Finally, do not put the cover back on the unit until you are sure everything is working. This means completing steps 5–8, plus loading your operating environment before the cover goes on.

**5.** Configure the ROM BIOS setup program to conform to the device.

There is no way in the world that every BIOS is going to know the parameters of every drive. That is why they have fill-in-the-blank setup menus. Where do you find the parameters? Well, it could be on that documentation you didn't throw out, or on the drive/device itself.

**6.** Low-level format the drive.

The low-level format not only tests the disk medium, it will also write out the sector IDs. Most drives only have the tracks and/or cylinders defined during their manufacturing process. It also matches the drive to the controller (older technology). In the IDE and SCSI environments, the drives are actually drive and controller combinations. So it is not necessary to low-level format IDE, EIDE, or SCSI drives.

*CAUTION:* *Some older IDE drives cannot be low-leveled formatted without destroying the positioning information that the drive uses to move the heads. Check the drive label or specification sheet.*

**7.** Partition the drive.

You must partition a drive, even if you intend to use it as all one environment. Some of this comes from the older technology, when the largest viewable partition that the DOS (Disk Operating System) could see was 32Mb. Can you imagine trying to work today with only 32Mb? When you partition a drive, you either designate it as one logical device (drive C:) or many logical devices (C:, D:, A:). Something else that comes into play with partitioning is the efficient use of partitions. The name of the file system in all versions of DOS and Window is called the File Allocation Table (FAT). A "FAT"-based system allocates space to files in units called clusters. This unit can range from 2K on a 100MB drive, up to 64K on a 2G or greater size drive. For example, if you save a 400-byte file on a 100MB disk drive using 2K clusters, you will only use up 400 bytes of a 2,048-byte cluster (2 x 1024). That is a waste of 1,648 bytes in that cluster, which will remain unused. Do that on a 3G drive where the clusters are 64K (65,536 bytes) in size, and you are wasting 65,136 bytes. However, because many programs today contain graphics and sometimes sound, you may not be wasting as much storage as you think.

Let's get back to the meat of this matter. How do I partition the drive? DOS provides a program called FDISK. When invoked, FDISK will look for the drive (by the way, this can be used as a diagnostic aid if you are having hard-drive problems). The menu will show the following:

Current fixed disk drive: 1

Choose one of the following:

Create DOS partition or Logical DOS drive

Set active partition

Delete partition or logical drive

Display partition information

Change current fixed disk drive

Enter choice: [1]

Press ESC to exit FDISK

**NOTE:** *Option 5 only appears if you have more than one disk drive installed in your system.*

Please be sure to follow all manufacturer instructions because many designate a small space on the hard drive dedicated for their own use. This can and will vary from vendor to vendor.

8. High-level format the drive.

Finally, a high level format is performed by running the DOS FORMAT program. The FORMAT command creates the DOS boot record, FATs, and root directory.

Now that is the generic approach, let's examine some specifics with IDE and SCSI.

**IDE**  Earlier in the book, we spoke about the different disk drive control electronics. Now, we will look deeper into the IDE interface. The integrated drive electronics (IDE) interface incorporates the controller directly on the hard drive. You may be familiar with some of the early IDE configurations, known as "hard cards." This arrangement simplified installation because there were no separate data/control cables to attach. One cable provided the necessary signal interface to the main system.

There are three types of IDE interfaces, based primarily on the architecture of the systems where they are used:

- XT IDE (8-bit)
- AT Attachment (ATA) IDE (16-bit)
- MCA (Micro-channel) IDE (16-bit)

IDE drives have an inherent reliability that drives with separate controllers do not have. Less circuitry, less cabling, and a reduced number of connections increase reliability. The XT and ATA configurations have standardized with 40-pin connectors and cable, but because they have different pin-out arrangements, they are incompatible with each other. Our discussions here will be with the ATA type because XT and MCA are no longer in production and are considered to be obsolete technology.

Most systems today, including ISA and EISA, will provide an ATA connector on the system board or in some cases, an adapter card. The adapter card is nothing more than a buffered cable that may be added to the system. There are a couple of versions of the ATA standard. ATA IDE developed in 1989 and ATA-2 developed in 1995. ATA-2 is more commonly referred to as Enhanced IDE.

For an IDE or EIDE installation, you will need to know the following information, which can usually be located in the documentation that came with the drive or on the drive itself. This information includes:

- Number of cylinders
- Number of heads
- Sectors per track
- Location of master/slave jumpers
- Write precompensation cylinder

The CMOS setup menu requires the previous information for the computer. In later models like Enhanced IDE, you can select Auto-Detect, which will determine this information automatically.

Unlike using older drive systems, you do not need to worry about terminating resistors or drive select jumpers with an IDE/EIDE installation. The only addressing to worry about, if there is more than one drive, is that for the master/slave jumpers. These jumpers designate the primary and secondary drive. With an IDE drive, each has its own controller, and the board they plug into is just a bus interface. The setting of the jumpers to determine one master and one slave basically allows one of the controllers, the master, to control both IDE drives. In summary, one drive is set to master, and the other is set to slave. Because the location and labeling of these jumpers vary from manufacturer to manufacturer, please be sure to refer to the documentation that came with the drive.

**NOTE:** *You may notice the repetitiveness of the statement, "Review the documentation that came with the drive." We cannot stress enough the importance for doing so.*

The cable connection to the IDE drive is a single 40-pin cable that has three pin-header style connectors on it. One of the connectors goes to the IDE interface connector, and the others plug directly into the drive(s). Again, there will be no terminator resistors to concern yourself with. Also, it does not matter which drive is the primary or secondary (master or slave), as long as they are both connected if they are present. Some cable arrangements placed the interface connector in the middle of the cable while the drive connectors were at either end. In some of these cases, the cable controlled the master/slave designation of the drives. Again, refer to the documentation.

As we mentioned earlier, it will not be necessary to low-level format an IDE/EIDE drive because the controller is part of the drive. So the next step after the drive and cabling are installed is to partition and format the drive. You are now ready to load the operating environment.

**SCSI**  The small computer system interface (SCSI, pronounced "scuzzy") is not a disk interface, but a systems-level interface. This interface allows you to plug up to eight controllers into a single SCSI system so they can communicate with each other. One of these controllers must be a host adapter, which functions as the main interface to the system.

When you purchase a SCSI drive, you are getting the drive, controller, and SCSI adapter in one circuit. This is usually referred to as an embedded SCSI drive. Embedded SCSI drives allow you to attach seven hard-disk drives to one host adapter.

SCSI is a standard in the same way that RS-232C is a standard; however, the SCSI standard defines only hardware connections, not any driver specifications. SCSI-2 was introduced in 1991, and added new commands and functionality. These enhancements, which include caching, command queuing. and power management, increased its performance and flexibility. Several variations have been defined in SCSI-2:

- Fast SCSI: doubles the data transfer rate. SCSI-1 8-bit transfers are 5MBps, while Fast SCSI 8-bit transfers are 10MBps.
- Wide SCSI: utilizes an extra cable to increase the data path to 16 or 32 bits. Using non-differential cables and interface will increase the data transfer rate to 20MBps.
- Fast-Wide SCSI: gives a greater transfer rate over a wider cable, supporting data transfer rates up to 40MBps.

The majority of SCSI systems use an electronic-signaling method called "single-ended," although there are systems called differential SCSI. In a single-ended environment, each signal utilizes a single wire to carry the signal. In a differential-SCSI environment, each signal utilizes two conductors or wires to carry it to the device. The first carries the same type of signal that the single-ended SCSI would, while the second conductor carries the logical inversion of the signal. The receiving device takes the difference of the pair, which makes it less susceptible to noise and allows greater cable length.

Because SCSI is a bus, multiple devices will reside on it and each must be distinguished from the other by the use of a SCSI ID. This ID, for SCSI-1 and SCSI-2, is a number from 0–7. Please note that the SCSI host adapter will take up one SCSI ID. Setting the ID will typically involve the changing of jumpers on the drive. If it is an external type, it may have an accessible set of switches for ID configuration. If no external selector is available, the external chassis must be opened to access the drive.

The nature of SCSI requires that both ends of the cable, or chain, be terminated. In many older systems, this was a passive terminator; although in many newer environments, this terminator could be active. A typical passive terminator will allow signal fluctuations in relation to the terminator's power signal on the bus. Active terminations have one or more voltage regulators to produce the termination voltage, rather than resistors being the voltage dividers. Active termination is required with Fast SCSI.

Other configuration concerns with a SCSI device include:

■ Start on command

In multiple drive systems, it is not a good idea to have all the drives come spinning up at the same time because this can be a large drain on the power supply. Many SCSI drives provide a way to delay drive spinning to see that this does not occur. During initialization of the SCSI adapter, it will send out a "start unit" command to each of the drives. If the jumper is set properly on the SCSI drive, it will wait for the adapter to issue this command before it will begin to spin up to speed. This string of commands is usually sent from the highest priority drive (ID7) to the lowest (ID0). In the event that the host adapter does not send this command, some drives may delay startup for a fixed number of seconds.

■ SCSI parity

Because most SCSI adapters support parity, this should be enabled. Parity is a form of error-checking that ensures that data transfers are accurate and reliable.

■ Terminator power

Both terminators at each end of the SCSI cable require power from one of the devices. This is usually provided by the host adapter.

■ Synchronous negotiation

SCSI can run in two modes, asynchronous and synchronous. Before data is transferred, the sending device, the initiator; and the receiving device, the target, negotiate how the transfer will occur. If both devices support synchronous communications, they will determine this during the negotiation stage and communicate at the faster synchronous rate.

There are SCSI devices that also support the PnP (Plug and Play) standard that allows the automatic configuration of devices when they are detected in the system for the first time.

Finally, when configuring SCSI devices, make sure you add one device at a time rather than installing many at one time. This will avoid a lot of confusion if you run into any problems. Keep a log or good documentation of your installation, and only use high-quality, shielded SCSI cables.

Many decisions must be made when deciding about upgrading a microcomputer. When it is time to do an upgrade for one portion of the system, it is sometimes best to buy a new system. A prime example of this was the 75Mhz Pentium system we purchased back in 1995. During its three-year reign, the only upgrade we had done was to install more memory. When it came time for a larger hard drive and faster modem, it was discovered that an entire machine replacement was probably the best move. Along with needing more storage and quicker communications, we also needed more processing power to run the new applications we had bought. So instead of upgrading, we went to a 300Mhz Pentium II system.

You will typically find two types of customers out there: those who stay technologically current and those who keep a system until its clock stops ticking. I must add that if their applications have never changed, this is probably a good move. It is simple economics.

## Monitors

Refer to Figure 4-18. Although there are many display technologies available, the most widely used, except in the laptop environment, is the Cathode Ray Tube (CRT) type monitors. This is the same technology we see in our television sets, which contain a large glass vacuum tube. At one end is a set of electron guns; the other end contains phosphors that will glow when struck by the electron beam. It is beyond the scope of this book to discuss the technical details of a monitor. Please refer to the appendices for information on other publications that can provide you with details.

**Figure 4-18**
A standard monitor.

Other technologies available include the Liquid Crystal Display (LCD), which was typically employed by the laptop computers. Some of this technology has made its way to the large monitors that we see in some of the new flat panel designs. They have viewing screens that are equivalent to larger monitors, but require very little depth. In an LCD, a light wave passes through a liquid crystal cell. Note that each color segment, RGB (Red, Green, Blue), has its own cell. It allows light to pass through, but by applying an electrical charge the orientation is altered, which, in effect, will alter the orientation of the light passing through as well.

The three LCD types are

■ Passive-matrix monochrome

■ Passive-matrix color

■ Active-matrix color

In passive-matrix designs, every cell is controlled by an electrical charge transmitted by a transistor circuit, according to row and column positions on the screen's edge. In an active-matrix environment, every cell is controlled by its own transistor, which gives it a brighter image, but requires more power. Regardless of the video monitor display type, our primary concern is matching the monitor to the video output present in the computer system.

When configuring, installing, or upgrading video cards and monitors, you may find yourself dealing with many different video standards. These include:

■ EGA (Enhanced Graphics Adapter)

■ VGA (Virtual Graphics Adapter)

■ SVGA (Super VGA)

As we mentioned earlier in the book, the EGA standard was a digital output; the VGA and SVGA were analog outputs. This is important to keep in mind when updating an old system because it may be necessary to change the monitor as well as the video card.

**VIDEO ADAPTERS**   As with most computer devices, the video monitor requires a set of input signals to display a picture on the screen. With many system boards today, this video circuitry is integrated into the system board, and is not a separate adapter. Regardless, the output is the same.

Observation is key to identifying the type of video output you have. If you have an earlier digital type output like CGA (Color Graphics Adapter) or EGA (Enhanced Graphics Adapter), you will have a 9-pin, D-type female connector on the back of your computer. If you have a VGA (Virtual Graphics Adapter) or SCGA (Super VGA) the connector will be a 15-pin, D-type female connector. Figure 4-19 shows the male counterpart of the VGA style that is connected to the cable of the video monitor. Because technology today is centered on the analog VGA/SVGA outputs, that is what we will concern ourselves with. As we mentioned earlier in the book, the analog signal gave a greater number of colors that could be displayed, which, along with increased resolution, gives us more realistic images.

We are always looking at ways of improving the video in a microcomputer environment. The areas we must be concerned with are processor, RAM (type and amount), and the bus interface. There are many adapters out there and it is necessary to be familiar with them.

Many video boards incorporate their own video processor. There are three types of processors, or, chipsets that are used:

■ Frame-buffer

One of the older technologies is the frame-buffer, where the video card displays individual frames of an image. Even though each frame is maintained by the video card, the main CPU on the system board provides the computing to create the frames. This places a heavy burden on the CPU.

■ Co-Processing

Another arrangement is co-processing. In this arrangement, the video card has its own independent processor that performs all video-related functions. This is the fastest method of all.

■ Accelerator

Between the frame-buffer and independent processing is a fixed function accelerator chip. This scheme has the video board doing many of the time-consuming tasks, but still relies on the CPU for commands from applications.

When choosing a video adapter, it is important to know the difference between the processor types because many applications can be sped up or slowed down with different video adapters.

**Figure 4-19**
Two views of a 15-pin connector.

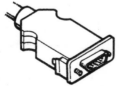

Memory, as we know, can have a major effect on the performance of our microcomputers. Too little, and the computer will run slowly and may have many intermittent errors. Modern video adapters need high data-transfer rates to and from the video memory.

There are several memory technologies that have emerged to meet these performance needs, including EDO and VRAM.

**EDO (EXTENDED DATA OUT)**   This memory is used in both system memory and video circuitry. EDO provides a wider bandwidth by offloading memory pre-charging to separate circuits. This allows the next access to begin before the previous access has completed, offering a 10 percent boost over earlier DRAM (Dynamic Ram) technology.

**VRAM (VIDEO RANDOM ACCESS MEMORY)**   VRAM is dual-ported, which allows the processor/accelerator chip and the main CPU in the system to access this memory simultaneously.

Finally, when installing and upgrading, there is the question of bus design. You must choose an adapter that is compatible with your system's bus design. There are video adapters that will plug into your standard ISA, EISA, or MCA bus; while others will incorporate VESA or PCI technologies. Those that plug into the standard ISA, EISA, or MCA busses are the slowest because they are limited to the speed of that particular bus. ISA, for example, is limited to a data-path width of 16-bits and speeds of 8.33 MHz. EISA and MCA will allow for a 32-bit data path with speeds of 10 MHz.

The VESA local bus (VL-bus) allows the video card to communicate directly with the processor's local bus, which in an ISA systems can allow the board to communicate on the 16-bit data path at speeds up to 40MHz.

PCI video cards add processor independence; faster local bus speed; and, by design, are meant to be Plug and Play (PnP), which requires little or no configuration. For the most part, PCI is what you will see currently and into the future because it is the fastest and easiest to install.

Refer to Figure 4-20. Many older adapters and even some newer ones have an extensive number of jumpers and switches on them. When installing these boards, it is extremely important that the configuration components be set properly. Improper setup may cause video malfunction or cause damage to your system. As always, refer to any documentation that accompanies the video board you are installing. In Chapter Five, we will discuss setting up a video monitor and adapter in the Windows environment.

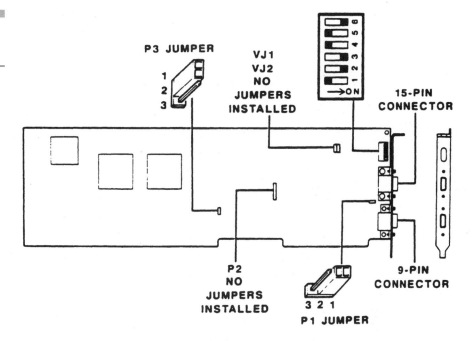

**Figure 4-20**
Various connectors
and jumpers.

## Modems

A modem is a device that converts electrical signals from a computer into an audio format that is transmitted over telephone lines, or vice versa. It accomplishes this by modulating or transforming digital signals from a computer into an analog signal that can be carried successfully on a phone line. It also demodulates analog signals received from the phone line back to digital signals before passing them to the receiving computer. (Thus, the name, "modulator/demodulator" or "modem.") It must do all this in conjunction with a software communications package.

Most computers today have a modem, a necessity in the mobile and laptop environments. When installing a modem, you must first select a location where the board may be connected to the system bus. Some areas to observe are the rear panel access for the telephone line and any physical limitations due to surrounding circuitry.

The typical hardware configuration involves selecting port address and interrupt levels. Modems must be configured to use the serial ports (COM ports) and a particular interrupt request (IRQ) level. It is important that the modem have a unique address to avoid any conflict on the bus with other devices. Please refer to our previous section on I/O Addresses and Interrupts for COM port addresses and recommended interrupt levels.

Most modems today conform to the standards set by the CCITT (Consultative Committee on International Telephone and Telegraph). In the early 1990s, this organization was renamed the International Telecommunications Union (ITU). The ITU is the international body of experts that is responsible for developing the data communications standards that we have today. This organization falls under the umbrella of the United Nations, and its members include representatives from major modem manufacturers, common carriers, and governmental bodies.

Modem standards can be grouped into three areas:

■ Modulation

Modulation is the electronic signaling method used by modems. If two devices are to understand each other, they must use the same modulation method. Three popular modulation methods are FSK (Frequency Shift Keying), PSK (Phase Shift Keying), and QAM (Quadrature Amplitude Modulation).

■ Error-correction

Error correction refers to the capability to identify errors during a transmission. If an error is identified, the modem will automatically resend the data that was incorrect. For error correction to work, both transmitting and receiving modems must adhere to the same correction standard. Xmodem, Ymodem, and Zmodem are a few of the error-correction standards used today.

■ Data compression

Data compression refers to the modem's capability to compress the data, thus saving time and money. Data can typically be compressed to its original size.

Refer to Table 4-13 for Modem Standards.

*NOTE:* *Baud rate and bits per second (bps) are often confused. Baud is the rate at which a signal between two devices changes, within one second. Sometimes a modulation change is used to carry a single bit. In such cases, 1200 baud would equal 1200 bits per second. If a modem could signal two bit values for each signal change, the bps rate would be twice the baud rate, or 2400 bps at 1200 baud. The true gauge of communications speed is bps.*

There are a few proprietary standards used in the industry, too. Please refer to the additional reading section in the appendices for more information.

Most modems that are used today are of the internal type, either in a desktop ISA slot or as a PCMCIA card in a laptop. However, there are still external modems in use. For that reason, we will briefly explain what the LED (light emitting diode) indicators are showing you.

■ AA (Auto Answer)

Indicates that the modem is ready to respond. You must also have a communication program installed and ready to respond.

■ CD (Carrier Detect)

Indicates that the microcomputer and the modem have recognized each other and that a carrier connection has been established.

■ HS (High Speed)

If on, indicates that the modem is ready to transfer data at its highest speed.

**Table 4-13**

Modem Standards

| Modem Standard | Definition |
| --- | --- |
| V.22 | Provides 1200 bps at 600 baud (state changes per second) |
| V.22bis | Provides 2400 bps at 600 baud |
| V.32 | Provides 4800 and 9600Bps at 2400 baud |
| V.32bis bps | Provides 14400 bps or fallback to 12000, 9600, 7200, and 4800 |
| V.32terbo | Provides 19200 bps or fallback to 12000, 9600, 7200, and 4800; can operated at higher data rates with compression; was not a CCITT/ITU standard |
| V.34 | Provides 28800 bps or fallback to 24000 and 19200 bps and backwards compatible with V.32 and V.32bis |
| V.34bis | Provides up to 33600 bps or fallback to 31200 or V.34 transfer rates |
| V.42 | Same transfer rate as V.32, V.32bis, and other standards but with better error correction |
| V.90 | Provides up to 56000Bps. Derived from US Robotics x2 technology and Rockwells; K56flex technology |

bis stands for second version and terbo stands for third version

bps = bits per second

■ MR (Modem Ready)

If on, indicates that the modem is ready to operate.

■ OH (Off Hook)

If on, indicator tells you that the phone line is ready for use.

■ RD (Receive Data)

When flashing, indicates that the modem is receiving data from a remote system.

■ SD (Send Data)

When flashing, indicates that the modem is sending data to a remote system.

■ TR (Terminal Ready)

This indicator, when on, signals that your computer's communications program is active.

The last type of modem we will discuss here is the ISDN (Integrated Services Digital Network). ISDN is a network with an infrastructure designed to integrate voice, data, video, images, and other applications or services. Narrowband ISDN can provide speeds from 56 to 2Mbps (megabits per second), while Broadband ISDN can provide speeds from 2 to 600Mbps. It is different from traditional telephone networks because it is digital from one end of a connection to the other. It also defines a small set of internationally standardized interface protocols, which allows all ISDN devices to use the same type of physical connection and the same set of signaling protocols to request services.

There are many things to consider when installing or upgrading a system's modem. First, you must verify that whoever or whatever you are communicating with has the same standard modem that you are using. If it is the 56K standard or an ISDN type, both ends must have the same capabilities. Make sure that all firmware or associated drivers have been installed on the system. Again, please refer to all documentation and software that comes with the modem. In the case of PnP, this installation is relatively easy, and will be handled quickly and efficiently by the Windows environment. In order for a modem to work, it must have an I/O address like COM1 or COM2, an interrupt request dedicated to it, and a communications program to facilitate communicating with your ISP (Internet Service Provider) or company network.

# Floppy Disk Drives

There are four basic items to keep in mind when configuring floppy disk drives:

- Drive select
- Terminating resistor
- Pin 34—Disk change signal
- Media sensor—sensing low or high-density media type

**DRIVE SELECT**   The drive select is set to give each disk drive in the system a unique address. Floppy drives usually have jumpers labeled 1 through 4 for the drive select. Keep in mind that some disk drive manufacturers label their drive selects 0 through 3. This means that drive select 1 and drive select 0 could each indicate the first drive in the system.

The hardware refers to the drives as 1 and 2, or 0 and 1; whereas the operating environment, such as MS-DOS, refers to them with an alpha character, typically A and B. Each floppy drive must have a unique address. Bear in mind that interface cables can affect addressing. For example, in the early PCs, a standard 34-conductor flat cable connected the floppy drives to the controller card. In later models, IBM added a physical twist to its 34-conductor cable to switch the drive select lines. Drives hooked to this type of cable are both addressed identically, and the drive select signal is "swapped" in the cable.

**TERMINATING RESISTORS**   Terminating resistor packs prevent random signals that are generated on the cable from going to the disk drive. Typically, these are pull-up resistors that hold the signal lines at a +5-volt level, and the active state of the various signals is active low. In this way, when a signal line is asserted, you get a clean transition from high to low.

The rule of thumb for terminating resistor packs is to place them on the drive that is the last on the cable run, coming from the controller. Most drives have an empty integrated circuit socket where this terminating pack is installed. Some manufacturers use dip-switch devices for these termination resistors.

Most 3.5" drives use what is called the distributed termination technique. This means that the terminating resistors are permanently installed. The resistor value in these drives is adjusted appropriately so that the termination is distributed between both drives.

**PIN 34 DISK CHANGE SIGNAL**   This signal, emanating from Pin 34, is used to tell your system that the diskette has changed from one floppy to the next. The basic rule for the disk change signal is simple. For 360K drives only, Pin 34 can be open or disconnected. For any other type of drive, the disk change should be connected. In the early XTs, the Pin 34 signal was always ignored and unused.

**MEDIA SENSOR**   The media sensor setting is easy to describe. Only 1.44MB and 2.88MB disk drives have this sensor. Always enable this sensor. It could be a jumper or a switch, so refer to the disk drive manual. This media sensor detects whether high- or low-density media are being used; and adjusts the recording mode, which adjusts the drive's write current level.

# Hard Drive

To most people, the hard drive is the most vital component in their system. It contains their programs and, most importantly, their data. In contrast to the floppy drives, the hard drive has greater storage capabilities, faster speeds, and is more delicate.

Because of its delicacy, it is important that data on the hard drive be backed up. Surprisingly, many users are not familiar with the term "backup" and need to be educated about its importance. End users are responsible for backing up their own systems. (Keep in mind that we are all end users when it comes to our own systems.)

From a hardware standpoint, there are four items to pay attention to when dealing with hard disk drives:

- Drive select
- Terminating resistor
- Interface type
- ROM setup (drive type) (AT type systems only)

**DRIVE SELECT**   Setting the drive select jumper for the hard drive is almost the same as setting it for floppy disk drives. If multiple drives are being used, all drives must be set for the same select, depending on the type of cable being used. (See discussion of "swaps in the cable," in the previous section.)

**TERMINATING RESISTOR** As with floppy drives, the terminating resistor pack should always be installed in the drive that is last on the cable or furthest from the controller. Do not discard any terminating packs because they may come in handy later.

**INTERFACE TYPE** Several types of hard disk drive interfaces can be used in the microcomputer environment:

- ST-506/412
- ESDI
- IDE
- SCSI

The ST-506/412 interface, developed by Seagate Technologies in 1980, was the popular interface in most early PCs. This interface was used for the hard drive for the Seagate ST506, which was a 5.25", full-height drive, and had the capacity to store 5MB of information when formatted. Later, Seagate developed the ST-412 drive, which was also a 5.25", full-height drive, but could store 10MB of information. The one thing that made this interface popular was its ease of installation. Cabling and hookups were the same between the 506 and the 412, and the only changes were to the drivers located in the setup menu for drive type selection.

Enhanced small device interface (ESDI) is a specialized hard disk drive and tape drive interface, developed in 1983 by Maxtor Corporation. ESDI is a high-speed interface, capable of transferring information at 24 megabits per second. (Most applications limited this to 10-15 megabits per second.) Unlike the ST506/412 interface, ESDI did not require use of a setup program for selecting the drive type. The ESDI interface enables the controller or motherboard ROM BIOS to read the parameters directly from the hard drive.

**TAPE DRIVE STORAGE MEDIA** Tape backup devices are available in configurations that support hundreds of MB and more. They may not be the quickest devices, but they can be set up to perform backups without operator intervention, allowing users to schedule nightly backups.

Tape backup devices can be classified by the type of media used, the interface used, or the software used.

The type of media include the following:

- DC-600 cartridges
- DC-2000 cartridges

- 4mm digital audio tape (DAT)

- Datagrade 8mm tape: Do not use video grade 8mm tape—it can cause permanent head damage.)

- Digital linear tape (DLT): a digital standard capable of storing 6GB on a linear tape, with a backup rate typically approaching 48MB per minute. High-end applications are also available in 20GB capacities.

Emerging technologies also include the Travan media, although these are not covered in the current version of the A+ exams.

The DC-600 units can store from 60MB to 525MB or more, depending on format and the quality of tape used. DC-2000 cartridges only store 4080MB and are suitable for low-end applications. The 4mm digital audiotapes are available up to 8GB; and 8mm cartridges typically come in two sizes: 2.2GB or 5GB. The 4mm digital audiotapes and the 8mm cartridges, because of their larger capacity, are ideal for network server applications.

- Interface

- Existing floppy controller QIC-02

- Small Computer Systems Interface (SCSI)

- Stand-alone QIC-02

- Parallel port (very popular in the small business and home market)

- Integrated Drive Electronics (IDE): (quickly emerging as a viable backup interface)

In early PC/XT environments, with their multiple drive floppy controllers, you could use the extra connector to hook up a tape backup device. Although economical, these were very slow, limited to about 40MB, and the tapes generally had to be formatted before use. The QIC-02 interface, available as a stand-alone interface, was designed exclusively for a tape backup environment. This interface can back up at a rate of 5MB per minute. SCSI allows faster backup rates; however, the speed is typically limited by the tape drive, the software data compression scheme, and the directory file structure.

**SOFTWARE**   A variety of software is used for backup on tape drives. Make sure that the software is capable of backing up an entire partition (a file-by-file backup). This should also include the capability to restore file-by-file. Other important features are the capability to run on a network and verification. Be sure that the software supports the drive and interface you are using. Many packages, because of their support complexities, now ship separate configurations for SCSI/IDE and floppy/parallel.

**TOOLS**  Having the correct tools not only assists you with the job at hand, but also provides the customer with the perception that they are dealing with a professional. Can you imagine what perception you would have if you went to the dentist and he was fumbling through an old rusty toolbox to find something to use on your mouth? You would probably find a reason to excuse yourself from the chair, and make a hasty departure toward the main entrance. It is no different in our field. A clean set of tools and test equipment give the customer a perception that we are A+ professionals, have the proper equipment to effect their repairs, and know what we are doing.

Here are some basic tools and supplies that every computer professional should be carrying. Obviously, there are some others, and possibly more elaborate pieces that could be required, depending on the equipment you happen to be working on.

| | |
|---|---|
| Screwdrivers (Phillips and flat-blade) | Small flashlight |
| Pliers (various sizes, including long-nose) | Hemostats/tweezers |
| Torx Drivers (commonly T10 and T15) | ESD anti-static kit |
| IC Chip extractor / inserter | Wire cutters and strippers |
| Small file | Parallel and serial wrap test connectors |
| Digital Multimeter | AC outlet tester (neon light type) |
| Diagnostic software | Small plastic wire ties |
| Compressed air | Contact cleaner and freeze spray |
| Soldering iron / Solder | Foam or cotton swabs |
| Electrical Tape | Heat Shrink insulating tubing |

There are many generic utility and diagnostics software programs on the market today. Many are very good and they complement your tool collection. However, do not forget about the software tools and/or utilities that are available from the manufacturers. Many have Web sites that allow you easy access to the latest and greatest ROM upgrades, diagnostics, and service bulletins/advisories. Some Web sites offer online registration allowing the manufacturer to alert you via e-mail regarding changes to the product. These changes can be service updates, technical bulletins, or just about anything that would effect how you service that product in the future.

Updating the system BIOS is a relatively easy task. Often, the BIOS needs to be updated to correct earlier problems, to allow the machine to work with newer hardware/technology, and to work with new software innovations.

We know that the BIOS is the interface between hardware, software, and the operating system environment. It is the BIOS that makes up for all the little peculiarities of an open architecture environment. Most importantly, the BIOS is the first software code that is available to the microcomputer upon power-up. It contains all the initialization routines, the POST (Power on self-test), and the Boot-strap program that instructs the systems to begin reading the storage devices in order to "boot-up."

Technical personnel often update the BIOS just because there is a new version. This is not always a valid reason. First, you need to know why there is a new version and what purpose it is going to serve. If it solves a problem that isn't affecting your customer, it may not be in their best interest to update it. There are customers who have customized software images or standards on the installed base, and they do not want any changes to that environment until they have had a chance to test it with their image. Always make sure that there is a reason to update the BIOS and that you are not updating just because there is a new version available. Discuss this with your customer prior to performing the upgrade.

In earlier systems, it was necessary to physically remove the old BIOS chip (or ROM chip) and replace it with one that contained the later version. That is no longer the case. With improvements in the EEPROM (Electrically Erasable Programmable Read Only Memory) technology, we can now do this as easily as executing a file command. These "FLASH ROMs," as many are called, can be updated without even opening the machine.

Most manufacturers have very extensive Web sites, where you can find all the latest information and updates that are available for their particular products. Some of these sites require that you have a log-on access code, and in many cases it can be provided by your employer. At these sites, you will find libraries full of downloadable software updates, BIOS updates, and even diagnostic software. Many are even including their service documentation so that you can download a service manual and print it yourself.

Once you have selected the BIOS update that you need, you can download it to your system. In most cases you will be given a choice about where you want to save it to, and in many cases a floppy disk is where you want it. You can, however, also save it to your hard disk. When these files are sent to you, they are typically compressed, or "zipped," into a self-extracting EXE (executable) file. Once this file is on your floppy, you can execute it and the file will "unzip" itself. The unzipped files will include an executable (EXE) file that will update the BIOS. Inserting the floppy into the machine that needs updating and then invoking the file command will automatically update the BIOS to the system.

It is always best to reboot a machine after the BIOS has been upgraded to ensure that all changes have taken effect. It's also a good idea to run some system diagnostics to be sure that all seems well with the system. Notice that I said, "seems." All potential problems are not always apparent. Only after putting the system through its normal paces, usually by the end user, will any other "bugs" be uncovered.

Users generally tend to think about systems optimization in one of two ways. On the one hand, you have users who never think twice about their system unless there is a specific need to change it. Other users want every new available innovation installed on their machine, whether their applications require it or not. I always refer to these users as the "desktop gearheads." Now please don't get me wrong, I believe that a system should be set up to run the most efficient way for the applications you have applied it to. But with the way technology changes, you could spend most of your time trying out new ideas. If this is your business, that is another story. However, I am sure you do not use your everyday computer to try out all new changes in software, hardware, or firmware.

We mentioned earlier in the text that it is extremely important to keep track of economics when attempting to optimize or update a system. Just look at the typical lifecycle of computer products today. A couple of months ago, as I mentioned earlier, we bought a 300Mhz desktop unit. This morning, when I was doing some Web research, I came across the ads for the new 400MHz machines. Talk about some fast changes!

From my own personal viewpoint, I believe that your dollars are best spent with hard drive and memory upgrades to existing machines. When you start looking at CPU updates, you had better be doing your homework. I am not going to get into bus speeds again, but if you replace or update the processor, is the rest of your environment going to let it perform as it should? And is the change in performance worth the money that is being spent?

In summary, there will always be products that claim better speed, efficiency, and performance. Just make sure these claims can be justified and be careful about using your customer's environment as the test case. Test it yourself first!

The hard drive technology is amazing. I am probably dating myself here, but I remember when I got my first 20M hard drive and couldn't imagine ever using all that space. Now I have a 2.1G drive and it is half full just with the applications I utilize on a day-to-day basis. Back then, I used it for some simple word processing, spreadsheets, and bulletin board access. Now, with report generating, project software, AS400 Service Tracking programs, and more, I wish I had a bigger drive.

This problem was solved by the addition of an Iomega Jaz Drive, which gives me an additional 1G removable capacity. When updating hard drives, please pay attention to size, speed, and type of interface. Review all possible choices, and provide a recommendation to your customer that best suits their needs. It is sometimes easier and more economical to buy a larger drive than you need so that you will have room to grow in the future. Most applications are not shrinking in size. Look to the future.

As these applications grow, they also require more memory. It is important that you have enough memory to work in the environments of today. The average memory size that I see with many customers these days is 32M and greater. Besides the hard drive, I feel that memory is one of the best investments in a computer system today. Especially when you consider the many windows you may have open, the size of the reports you may need to print, and the speed at which you want to get this done. At one time, we had patience and could wait 10 seconds for a job to run. Now, 10 seconds seems like an eternity. Having adequate memory ensures that you will not experience the frustration of losing files or seeing "not enough memory" error messages.

Although high-speed memory for caching is also a good idea, much of this is built into the microprocessors and system boards today. As with any upgrade, evaluate carefully before steaming forward.

In any microcomputer environment where errors are exhibited, you must be able to approach a problem and, by using your knowledge and skills, arrive at a sound and expedient solution. Diagnosing computer problems can be fun if approached with the proper state of mind. Look at the problem as a challenge or a case to be solved. Draw conclusions or inferences based on observation, facts, or hypotheses. Take what seems to be unrelated information and assemble it, like a puzzle, to form a solution. The key is observation. And remember that it takes effort to get your "clues."

All the information gathered during testing and operator interviews must be compiled to arrive at the solution or to a course of action that will reveal the solution. Your determination is the key. You will find it difficult to solve the problem without a little work. Take no shortcuts.

All system problems are found in one or more of the following four areas:

- Hardware
- Software
- Environment (ac power, temperature/humidity, etc.)
- Input error (commonly called operator error)

Today's computing environment in large companies is different from what it was many years ago. Those that have made heavy investments in their technological infrastructure have established complex technology support groups, or help desks, to assist users with both the hardware and software image that has been selected as the standard. These help desks take the first call from a user experiencing problems. It is their goal to first determine whether the problem is hardware or software in nature. They make a problem determination, and then pass it on to the appropriate group to resolve. It may be as easy as reconfiguring software or having to replace a system board.

The easiest diagnosis is usually the system that is totally dead. However, if the system does start up and exhibits an error, it is important to speak with the operator of that machine. Pay attention to what the user of the system tells you. The user may have already opened the machine and attempted a repair, so verify all configurations and any other settings that can be moved, relocated, or changed by the unknowing. A conversation with the end user can provide much other valuable information. Questions that should be asked include the following:

**Did you notice the error immediately at power-up or after the system has booted?** Some thermal problems exhibit themselves when the circuits are cold; others show up when the circuitry has been powered on for awhile. This question also lets you know whether the system failed the power-on self-tests (POSTs) or if some other software-related problem emerged after the system booted.

**Could you continue after the error occurred or did the system lock up?** This question helps determine whether the error is recoverable or nonrecoverable. This does not mean that the error is more or less serious; it could, however, lead to the next question.

**Did the system display an error message?** An error message can be looked upon as the computer "telling on itself." Usually, it indicates whether the error occurred in memory, processing, or during an input/output (I/O) operation. In addition, error messages may tell whether the error occurred in the operating environment or the application environment. See Table 4-14 for a list of common error messages.

The more familiar we are with microcomputer environments, the easier it becomes to recognize where an error message originates. An easy way to familiarize yourself with this environment is to examine operating system user guides. It will typically list the most common error messages. Refer to Table 4-14 for some common error messages.

It is critical to be able to identify the origin of an error message. Did it originate from the ROM BIOS of the computer, from the operating system, or possibly from the application you are currently running? Those listed in Table 4-14 typically come from the system BIOS. There isn't always an error message to help you along. At times, the machine may lock up or halt for no apparent reason. It may do this consistently or it may error intermittently. This is where diagnostic aids or tools will come in handy.

**Table 4-14**

Common Error
Messages

```
+++ ERROR: Please replace the backup battery! +++
+++ ERROR: Bad configuration information found in CMOS! +++
+++ ERROR: CPU failure! +++
+++ ERROR: ROM checksum failure! +++
+++ ERROR: Overflow! +++
+++ ERROR: RAM failure! Address: XXXX:YYYY, Bit: X, Module:
XXX +++
+++ ERROR: Parity Hardware failure! Address: XXXX: YYYY, Bit:
X, Module XXX +++
+++ ERROR: Parity failure! +++
+++ ERROR: Memory Parity Failure! +++
+++ ERROR: Timer Interrupt failure! +++
+++ ERROR: Base memory size error! setup: XXXK Actual: YYYK
+++
+++ ERROR: Extended Memory size error! Setup: XXXXXK Actual:
YYYYYK +++
+++ ERROR: Divide by zero! +++
+++ ERROR: Keyboard not responding or not connected! +++
+++ ERROR: Invalid/No keyboard code received!+++
+++ ERROR: Drive not ready! +++
+++ ERROR: Bad disk controller! +++
+++ ERROR: DMA overrun! +++
+++ ERROR: Disk not bootable! +++
+++ ERROR: Sector not found! +++
+++ ERROR: CRC error! +++
+++ ERROR: Invalid address mark detected! +++
+++ ERROR: Seek failure! +++
+++ ERROR: Invalid data read! +++
No system
Not a bootable partition
+++ Non-maskable interrupt! +++
+++ ERROR: Wild Hardware Interrupt! +++
FATAL: Internal Stack Failure, System Halted
```

**Can you reproduce the error?** Error duplication is a key area to explore. It may show that operator error is causing the problem. Even if it is not operator error, it can give you valuable information as to what was occurring at the time of the error.

**Is the error intermittent or does it happen repetitively?** Repetitive errors are easier to track than intermittent ones are. See if the error occurs during most operations or just certain ones. Even if an error occurs randomly during different operations, it may point to some common denominators.

**What operation were you involved in when the error occurred, or what task were you doing?** If the operator was entering data, it could be a keyboard-processing error. If the operator was attempting to print, there might be a problem with the printer or I/O port. An error while saving to file could point to a faulty drive. Questions like these can tell you where the problem may be and if it might be environmental or the of operator input.

When diagnosing a microcomputer, you may need to verify the power being fed into the computer, as well as the output of the internal power supply. As technicians, we cannot always rely on the light-emitting diode (LED) indicators, which may also be faulty.

Here is an instrument that may be of help. The most common instrument for measuring voltage is the DVM, or digital voltmeter. The voltmeter is also called a multimeter because it measures not only voltage, but also current and resistance.

Voltage is defined as a difference of potential. So when you measure voltage, it is always in reference to some point. That is why the multimeters have two leads, or probes. One is typically the color black for ground, or common. And the other is red for the hot, or positive, side.

When measuring an unknown voltage, always set the scale on the multimeter to the highest setting. You do not want to damage a meter if the voltage you are measuring is higher than the setting on the meter.

Place the black lead, or probe, on the ground or on the chassis of the machine, and put the red probe on the wire or the other point you are measuring. Once you see the voltage reading, you may adjust the scale setting downward to obtain a more accurate reading.

In the microcomputer system, the direct current (dc) voltages you typically see are ±5 Vdc or ±12 Vdc. The +5 voltage is used for most logic, and the ±12 voltage is used for disk drive motors and serial communications.

When verifying power from a wall outlet, make sure the meter is set for the AC (alternating current) mode. Otherwise, you may damage the meter.

If you are fortunate enough to have power, then some of the diagnostic aids that are available may come in handy. First, there is diagnostic software, or, as they more commonly known, diagnostics. All computers have some built-in diagnostics, which is known as the POST (Power on self-test). These simple tests are executed every time you cold-boot your computer or when the machine starts from a power-off condition. Other testing software can either come from the manufacturer of the PC or from third-party companies. Regardless of which one you choose, it is always important to have a copy of the latest version of the diagnostics.

Let's take a look at the different areas of the microcomputer system, and list some of the error messages or other indications you might see if there are problems.

## System Board/Processor/Memory

Error messages related to the following areas could indicate problems with the system board:

- Interrupt errors (including NMI)
- ROM Checksum
- Battery or CMOS failure
- Memory size error (CMOS mismatch)

- System Timer Failure
- Memory Parity Failure
- Cache memory errors

These errors will have more catastrophic effects on the system then other types of errors. Also, many of these errors are usually caught during the self-test part of the system startup sequence. Processor and memory errors are notorious for giving you random unrelated problems. It is best to test for these by using diagnostic software, providing the machine will allow you to load it.

## Keyboards/Mouse/Track Ball/Pen/Touch Pad

The first indication that there is a problem with one of these devices is when you try to use it and it doesn't appear to work. However, in many cases it may have told on itself when the machine was booting (for example, a quick message that says, "No mouse found" and therefore, does not load the software driver necessary to operate the device). Depending on the type of device, some may utilize a COM port, while others may use a dedicated input port.

It is important to know the type and the software necessary to control it. Usually, the easiest test is to try another one. If a new one works, then run some diagnostic tests and be on your way. If a new one does not solve the issue, then you have to examine the situation more thoroughly and check all other possibilities. This would include any and all connections along with any configuration items, both in hardware and software. Depending on the operating system you are running, there are different ways to load and configure devices. We will deal with this more in Chapter 5, when we discuss the DOS/Windows environment.

## Floppy Drives

When diagnosing any failure of storage media, you must take into account everything involved with the operation you were performing when the error occurred. In the case of a floppy drive access, whether read or write, a number of things are involved:

- Diskettes
- Disk drive
- Interface cable
- Power cables
- Floppy controller card
- System board
- Operating environment configuration
- Software setup
- Firmware setup (code in the ROM)

Hardware failures can involve any circuitry within the disk drive itself or the controller card that is plugged into the expansion slot of a microcomputer. The disk drive is comprised of electronic circuitry, mechanical assemblies, and drive motors. That is why, with any diagnosis, the first step of observing is so important. Look for loose cable, broken belts (on some earlier drives), or even dirty read/write heads. Often, a few minutes spent observing can save you hours of effort.

Any time you encounter a floppy drive error, the easiest test is to try another diskette. Diskettes can be corrupted, both magnetically and physically. Or, if they were written to by another device, there may be some incompatibility between the two devices. Next, check another simple thing: are the devices getting power? Check to see if all related boards and/or modules are properly seated in their connectors and that the contacts are not dirty, causing a bad connection.

If everything is connected and properly installed, including any software, and the errors occur with more than one diskette, the problem may be with the disk drive or the controller. If there is more than one floppy drive and the other drive works, it is less likely that the controller is at fault.

## Hard Drives

In the case of a hard drive, the elements to consider include:

▪ Hard drive

▪ Interface cable

▪ Power cables

▪ Hard drive controller card if applicable

▪ System board

▪ Operating environment configuration

▪ Software setup

▪ Firmware setup (code in the ROM)

The hard disk drive is comprised of electronic circuitry, mechanical assemblies, and drive motors. Unlike the floppy drive, the hard disk drive is a sealed unit and cannot be opened outside of a special "clean room." However, you can and should make sure that all cables and connections are properly made. If any connections are in doubt, remove the cable and/or connector and remake the connection.

If the hard drive fails to boot, take a bootable floppy disk and boot the system on the floppy drive. When you get to the A> prompt, try to log over to the hard drive. If that is successful, it is likely that only the "boot track" on the hard drive is bad, or corrupted. If this is not successful, the problem may lie in the hard drive itself, or possibly the ROM setup code. As always, verify any configuration settings before replacing any hardware components.

In the Windows 95 environment, you need a boot disk, also known as a Startup diskette. Remember when you installed Win 95, it asked you if you wanted to create a Startup diskette. Of course everyone said yes and made one. Didn't you?

## Tape Media

In the case of tape media, the elements to consider include:

- Tape cartridges or media
- Tape drive
- Interface cable
- Power cables
- Interface or controller card
- System board
- Operating system environment
- Software setup
- Firmware setup (code in the ROM)

The tape drive is comprised of electronic circuitry, mechanical assemblies, and drive motors.

Any time a tape drive error occurs, the easiest test is to try another tape cartridge. Like diskettes, tape cartridges can be corrupted, both magnetically and physically. Or, if they were written to by another device, there may be some incompatibility between the two devices.

If another tape cartridge works, then discard the previous one that caused the error.

If the tape cartridge is not the problem, carefully inspect the interface and power connections. Verify the configuration of the installed hardware. Finally, if necessary, replace any defective components.

## Video Monitors

Many video-related errors are easy to spot. Either you have a correct display with all the colors you expect; or the picture is distorted, missing, or not in color. Other display-related errors could revolve around video memory errors or I/O-addressing concerns. These more-complex errors could cause your machine to lock up, or cause memory or I/O-related error messages. Usually disk-based diagnostics can help to uncover these.

The first thing to check is the most obvious. Someone may have turned the brightness and contrast controls all the way down on the monitor. The customer may be sure he has a dead monitor. A simple readjustment will bring this "dead" video monitor back to life. Refer to Figure 4-21.

**Figure 4-21**
Various monitor
controls, including
power LED, contrast,
brightness, and
power switch.

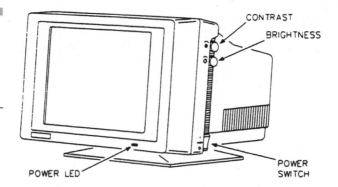

**Figure 4-21**
Various monitor controls, including power LED, contrast, brightness, and power switch.

The next question you need to answer with video displays and/or adapters is whether the problem is in the video adapter, the computer system, or the video monitor itself. Usually, the quickest way to find the answer is to replace the video monitor with another of the same kind. If the problem is solved with the new monitor, most likely the previous video monitor has a fault.

If the problem is in the video monitor, you must know what type of maintenance support is available for that device. Many monitors are what is known as "whole unit swap," and cannot be fixed on-site. In these cases, the monitor is exchanged with a whole working unit, and the defective one is returned to the manufacturer for repair.

Specialized knowledge is needed to go inside a video monitor to repair it. The inside is a high-voltage environment, and inexperienced repair people can cause harm to themselves or to the equipment.

If you have never been trained in video monitor service, leave it to an experienced individual. Problems with video adapters are easily solved by replacing the adapter card. However, before replacing the card, verify all related configurations, because a setup error or jumper/switch setting can give you the same result.

Refer to Figure 4-22 for a typical troubleshooting chart on video monitor.

## Sound Card/Audio

I couldn't imagine a computer today without a sound card. Whether you are utilizing it for your multimedia applications, or listening to your favorite CD, it is likely that your computer contains an audio component. How can you tell if it is working, and what effect can it have on any other components in the system?

**Figure 4-22**
A typical
troubleshooting
chart.

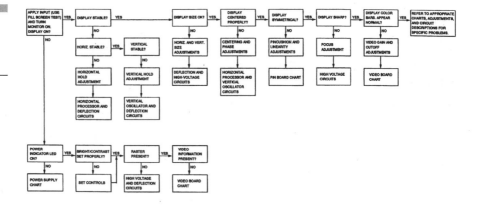

There are two types of sound card problems. Those that were working and now don't. And those new installs or upgrades that don't want to work. Typically, it is quite easy to know if your sound card has failed. Either you hear sounds coming from it, or you don't.

One of the most common problems occurs during upgrades and new installs. When a sound card is installed, you need to select IRQs (Interrupt requests), I/O addressing, or DMA channel selection. The problem you may run into is a conflict of resources between other devices installed in the system. One of the safest methods of installation is to take the other option cards out and let the sound card have first choice of the interrupts and I/O addresses. Then configure everything around that.

Here are some helpful hints with regard to other problems.

No sound: Make sure that the speakers are connected; if they are the amplified type, make sure that they are powered and/or the volume control is turned up. Also, make sure that any multimedia application settings are not keeping you from hearing the sound.

One-sided sound: Check all connections and make sure the proper device driver is loaded.

Scratchy sound: This could be caused by interference from other cards in the system, or the speakers may be too close to the video monitor. This can also be caused by poor quality sound cards or add-ons.

Another thing to keep in mind is that many sound cards include connections for both the CD-ROM and its audio cable. You may have a problem where the sound is working fine, but the CD-ROM appears to be acting up. Don't discount the sound card.

# Modems

When diagnosing modem problems, some easy spot-checks may save you a significant amount of time. Make sure that all external cabling is properly connected. This includes the connections of the phone line, both at the computer and wall receptacle. Is the phone line active?

Beyond these basics, you will want to have diagnostic software that is capable of testing the communications ports on the system. The modem is installed as a COM device (serial port), and some simple diagnostics will determine if that particular I/O port is functioning.

A number of disk-based diagnostic programs are available, including Check-It and QA-Plus. However, please realize that the diagnostics are limited to testing the particular I/O port that the modem is connected to.

If the I/O port is all right, the best test for the modem is to use whatever communications software you have, including the Terminal program available in Windows, and attempt to communicate with the modem or send a fax. Be sure you have the correct settings for baud rate, number of bits, and communications protocol.

Once it has been determined that the modem is at fault, the only repair step is to remove and replace the modem. Again, pay attention to all cabling and/or other devices that are moved during the replacing of your modem.

# BIOS

If there is ever a failure with a BIOS ROM, the POST test should pick this up and report a checksum error. When a BIOS chip is programmed, all the locations in ROM are summed together, ignoring the carry bits. The subsequent value is called its checksum and is stored at a location in ROM. During POST testing, all locations of ROM are summed together and the resulting value is compared to the value, or checksum, that was stored earlier. If there is a match, no problem. If the answers do not compare, then a checksum error is reported. This tells you that something within that ROM changed. Because no values in ROM should be changing, it is important that you replace the ROM, or if necessary, the system board.

# Device Drivers

The only way to correct a faulty device driver is to reload it. Often, it is the only way to discover it was bad. Never take anything for granted: if you have checked everything else, and the device still does not work, re-load the device driver.

## Repairing Displays

Today, video displays are typically swapped out as whole units and sent back to the original manufacturer for repair. Before sending any video display back for repair, diagnose whether the problem is in the video display or the video board of the computer. This can be accomplished by trying another video display in its place, or there are various test devices on the market that will provide various video outputs and test patterns.

If you are in a company where repair is done to the field replaceable unit (FRU), it is important that you know the various modules you may find inside a video display. The most common modules in a video display are:

**Interface logic board:** The interface module handles the input video signal from the computer, and amplifies and modifies it to drive the red, green, and blue electron guns of the CRT. This module also assists in handling the horizontal and vertical sweep signals.

**Horizontal oscillator/high voltage power supply:** The horizontal oscillator assists in developing the high voltage required by the CRT.

**Power supply:** A power supply is required to supply all necessary circuit and reference voltage for both the digital and analog portions of the internal circuitry.

**CRT (Cathode Ray Tube):** The CRT is the large display tube that actually forms the final display that is viewed. It is a glass tube sealed in a vacuum. Some of the main components of the tube include the electron guns, horizontal/vertical yokes, and anode (high-voltage) lead input. Because the high-voltage levels in color video displays can run anywhere from 20,000 to 25,000 volts, it is extremely important to understand the proper safety measures. Always refer to any service documentation on a video display before opening the unit.

**Parallel ports/scanners:** In this scenario, we have a device connected to the parallel port of the computer. One thing to keep in mind when diagnosing any computer-related problem is that it is important to imagine all the possible components in the machine that could cause a problem. For example, if your scanner does not work and it is connected to a parallel or serial port, here is a list of items that could cause a problem:

- The scanner itself
- Cable from scanner to computer (including any internal cabling)
- Parallel or Serial port problem
- Hardware of Software Configuration

Please keep in mind that there could be a number of things pointing to the specific area that needs to be addressed. The scanner may appear to work, but distort the image it is reporting to the computer. Or it may halt during the middle of an operation. Paying attention to this detail will reveal to you some insight into the problem. As with most problems, eliminate the obvious first. A simple diagnostic program with a wrap-around test plug could easily indicate to you whether or not you have a problem with the parallel or serial port. Many printers and scanners today have self-tests that could help you determine whether the device or communications to the device could be the problem. By dissecting it one piece at a time, you will not leave any stone unturned.

## CD-ROMs

Some CD-ROM drives and controller boards are provided with diagnostic programs. Read the information that comes with your hardware and software components to know what is available. If diagnostics are provided, run them and view the results.

Some of the common symptoms or errors are as follows:

- Computer does not start
- Computer starts but does not recognize CD-ROM
- CD-ROM drive cannot read disk correctly

**COMPUTER DOES NOT START**   When a working computer stops working after an upgrade, it is typically due to a cable or connector problem. Verify all connections that had to be added or disconnected and re-connected.

**COMPUTER STARTS BUT DOES NOT RECOGNIZE CD-ROM**
There are a few possible causes here. First, you may need to check the installation of the software device drivers. If any are not loading, the computer will not communicate with the CD-ROM. Second, verify that the settings of your controller card are not conflicting with any other boards in the system. Many utility software packages contain audit programs to show you how your particular system is utilizing its resources.

**CD-ROM DRIVE CANNOT READ DISK CORRECTLY** Verify that there is a disk in the tray and that it has the correct side facing up. Are you using a CD of the correct data format? Check cable connections. Verify the configuration settings of the controller board.

When problems occur with your CD-ROM, there are only a few things that might need replacing or reinstalling: your CD-ROM drive, controller card, cabling, or software installation. If you are replacing the drive, keep the drive rails off the defective drive.

## Summary

Once the microcomputer environment has been diagnosed, you must make a hypothesis or an educated guess about to what is causing the problem. In any repair environment, it is important to be cautious as you disassemble the microcomputer. Follow ESD procedures. Also, before you start to remove any components from a system, be sure you know the placement of every module within the enclosure and the routing of any cabling. Many times, modules have to be removed in order to gain access to others. This is especially true in the laptop/notebook environment.

You must be concerned with all fasteners and their size, internal shielding, cable routing, and external case pieces. Take no shortcuts—a misplaced fastener or shield might cause improper operation once you reassemble the unit. If necessary, keep a piece of paper with you, and make notes or drawings as you disassemble so there is no guesswork when you have to reassemble.

After you replace the suspect module, power up the system and verify the proper POST, system initialization, and booting of the operating environment. After the system has booted, load a disk-based diagnostic and run a complete system check to ensure that the original problem has been solved, and that any other modules or cables that were removed have been properly replaced. This includes all peripherals disconnected during your analysis process.

If the problem appears to be solved, it is time to load the customer's applications, and ask the customer to run the computer through its paces to uncover any latent software or configuration errors. If the problem persists, it is time to re-diagnose the situation and make another educated guess.

If the customer is still experiencing errors, take a closer look at his or her software. Does the error occur in all applications or just one? What type of error is occurring? If it involves communicating with a printer or other peripheral, it may be nothing more than an incorrect or corrupted device driver. If the error involves memory-type errors or system lockups, it may be related to memory management and/or high memory type drivers. In the case of brand new software, it could be insufficient memory. It is important to methodically wade through all possible scenarios to uncover the source of a problem.

However, do not discount the possibility that the parts you have used for replacement could be defective. Although manufacturers have many quality procedures in place, there are times when even new parts fail.

## Microcomputer Safety

When dealing with electronic circuitry, whether at a component level or a module level, it is important to understand all areas of safety. If you do not follow safe practices, you could damage the computer system and injure yourself.

Typically, two labels are used on electronic equipment to inform service personnel and end users about the possibility of equipment damage and threat to personal safety. A Caution will typically alert you to potential equipment damage; a Warning will alert you to the danger of personal injury that could result from not following a set of directions. See Figure 4-23 for an example.

Electronic equipment offer many opportunities for accidents. Not only do they pose an ever-present danger of electric shock, but many components get very hot and can burn you. In addition, some components can actually explode if wired incorrectly or if neighboring components fail. Thus, you must protect yourself to avoid eye injury or other physical harm.

The following precautions form a foundation for safety. Following them will not prevent all accidents from occurring, but it should help reduce the likelihood to an acceptable level. You must constantly be aware of potential hazards and periodically check your actions against these safety precautions.

**Figure 4-23**
The Caution symbol appearing on electronic equipment.

Do not wear jewelry such as rings, watches, and bracelets at the workplace. Most of these objects are conductive, and will cause a shock if they contact both you and the energized circuit. In addition, they pose the hazard of catching on components or on moving electromechanical devices.

Always be aware of possible electrical paths through your body. If you must work on energized equipment, use one hand at a time. This prevents a current from passing from one hand, through your body to the other hand. Often it is wise to rest part of your hand on the chassis while supporting a test probe. This way, if there is a shock, it will go through your hand and not your heart.

Be aware of the threat of burn. Components such as transistors and resistors may become very hot. Don't touch them with bare hands, even after the power has been turned off.

Plug the test equipment into the same outlet used by the computer and peripherals. Otherwise, you risk the danger of connecting to the opposite phase of the power line. This would result in a 220-volt difference in power connections. Although this is normally not a problem, there is a possibility that one outlet is out of phase with another.

Never remove circuit boards from any computer system while the power is on. Removing boards with the power on may cause serious damage to the computer system.

## Electrostatic Discharge (ESD)

Static electricity is a stationary form of electrical charge. It is a transfer of electrons from one body to another. The magnitude of the charge depends on the size, shape, composition, and electrical properties of the substances that make up the bodies. This transfer is called electrostatic discharge (ESD).

The transfer of a static charge cannot be felt by a person if it is less than 3,500 volts. However, most electronic components are sensitive to static charge well below this level. Industry experts believe that hundreds of millions of dollars worth of damage is caused each year by static discharge. Two types of damage can result from ESD: catastrophic damage, when a component is rendered totally ineffective from a static discharge; and degradation, when a component is weakened by static discharge.

Degradation is by far the bigger nuisance because it may cause premature failure of a component—sometimes days, weeks, or even months after the static discharge.

Another problem with degradation is that it can affect the operating characteristics of an electronic system. The component may pass diagnostic tests, but still cause many intermittent failures. Modules or boards that have suffered degradation end up costing more because it is too difficult to spot them in inventory, and these modules will typically pass most basic diagnostics.

Degradation is so common because of the prevalence of static electricity in the environment. To give you an example of the voltage that can be generated, a person walking across a carpet in a room with 55% relative humidity can generate up to 7,500 volts. Lower the humidity to 40% and the voltage may increase to 15,000 volts. Keep in mind that you will not typically see a spark until the discharge reaches a 5,000-volt level.

Anyone who handles an electronic component without following ESD procedures can cause damage, and many people handle each part during its manufacture and shipping process. By the time you, the technician, receive the part, it has passed through many hands. Anywhere along the line, if someone mishandled the device, ESD could have caused degradation. And if everyone else followed their procedures and you do not, problems can still result.

When we speak of ESD procedures, we refer to the material used in packing as well as to the special techniques used by the personnel of these various concerns. As a service technician, you should use a static wrist strap when dealing with the circuit boards within the electronic environment where you are working. But do not use a static strap when working on high-voltage devices, such as video displays.

The best rule of thumb when dealing with any service situation is to take your time and use common sense. Never rush!

## Video Display Safety

Because high voltage runs in the display, the display should only be opened by service personnel who are experienced in this type of repair. For this reason, many manufacturers do not distribute internal parts and service information for their video monitors.

Video adapters should be treated like any other electronic component that is static-sensitive. Improper handling could result in immediate or premature failure of components on the adapter.

Be careful when discharging a cathode ray tube (CRT). An old CRT is like a giant capacitor. It is capable of holding a charge for an extended pe-

**Figure 4-24**
Anode lead on CRT.

riod of time. Even though many video monitors have what is known as a bleed-off circuit, it is always best to perform a discharge procedure on the CRT before removal and handling.

Make sure that power is removed completely from the monitor you are working with.

To perform the discharge, first locate the anode lead where it connects to the CRT. This looks like a suction cup plug at the end of a wire connected to the glass body of the CRT. Refer to Figure 4-24.

Connect a jumper wire from a ground and connect the other end of the jumper wire to the metal shaft of the screwdriver. Take the tip of the screwdriver and pry it under the rubber cup where the anode lead connects to the CRT. Be sure that your fingers are not touching the metal part of the screwdriver, and that the screwdriver you are using has a well-insulated handle.

If there is any built-up charge, you will hear a small popping sound. Once this is complete, it is safe for you to remove the anode lead from the CRT. If you don't hear the pop, make sure that the screwdriver is touching the metal conductor of the anode lead.

Because of stricter environmental laws today, it is illegal to toss many batteries and CRTs in the garbage. Many of these items are labeled "hazardous waste" in several states. The manufacturer may have included a fact sheet with the new CRT and batteries, explaining safe disposal methods for the old CRT and batteries. If not, you may either contact the manufacturer directly for suggestions on disposal or check with a salvage company in your area, which may provide you with a safe avenue for disposing of these items. Also, if you surf the Web, there are many recycling companies that offer recommended procedures and drop-off points for hazardous waste. In your area, look for the EPA (Environmental Protection Agency) and check the Web site of your local county.

## Storage Media Safety

Storage media should be handled with the same adherence to ESD practices that you would use with any electronic component. If the device is to be transported, make sure that it is properly packaged and shipped. See that the hard drive heads have been parked. Older PCs use a utility called "park" or "ship," but for systems made within the last six or seven years, the drives automatically go to a safety zone when power is turned off.

## Printer Safety

When working with printers, there are a few things to keep in mind. The first is clothing. While it is professional for a man to wear a tie, it is also a good idea to tuck it into your shirt when working on mechanical devices. Otherwise, you may find your tie caught on moving parts inside the printer.

Second, you are dealing with a dirty environment inside the printer, so you want to be careful with your hands around your own clothing and the customer's work area. There is nothing worse than leaving your mark wherever you go.

When working with laser printers, there are specific tools and measurement equipment provided by the manufacturers to verify that the laser is working properly. Never take any shortcuts with the recommended procedures. Also, as with any electronic components, please keep ESD procedures in mind.

# Preventive Maintenance: Maintaining Microcomputers

Any equipment needs some maintenance for continued reliable operation. Routine maintenance for the microcomputer focuses on air passages and cooling fans to ensure proper ventilation; floppy disk drives with their motors and read/write heads; and some peripheral devices, such as tape drives, which are used for backup of the mass storage devices.

Any time a system is opened, all internal components such as cables, fastening hardware, or board installation should be inspected. Cables could be loose, cut from the last cover re-assembly, or even crimped between some areas. Integrated circuits (see Figure 4-25) and modules that are not properly fastened have a tendency to "walk out" of their sockets or connectors.

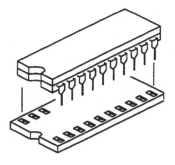

**Figure 4-25**
Standard integrated circuits.

Take any electronic circuit card that contains socketed components, such as add-on memory cards, and start pressing down on the memory devices. You will often find one that seems to snap back into place. We are not recommending that you remove every module and press on its components; however, if a module is removed for any reason, and it is in your hand, why not check it?

Preventive maintenance responsibilities are limited for video displays and adapters. For monitors, ensure that all air passages are clear. Many monitors are used as bookends, or bookshelves. They may block an air inlet, and could cause a temperature build-up inside the monitor, resulting in electrical failure of some components.

Whenever you clean a screen, check with the owner's manual; some monitors have a protective coating that could be damaged by certain household cleaners. A soft cloth dampened with water is the safest bet for cleaning any monitor. Do not spray any fluid at the screen because it may run down into the monitor circuitry. Also, it is best to have the display powered down when doing this.

## Maintaining Storage Media

Floppy drives can be treated pretty much like cassette tape decks. An occasional cleaning and lubricating is a good practice. The read/write heads can be cleaned by using a special swab with some 90% isopropyl alcohol. Do not use rubbing alcohol because this usually contains lanolin and may coat the read/write heads.

If you are not experienced with the workings of floppy drives, find some defective units to practice with. Never use the customer's drives for your education. Many heads on floppy drives have very fine wires connected to them, and if you are not aware of their presence, you could inadvertently damage them. The best insurance before performing any type of preventive maintenance is to review any literature supplied with the drives. And if you are not sure that a lubricant is safe to use, don't use it.

For most hard drives, it is critical to keep a current backup of the system, and software utilities are needed to defrag the drive from time to time. It is also a good idea to make sure that the customer has a current backup of the hard drive before performing any work.

Normal microcomputer preventive maintenance will ensure that all air vents on the computer are free of any obstructions, including dust and dirt, and so ensure that the hard drive is getting proper ventilation. Improper ventilation will cause the computer to run at unsafe temperatures.

Never assume that it is all right to run an enhancement utility on a customer's drive. Usually it is best to leave the software side of things to the customer, unless you are instructed otherwise.

With tape media, it is always important to keep the read/write heads clean. Dirt accumulates as the tape media are used, and can cause problems with read/write operations.

It is very important to follow the manufacturer's recommended procedures and to use manufacturer-recommended cleaning kits when cleaning various tape media. Materials and procedures that are safe for one system will not necessarily be safe for another.

Aside from their printing method, printers can be discussed in terms of their internal software control (ROM), hardware interface between devices, and mechanical operations.

**SOFTWARE CONTROL**  As with any computer, the microprocessor within a printer must have programs to execute. Many operations, if not all, are under software control. The instructions or programs can come from the external computer via the interface or from a set of programs located within ROM in the printer's internal circuitry. The RAM internal to the printer is used to store any externally generated instructions, as well as the characters to be printed.

In addition to the data received from the computer, the printer's microprocessor receives input from a variety of sensors located within the printer. These include configuration switches, paper sensors, and toner sensors.

**HARDWARE INTERFACE**  The hardware interface or physical connections between the printer and computer include the I/O ports, cabling, and the printer's interface board.

**MECHANICAL OPERATIONS**  Mechanical operations of the printer involve the mechanical assemblies that ensure proper movement of the paper, as well as movement of the printhead. Paper movers include the platen motors, tractor-feed assemblies, and various sensors.

The printer's main purpose is to transport paper and transfer images to the paper. It is the method of image transfer that distinguishes the main categories of printers: dot-matrix, thermal, inkjet, and laser. Each image-transfer technology has its own methods of repair and maintenance, and each is discussed in the following sections.

When installing any new printer, set it up and test it locally before connecting it to the computer system or network. Unpack it, connect the power, load the paper, and run self-tests. If these tests are not successful, there is no use hooking it to the system and adding more variables to the problem. There are several steps to keep in mind during the initial installation and configuration of any printer, as follows:

- Initial examination of systems (or peripherals) and preliminary tests
- Identification of components
- Physical installation
- Verification of configurations and connections
- System (or peripheral) power-up verification
- Software installation or ROM setup, if necessary
- Final diagnostics of entire system

**DOT-MATRIX PRINTERS**   All dot-matrix printers form characters by combining groups of dots. They operate in one of two modes: the font mode or the dot-addressable mode. In the font mode, the printhead's activity is controlled by a character-coded table in ROM, located within the printer's internal circuitry. The computer transmits the data, which is accepted and processed by the printer's electronic interface. Each bit of this data points to a block of matrix data within this ROM. Using this technique, a complete character can be generated from a single unit of input data. It's also possible with this method to define not only the character, but the font type by using a table within this ROM.

In the dot-addressable mode, a separate input is required for each printed dot within a single character. For dot-matrix printers, the dot-addressable mode is more flexible than font mode because users are not limited to the font defined by ROM, but can define fonts by their own dot-addressable data. The disadvantage is that dot-addressable mode operates at reduced speeds. Most printers can be operated in either dot-addressable or font mode, but most are typically used in the font mode.

The printhead on a dot-matrix printer is a series of pins arranged vertically and driven by a solenoid (a resistive coil). Early dot-matrix printheads had seven pins; the later models have as many as twenty-four.

As the solenoids that drive these pins on the printhead are energized, they extend out from the printhead and strike the print ribbon against the paper, thus producing a dot where the strike occurs. The printhead traverses the paper horizontally and strikes dots as it goes. It takes several passes to form one character line. These lines are similar to the scan lines on the video display, but are obviously much slower.

The color of the output produced is dependent on the color of the print ribbon installed in the printer. Early models of dot-matrix printers had a single-color ink ribbon; many of the later models have multiple color ribbons with the capability to produce color output.

**THERMAL PRINTERS**    Like dot-matrix printers, thermal printers also have a printhead with many vertical dots; however, instead of being an electromechanical device, they are heat-generating. Printheads in these devices use an electrical potential and a resistive element to produce heat on the printhead. The heat, when applied to paper of a special type, transfers characters without the need of an ink ribbon.

All dot-matrix and thermal printers incorporate the use of electric motors. Typically, each printer requires two motors: one for paper transport and one for printhead movement. Depending on the type of paper feed, the paper motor rotates either the platen or the tractor-feed assembly to move paper through the printer.

**INKJET PRINTERS**    Unlike dot-matrix and thermal printers, where contact with the paper is required, the inkjet printer is a no-impact technology. Instead, ink is "spray-painted" onto a page. Two methods can be used to accomplish this. One is continuous feed; the other is drop-on-demand. In a continuous-feed printhead, the ink is fed to the printhead through a pressurized supply line.

An oscillating chamber breaks up the ink flow and shoots from a single nozzle, one droplet at a time, at very high speed. The droplets are electrically charged so that they can either be deflected out of the printhead or recycled back into a main reservoir through an ink-recovery port. Deflection is accomplished in the same manner that a CRT electron beam is deflected, by using deflection plates. Continuous flow is typically limited to industrial applications.

Drop-on-demand technology is a much simpler and more reliable printing method. Ink droplets are only produced where and when they are needed. This eliminates the need for filtering, solvents, vacuum, and pressure. These printheads are a series of fine nozzles, each about one-third the diameter of a human hair that are arranged in vertical sets of 9, 12, or, 24—similar to the arrangement of pins on a dot-matrix printer.

Ink reaches each nozzle through a set of open channels and is gravity-fed from a small ink reservoir. In many cases, this reservoir is built into the printhead. Ink pumps in each channel break up the ink and form individual droplets that eject onto the paper. Many of today's disposable printheads are of this type.

**LASER PRINTERS**  Laser printers differ from the others in that they use a process that involves light, electricity, chemistry, pressure, and heat. This process is referred to as electrostatic. The main components used in the electrostatic process are as follows:

- Photosensitive drum
- Cleaning blade
- Erasure lamp
- Primary corona
- Writing mechanism
- Toner
- Transfer corona
- Fusing roller(s)

Figure 4-26 shows that the photosensitive drum and the cleaning blade are inside the print cartridge. The erasure lamp is a part of the printhead, and the writing mechanism is the printhead. The primary corona and the transfer corona are part of the lower frame assembly. Toner is included in the print cartridge, and the fusing roller is a part of the fuser.

Complete image development is a six-step process, involving all of the components listed previously. The six steps in the cycle are as follows:

1. Cleaning
2. Conditioning
3. Writing
4. Developing
5. Transferring
6. Fusing

**Visual Index**

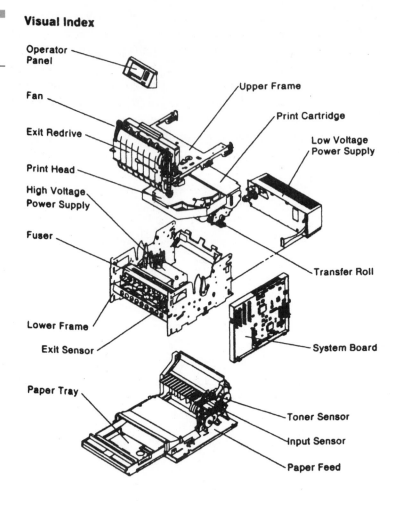

Operator Panel

Upper Frame

Fan

Print Cartridge

Exit Redrive

Low Voltage Power Supply

Print Head

High Voltage Power Supply

Fuser

Transfer Roll

Lower Frame

Exit Sensor

System Board

Paper Tray

Toner Sensor

Input Sensor

Paper Feed

During the six steps of the cycle, the laser printer charges a photosensitive drum. (The drum is an aluminum cylinder coated with a nontoxic organic compound that conducts electricity when exposed to light.) The charge on the drum attracts toner from the toner cartridge. As paper is fed through the printer, the photosensitive drum rotates and comes in contact with the paper. Because of the unlike charges between the drum and paper, the toner transfers from the drum to the paper. Then, the fuser assembly presses and heats the toner to bond it to the paper.

Now let's look at the process in more detail:

**CLEANING**  To begin the cycle, the photosensitive drum must be cleaned and electrically erased.

Cleaning is accomplished with a rubber blade, applied across the entire length of the drum to gently scrape away any residual toner. If this were not done, you would see random speckles or dots on your printed pages. It is important that the cleaning step not cause any damage, no matter how minor, to the drum. Toner that is scraped away in this process is deposited in a debris cavity or recycled back into the main toner supply area.

Electrical erasing is accomplished by a series of erasure lamps, placed in close proximity to the drum's surface. Erasure lamps leave the drum in a neutral state so that it no longer attracts toner.

A neutral drum is no longer receptive to light from the writing mechanism or from the laser, so the drum must be charged again.

**CONDITIONING**  This is where the primary corona comes into play. This solid wire has a large negative voltage applied to it, often more than -5,000 volts. Because it is close to the surface of the drum, and the drum and the high-voltage power supply share the same ground, an electrical field is established between the corona wire and the drum.

With low voltages, the air gap between the corona and drum would act like an insulator. However, with thousands of volts of electricity, the insulating strength of air breaks down and an electric corona is formed. The corona ionizes the air molecules surrounding the wire, and negative charges migrate to the drum's surface.

In addition to the primary corona, the laser printer has a primary grid between the wire and drum. By applying a negative voltage to the grid, the charging voltage and current to the drum can be regulated. Once the drum is conditioned, it is now ready to receive a new image.

**WRITING**  In order to form an image on the drum surface, the negative uniform charge that has conditioned the drum must be discharged in the precise area where images are to be produced. The discharging produces an array of electrostatic charges that are not visible.

Images are written to the drum's surface as horizontal rows of electrical charges. A dot of light on the drum's surface will cause a positive charge at that point, which will correspond to a visual dot on a completed page.

**DEVELOPING**  This pattern of charge must be developed into a visible image before it can be transferred to paper. Toner, which is an extremely fine powder of plastic resin and organic compounds bonded to iron particles, is used for this purpose. Toner is attracted to the charges on the drum in the areas exposed to the laser and not to the other areas of the drum.

**TRANSFERRING**   Once a toner image has been created on the drum, it must be transferred onto the paper. Because the toner is attracted to the drum, it must be pried away by applying an even larger charge to the paper. A transfer corona wire is used to positively charge the paper, thus attracting the toner particles. Once the toner is on the paper, it is held to the page by gravity and a very weak electrostatic attraction.

**FUSING**   In order to permanently affix the toner to the paper, fusing must take place. This is accomplished with the use of a high-intensity quartz lamp that heats a nonstick roller. By applying heat and pressure, the toner particles are now bonded to paper.

**DIAGNOSING PRINTERS**   With the printer (or any other peripheral device), the first step in analyzing difficulties is to determine if the problem is actually in the printer, or if it is in the software or the computer system. The typical complaint heard by the service engineer is, "I can't print." It is important to keep in mind all the areas that could affect the capability to print. These areas include the following:

- Software
- Computer systems or its I/O ports
- Cabling and other connections
- Printer interface
- Printer control electronics (see Figure 4-27)
- Printers' mechanical assemblies
- Paper faults, for example, moist paper or low-grade paper quality

One good rule of thumb, when working with printers and other mechanical-type peripherals, is to make sure that everything is clean. Printers operate in environments that contain paper dust, ink, and oils from mechanical assemblies. These can cause paper paths to become jammed, slide rails to start resisting the movement of printheads, and other problems.

Many service shops instruct their technicians to completely clean and lubricate any printer to the manufacturer's specifications before beginning any major diagnostic analysis. In many cases, the problem is solved with cleaning, but if the printer was extremely dirty, the dirt may have caused a component failure.

If you cannot print at all or if the output appears to be nothing but random character generation, then software configuration is a likely suspect.

Often, printer drivers get corrupted or are inadvertently changed by the operator. Within the Windows environment, it takes only a few seconds to

**Figure 4-27**

A typical layout for a laser printer board.

## System Board Connector Locations (Model 4029-02X)

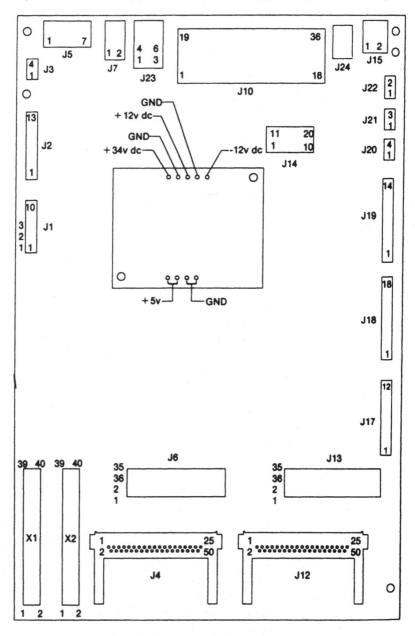

verify the type of print driver that is installed. Accessing through the printer section of the control panel will tell you immediately.

After checking the software, it is usually a good idea to run some quick integrity tests (disk-based diagnostics) on the computer system itself. Often, you can run these tests and inspect the cabling or the printer at the same time. It is not uncommon to find problems with interrupt circuits, memory circuits, or other related areas that could disrupt proper instruction and/or data flow to the printer or other peripheral.

Always inspect the cabling when diagnosing problems with external peripheral devices. You may find them stretched, crimped, or even broken.

All printers have a self-contained program in ROM called a self-test. This self-test is capable of testing all printer circuits, except for the printer's interface to the computer. Usually, the self-test executes some basic electronic diagnostics, such as CPU and memory tests; the self-test will attempt to print the character sets to determine whether hard copy output is possible. The output portion of the self-test also allows us to observe whether the mechanical assemblies are functioning as they should.

**REPAIRING PRINTERS**  As with the repair of any peripheral, it is important to be sure that the error is in the peripheral, and not in the computer or other areas. The computer can be diagnosed with disk-based diagnostics, and the printer can be diagnosed with the self-test. Once we are certain the printer has a problem, we must look at each of the printer's major components.

These components are the power supply, logic boards, sensors, and mechanical assemblies. Always refer to any manufacturer documentation before proceeding with a disassembly to replace a field-replaceable unit, and follow all safety guidelines.

**MAINTAINING PRINTERS**  Preventive maintenance for a printer is probably the most important and most neglected step to ensure trouble-free operation. Taking 5–10 minutes every couple of months could save you from expensive downtime when you least need it. When performing any type of preventive maintenance, always refer to any recommended procedures listed in user and/or service manuals.

Common steps in most preventive maintenance include vacuuming, cleaning, lubricating the interior, and also wiping down the external case. You will also want to make sure that all air passages required for proper cooling are clear. You cannot treat a dot-matrix like a laser or vice versa. Each has its own unique requirements for proper preventive maintenance. For example, years ago, some dot-matrix printheads used graphite bearings that could be damaged if oil was used on them.

# Portable Systems

The popularity of the portable systems continues to increase as we write these words. Sales, consulting, and many other disciplines that require travel also require portability and the equivalent power found in a desktop machine. In this section, we will review the main components of a portable system and highlight some of the problem areas that can be encountered.

Portable systems come in a variety of sizes or form factors, which describe their size and weight. They are as follows:

- Laptops
- Notebooks
- Sub-notebooks

Laptops are considered the largest of them all and usually weigh seven pounds or more. They typically have a clamshell design, which opens to reveal the screen and keyboard (see Figure 4-28).

Notebook computers are designed to be smaller, and generally fit into the under-seven-pound category; the sub-notebooks weigh in at four to five pounds. Please keep in mind, however, that what you gain in smaller size and portability may also cost you in features (although with today's technological advancements, the smaller packages pack a decent wallop).

When we speak of processors, memory, video outputs, and I/O ports, there are few differences from a functional point of view between portables and the desktop environment. What comes into play in the portable environment, more than anything else, is the packaging and the low power type components. See Figure 4-29 for an internal view of a laptop computer.

The basic components of a laptop computer are as follows:

**Figure 4-28**
Typical laptop computer.

**Figure 4-29**
Internal view of
laptop computer.

- Main board or System board
- Processor board
- Video display (LCD screen)
- Power supply board
- Battery
- Memory modules
- Adapter cards (modems, network interface, SCSI, etc.)
- External
- AC adapter

Upgrading and repairing portable systems is very similar to desktop systems, except that some manufacturers may not allow the use of generic components. However, standards like PCMCIA have decreased that possibility. Also, many third-party vendors produce hard drives, memory modules, and interfaces that connect to the I/O ports. Before adding a component to a portable environment, it is important to make sure that it is going to physically fit in the case of the unit you are working on. If the component is from the manufacturer of the portable system, there should be no problem. Third-party components, however, could be a problem. Many third-party vendors indicate what systems will accept their components, reducing the need to research this.

There are three types of PCMCIA interface cards: Type I, Type II, and Type III. The primary difference between the cards is their thickness. Type I cards are credit-card size (3.4 x 2.1 inches, and 3.3mm thick. The Type II cards are 5mm thick, and are commonly used for modems and network interface cards (NICs). Type III cards are 10.5mm thick, and are generally used for PC card hard drives.

PCMCIA cards are, by definition, "hot-swappable." This means a card can be replaced with a different one without having to reboot or turn off the system. Additionally, if the PCMCIA card conforms to the Plug and Play (PnP) standard, the appropriate software drivers will be loaded and configured automatically. To make this possible, there are three software layers that are required: Socket Services, Card Services, and Enabler.

Socket Services software isolates the proprietary aspect of an adapter from all of the software operating above it. Communications between the device driver and the adapter may be unique, but the other interface between the Socket Services driver and the Card Services software is defined by the PCMCIA standard.

Card Services software is responsible for assigning the appropriate hardware resources to the PCMCIA card. In Windows 95, Card Services obtains the hardware resources that it assigns to a PCMCIA card using Plug and Play.

In spite of their other capabilities, neither Socket Services nor Card Services are capable of configuring the hardware settings of the PCMCIA card. This is accomplished through a software module called an Enabler.

The Enabler receives the configuration settings assigned by Card Services, and actually communicates with the PCMCIA card itself to set the correct values.

Perhaps the biggest difference in portable systems is found in the display. LCD (Liquid Crystal Display) technology solved the portability issue of the large, cumbersome CRT display; and advancements in technology have made it just as feature-rich as the CRT.

The most popular type of LCD screen is the active matrix, which is also known as TFT (thin film transistor). In this arrangement, each pixel (picture element) on the screen has its own transistor to control it. Having a transistor at each pixel means that the electrical current that triggers pixel illumination can be smaller and can be switched at a more rapid rate. However, when you add up all those transistors (480,000 in some cases), the result is increased battery drain and increased cost. Regardless of these negative factors, the positive side is a crisp fast-switching display.

## Power in Portable Systems

Power consumption is a critical factor to deal with in the mobile environment. Because you often must rely on battery power, increased battery efficiency and low power consumption are very important. Another important area is power management, which allows the processor in the portable system to turn different areas of the circuitry on or off to reduce the drain on the batter. For example, if you are on an airplane and not using the parallel port, the power management circuit can actually remove power from the parallel port circuits, thus reducing the power drain. No need to power a circuit that is not being used.

We have seen the evolution of batteries across three main technologies:

- NiCD (Nickel Cadmium)
- NiMH (Nickel Metal Hydride)
- LiON (Lithium-Ion)

Nickel Cadmium is probably the most durable of all three. These batteries are quick to charge, last approximately 800 charge cycles (over 2 years), and work well in extreme temperatures. The downside is that that NiCD batteries are prone to the "memory effect" if they are not completely discharged in each cycle. The memory effect reduces the overall capacity and runtime of the battery.

Nickel Metal Hydride batteries have become very popular because they do not suffer from the memory effect. They are also capable of running 30% longer on each charge then their NiCD counterpart. In addition, they are manufactured from non-toxic metals, which makes them more environmentally friendly. NiMH batteries typically last 400 charge and discharge cycles (a little over one year).

Lithium-Ion offers the highest energy-to-mass ratio of any battery on the market, and they do not suffer from the memory effect. Compared to a NiMH battery of equal size, a LiON battery will deliver twice the runtime from each charge. LiON batteries have a life expectancy of 400 charge and discharge cycles.

## Infrared Technology

Infrared technology has become very popular in the portable systems environment. This technology allows wireless communication between PCs and various peripheral devices such as printers and keyboards.

The IrDA (Infrared Data Association) is an industry-sponsored organization, set up in 1993 to create standards for hardware and software used in infrared-communication links. In this special form of radio transmission, a focused ray of light in the infrared frequency spectrum (measured in terahertz) is modulated with information and sent from a transmitter to a receiver over a short distance. This is the same technology used in the remote control for your television set. Infrared is a line of sight transmission, so in most environments, you may be limited to three feet or less, with no interference in between.

Some points of safety to remember with infrared:

If you are not qualified to service infrared devices, refer service to an authorized servicer of that product.

Do not attempt to make any adjustments.

Avoid direct eye exposure to the infrared LED beam. (NOTE: This beam is invisible and cannot be seen.)

Do not attempt to view the infrared LED beam with any type of optical device.

# Docking Station

The docking station is a device that is used to "dock" the portable system into a cradle. The docking station allows the use of a full-size monitor, keyboard, and any other peripheral hookup that is needed in the office, but it is not feasible in the portable environment. For example, when hooked to a docking station, a user may have more adapters than when traveling. A docking station can support standard PC-size adapters and provide all the necessary I/O port connections. Before the advent of docking stations, the user had to hook up printers, external monitors, and any other devices he wanted to use in the office. Now, by just sliding the portable system into the docking station, all connections are automatically made.

Because of the docking station, another element is added to diagnosing errors. It is critical to know when the user is experiencing problems —whether the problem occurs when the system is out of the docking station, in the docking station, or both. Keep in mind that the system may operate error-free out of the docking station, or vice versa.

# Common Problems

Portable systems offer a unique computing environment, and along with that, a unique set of problems. You are dealing with a computing environment that is prone to more abuse than that of the standard desktop environment. When a computer system is on the move or traveling, it is more likely to be bounced around, exposed to temperature extremes, and attached to many different peripherals (different configurations). That is why it is important to always second-guess connection and configuration information. Many problems that are called into customer help desks consist of improper use, handling, or configuration.

Besides these considerations, it is important to have knowledge of the users and the way they care for the batteries. Earlier, we mentioned that NiCD (Nickel Cadmium) batteries could produce a memory effect. Many users will use these batteries for a short time and recharge them, use them again for a short time, and recharge them again. If you do not allow the battery to drain completely, it will lose its full charge capability, regardless of what the battery specification says. Even those batteries that do not have a memory effect should be allowed to be used to their full capability. Many batteries are rated by the number of charge and discharge cycles they can provide; if you charge them too frequently, you may shorten their life spans.

As new technology emerges, we are finding that the ESD (Electrostatic Discharge) safety practices are becoming more important than ever. Never take any shortcuts when it comes to ESD practices. You will see this caveat get added attention in all new training programs and service literature. Long gone are the days when you could "get by" without your static strap or anti-static mat. The new systems are extremely sensitive and will not allow any tolerance for "shortcuts."

Always pay attention or make a diagram when disassembling or reassembling a portable system. Not all screws are created equal, as we have found in many desktop products. Pay special attention to the routing of cables and the securing of all connectors. Many are flexed during the normal operation of a portable system, as in the cables between the system board and the LCD screen. If these are not properly secured, they will become loose and cause problems.

# Basic Networking

Even if your job responsibility doesn't include network service or repair, it is extremely important that you have a basic understanding of networks and the methods used to isolate problems. There are few businesses today that do not network their computer systems, so in most cases you will find yourself working on a system that is connected to a network.

It is not difficult to understand why networks are so popular. They are all about sharing: files, resources, and programs. If you have ever used an e-mail program, it is difficult to comprehend how you ever got along without it. Years ago, when we wanted to share files with others in our office we used the infamous "sneaker" net. This consisted of copying your file, spreadsheet, letter, or other document to a floppy disk. You then walked this floppy disk to your co-workers and they copied it onto their machines. It wasn't very high-tech, but it worked. Now we can send files, reports, memos and other important communications across the country, or even around the world, in minutes via e-mail.

This sharing of resources allows us to share printers, disk drives, and even computing power from other systems. In many cases, you could define a report or send in a request, and a mini- or mainframe system would do all the work and send the report to you within minutes. Generally, your system would not have the resources or power to do this.

There are primarily two classifications of computers on a network; file servers and workstations. The file server is more expensive, more powerful, and contains the resources that need to be shared. Workstations, on the other hand, are less expensive, less powerful, and connect to the file server. Typically, the file server is not a workstation, and a workstation is not a file server. At times in the past, servers were also used as workstations. This is not recommended, however.

Because the file servers are "serving" the entire network, they must be high-quality, heavy-duty machines. Therefore, they must have powerful processing power, large amounts of memory, high quality/fast hard drives, ample power supplies, and Network Interface Cards (NICs). When it comes to keyboards and display monitors, it is not necessary to have the best of these on the server. In fact, many server environments share a single keyboard and monitor for all servers through a special interface device.

Every machine that is attached to a network must contain a network interface card. All file requests and other network communications enter and leave the machines on the network through this adapter. Network adapters use Ethernet, Token Ring, ARCnet, or some other low-level protocol when communicating.

ARCnet, one of the oldest types, is very slow but highly reliable. ARCnet operates like a Token Ring network, but at a slower rate of 2.4Mbps.

The most widely used type of network adapter is Ethernet. Ethernet comes in three varieties, Thinnet, UTP, and Thicknet, depending on the type of cabling that is used. Ethernet typically has operated at a rate of 10Mbps, with the newer adapters raising that to 100Mbps. In an Ethernet environment, when two computers are trying to communicate with the server at the same time, a collision will occur. When this happens, the adapter will back off and try again. A certain number of collisions are considered normal and expected on an Ethernet network.

On a Token Ring network, an electronic token is passed from station to station. The station that possesses this token is allowed to transmit, while the others that do not have this token cannot transmit. This makes for a very regimented sharing of the network wiring. If the unit that has the token does not have anything to transmit, it just passes the token on to the next station. Token ring can operate at 4 or 16 Mbps.

Network adapter functions can usually be broken down into the following categories:

- Data transfer
- Buffering of data
- Frame formation
- Cable access
- Parallel to serial conversion
- Encoding and decoding
- Sending and receiving

## LAN Cabling

There are three distinct types of cabling:

- Twisted Pair (shielded/unshielded), also known as STP, UTP, or 10BaseT
- Coaxial cable (thick/thin), also known as 10Base2 and 10Base5
- Fiber optic

Twisted pair cabling is comprised of insulated wires within a protective casing, with a specified number of twists per foot. These twists reduce the effect of electromagnetic interference on the signals being transmitted. Shielded twisted pair refers to the amount of insulation wrapped around the cluster of wires. Unshielded twisted pair is standard telephone wiring.

Coaxial cable is the same cable that is used widely today in cable TV and audio installations. Thick and Thin refer to the diameter of the cable itself. The thicker cable has a higher degree of noise immunity.

Fiber optic cable utilizes pulses of light rather than electric signals. It is resistant to electromagnetic interference and attenuation ( the weakening of a signal as it travels along great distances). Fiber optic is the most expensive and difficult to work with.

Many companies are looking at utilizing infrared or radio communications to connect everyone together. Unfortunately, the speed and reliability needed for today's demanding network environments have yet to be achieved.

# TCP/IP (Transmission Control Protocol/Internet Protocol)

TCP/IP is a suite of networking protocols used by the Internet. TCP is the Transport layer, and IP defines the network protocol that transmits blocks of data. TCP/IP is a collection of Internet protocol applications and transport protocols that include File Transfer Protocol (FTP), Terminal Emulation (Telnet), and the Simple Mail Transfer Protocol (SMTP). The primary advantages of TCP/IP are as follows:

- Platform independence—allows it to be used with networks of all types.
- Absolute addressing—provides a means of identifying every system on the Internet.
- Open standards—publicly available to users and developers.
- Application protocols—allow dissimilar environments to communicate.

# Other Devices in a Network

Some other devices you need to be familiar with are:

- Repeaters
- Bridges
- Routers
- Gateways

A repeater is a device that gives network signals a boost so that longer communication cables can be used. Repeaters are used when the total length of your cable is larger than the maximum allowed for your cable type.

A bridge is a device that is used to connect two independent networks together, allowing them to act as one. They can also be used to connect one type of network to another, for example Ethernet to Token Ring.

A router is basically a very intelligent bridge. It not only knows the addresses of all computers on each side of the bridge, but also knows about other bridges and routers on the network. This way, it can determine the most efficient path to use to send each network message.

A gateway encompasses everything about repeaters, bridges, and routers. Gateways are usually used to connect a network to a mainframe computer or minicomputer. They are designed to connect different types of networks together and provide the translation between them.

## Repairs on the Network

Whenever repairing a system that is tied to the network, it is always a good idea to isolate that machine from the network. Before disconnecting a system from the network, make sure that the machine is powered down before removing any cabling from the back of the machine. If you suspect that the problem is in the network and not in the local workstation, do not attempt to find the problem yourself. Contact the network administrator at the site for consultation and more information. You do not want to reset any file servers or turn them off when users are logged into the network. Also, do not attempt any modification to the workstation software without consulting the administrator. Networks can be very complex and confusing. Take one step at a time and do not rush! If the server or any other part of the network must be reset, leave it to the network administrator. Never assume that a system has been backed up. You must always ask this question when dealing with your customer. If the system is not backed up, the customer may request you to do it.

During your diagnosis of a workstation, or server always make sure that your diagnostic software is free of viruses. Nothing will upset a customer more than having their network infected by a virus. As standard operating procedure, run any disks that you have used that day through virus scan prior to putting them on another customer's system. You may pick up a virus from one customer and relay it to the next.

When in doubt, don't!

## Customer Satisfaction

Even though this portion will be scored on your A+ exam, it will not affect your pass/fail grade on the exam. This section is probably one of the most important sections. All the technical skills in the world will not be of any value if you cannot deal effectively with people.

Have you ever listened to someone who was an authority on some subject matter, and everything that person said went completely over your head? Please keep this in mind when talking with your customers. You may be totally familiar with the subject matter of computer diagnosis, but you must be able to explain what you are doing, why you are doing it, and how much it will cost the customer. This requires some knowledge of communications. The most important fundamental in communicating is that you must be a good listener. I have heard it said that the reason we have two ears and one mouth is because we are supposed to listen twice as much as we talk. Listen to what the customer is saying and maintain eye contact. I do not mean that you should stare at them, but eye contact will let them know you are interested in what they are saying. Do not interrupt, and be prepared to ask questions. Even if you know what they are going to say, ask a question anyway. Asking questions says you are listening and trying to understand their situation. This will also give you an idea of the technical knowledge level of the customer, so that you can gauge your response appropriately.

When speaking with a customer over the phone, do not try to multi-task. Do not fill out your expense report, draw doodles on a pad of paper, or type on your computer. Give 100% of your attention to that person on the other end of the phone. They can tell if you are paying attention or not.

Professional conduct and appearance are important, as well as communication skills. How you carry yourself and how you look will effect how a customer responds to you. Until you get to know a customer and what type of personality they have, do not appear to be overly friendly or talkative.

# Sample Test Questions

What follows are sample test questions (and answers) for the A+ core exam. Each sample test question in this book comes from one of the following three sources:

**Self Test Software**. All questions from this company have been beta-tested to ensure that success with these questions is a good predictor of success with questions in the real A+ examinations. Note that the company has more than 200 questions in addition to those appearing in this book. They are available in a computer-based format and cover all three of the A+ exams. For pricing and information, contact Self Test Software at 1-800-200-6446, or 1-770-971-8940 (outside of the U.S. and Canada).

**CompTIA**. CompTIA provided sample questions and specified that they "are of the type found on the A+ Certification tests. They are for practice only, and will not appear on your test. They are similar to ones you will find there." These sample questions, contributed by CompTIA members, draw from those members' considerable service and support experience, as well as their familiarity with the kinds of questions presented in the A+ exams. The questions were written and beta-tested specifically for the A+ exam(s), but, for a variety of reasons, were not used in those exams. Therefore, CompTIA stresses that doing well on the practice questions is no guarantee that candidates will do well on the exam(s).

**The Authors.** The authors contributed sample test questions to this book. These questions draw from the authors' considerable familiarity with the kinds of questions presented by the A+ exams; however, these questions have not been beta-tested to objectively verify that those who do well on them will also do well on the real A+ exams. They are offered as an additional source of feedback about the candidate's skills, and are therefore a useful tool for study and preparation.

The source (Self Test Software, CompTIA, or Authors) for each question is listed with the question.

1. What type of output device should never be hooked up to a manual switch box? (Self Test Software)

   a. Dot-matrix printer

   b. Daisy wheel printer

   c. Inkjet printer

   d. Laser printer

2. How many interrupt levels are available in the typical AT-compatible system, including the NMI? (Authors)

   a. 32

   b. 16

   c. 8

   d. 17

3. The Extended Industry Standard Architecture (EISA) is also compatible with what? (Authors)

   a. MCA (Micro-Channel Architecture)

   b. S-100 Bus

   c. Industry Standard Architecture (ISA)

   d. IEEE488

**4.** Identify which statement is correct. (CompTIA)

a. To dispose of dead or old batteries, just place them in the trash can

b. Check the battery for label information on special disposal procedures

c. All batteries can be recycled

d. Batteries pose no problem to the environment

**5.** Choose two handshake signals used in a serial data transfer between a computer and printer. (Authors)

a. Data Terminal Ready and Select In

b. Busy and Error

c. Data Terminal Ready and Data Set Ready

d. Acknowledge and Busy

**6.** The term "ESD" refers to what? (CompTIA)

a. Environmentally safe data

b. Electromagnetic surge device

c. Enhanced switching device

d. Electrostatic discharge

**7.** What is the maximum length for a SCSI network? (Authors)

a. 20 feet

b. 24 feet

c. 28 feet

d. 30 feet

**8.** If, at system power-up, the only response is that the power supply fan is running, which of the following is not a likely suspect? (Authors)

a. System RAM

b. Power supply

c. BIOS ROM

d. Video

9. What product must be used to clean rubber rollers on a laser printer? (Self Test Software)

    a. Denatured alcohol

    b. Silicone spray

    c. Soap and water

    d. Glass cleaner

10. If, on power-up, the video display indicates a 300-series error code, which of the following is the most likely suspect? (Authors)

    a Main board

    b. Video

    c. Keyboard

    d. Floppy controller

11. A CAUTION will typically alert you to what? (Authors)

    a. Possible damage to equipment

    b. Possible harm to you

    c. Possible damage to software environment

    d. None of the above

12. What is the best device for transporting circuit boards? (Self Test Software)

    a. Vinyl container/bag

    b. Plastic foam container/bag

    c. Shielded container/bag

    d. Static shield container/bag

13. Carpeting can be one of the most static-prone surfaces in the office environment. Which type of mat will greatly reduce static problems? (Self Test Software)

    a. Rubber

    b. Nylon

    c. Plastic

    d. Vinyl

**14.** What is the first step when installing a new DOS upgrade? (Self Test Software)

    a. Delete the COMMAND.COM file

    b. Back up the existing operating system and data

    c. Reformat the currently formatted hard drive

    d. Copy the previous version of the operating system to a subdirectory call OLD_DOS

**15.** In inkjet technology, the droplets of ink are deflected toward the paper by what? (Authors)

    a. A multi-directional nozzle

    b. Electrically charged plates

    c. High pressure

    d. Gravity

**16.** If a microcomputer system prints under your spreadsheet application, but not under your word processing application, there is a good chance that the problem lies where? (Authors)

    a. Your operating system environment

    b. The Windows environment

    c. An incorrect printer driver selected for the word processor

    d. Your print spooler

**17.** The primary corona's main purpose is to do what? (Authors)

    a. Clean the photosensitive drum

    b. Charge the toner particles

    c. Erase the photosensitive drum

    d. Charge the photosensitive drum

**18.** The device that regulates voltage and current to the photosensitive drum is the what? (Authors)

    a. Transfer corona

    b. Primary grid

    c. Cleaning blade

    d. Laser

19. Networks allow the sharing of what things? Choose all that apply. (Authors)

    a. Computer systems

    b. Printers

    c. Software

    d. Disk drives

20. Which of the following are important for reducing the chances of ESD? Choose all that apply. (Authors)

    a. Personnel training

    b. Materials used in packing

    c. Discharging prior to handling a device

    d. Static workstations

21. The 80386SX CPU supports a _____ bit external data bus and 24 bits of addressing. (Authors)

    a. 8

    b. 12

    c. 24

    d. 16

22. Which component enables independent communication between the processor and the external printing device? (Self Test Software)

    a. I/O controller

    b. Expanded memory

    c. Video controller

    d. Hard drive controller

23. In the PC/AT-compatible environment, the BIOS program is located where? (Authors)

    a. Just above the 0000 address

    b. Just below the 640K address

    c. Just below the 1M address

    d. Just above the 1M address

**24.** A computer virus is what? (Authors)

  a. A hardware flaw that induces problems into other devices

  b. A program designed to corrupt data or cause damage

  c. Not transmitted in network environments

  d. A series of programs in ROM designed to slow down a network

**25.** One of your best resources for tracking down a nonthermal intermittent error is what? (Authors)

  a. A logic probe

  b. Disk-based diagnostics

  c. A can of circuit cooler

  d. A set of benchmark utilities

**26.** Network problems can be caused by which of the following? Choose all that apply. (Authors)

  a. Server

  b. Workstation

  c. Software

  d. Operator

**27.** Transferring an entire data word over several conductors at one time is called _____ communications. (Authors)

  a. Serial

  b. IEE488

  c. Parallel

  d. Network

**28.** The inductive and/or capacitive coupling of a signal from one conductor to another is called what? (Authors)

  a. Crosstalk

  b. Reactance

  c. FSK (Frequency Shift Keying)

  d. None of the above

**29.** The two main advantages of parallel communications are what? (Authors)

   a. Cost and efficiency

   b. Speed and simplicity

   c. Distance and simplicity

   d. Cost and speed

**30.** The device driver used to set up a RAM drive using the DOS CONFIG.SYS file is called what? Choose all that apply. (Self Test Software)

   a. VDISK.SYS

   b. MAKEDRV.SYS

   c. RAMDRIVE.SYS

   d. RAMDRIVE.EXE

**31.** Which of the following video monitors could accept either an EGA or CGA input? (Authors)

   a. IBM 8512

   b. NEC Multi-Sync

   c. Zenith Data Systems ZCM-1492

   d. IBM PS/2 8514

**32.** If a printer self-test passes and the user still cannot print, possible suspects include what? Choose all that apply. (Authors)

   a. Computer interface

   b. Software configuration

   c. Printer interface

   d. Printer off-line

**33.** The natural hierarchy of software is what? (Authors)

   a. Operating System, ROM, Application

   b. ROM, Operating System, Application

   c. Application, Operating System, RAM

   d. Operating System, Application, ROM

**34.** At power-up, the first code that the microprocessor has access to is available from what? (Authors)

   a. Disk

   b. RAM

   c. ROM

   d. None of the above

**35.** To limit the chance of ac line noise, you should do what? (CompTIA)

   a. Use extension cords

   b. Install the computer system on its own power circuit

   c. Install the computer system on a circuit with other high wattage units

   d. Avoid using a ground connection

**36.** The file that is the primary MS-DOS user interface is what? (Authors)

   a. DIR

   b. COMMAND.COM

   c. AUTOEXEC.BAT

   d. IO.SYS

**37.** Which of the following is not a resident command? (Authors)

   a. DIR

   b. COPY

   c. REN

   d. EDIT

**38.** Which of the following are examples of non-impact printers? Choose all that apply. (Authors)

   a. Thermal

   b. Daisy wheel

   c. Laser

   d. Electrostatic

**39.** Dynamic RAM (random access memory) must be _____ every 2 milliseconds. (Authors)

a. refreshed

b. written to

c. read

d. reloaded

**40.** Which of the following is not a transient command? (Authors)

a. FORMAT

b. EDIT

c. COPY

d. SHELL

**41.** In a laser printer, the photosensitive drum is typically connected to what electrical potential? (Authors)

a. Positive

b. Power supply ground

c. Neutral

d. AC reference

**42.** Which of the following best describes the six-step process involved with electrostatic printing? (Authors)

a. Paper feed, charging, writing, developing, erasing, transferring

b. Cleaning, charging, writing, erasing, developing, fusing

c. Cleaning, charging, writing, developing, transferring, fusing

d. Charging, writing, developing, transferring, erasing, fusing

**43.** Which of the following best describes the single beep heard after power on? (Self Test Software)

a. Has no meaning

b. The system has powered on

c. POST has successfully completed

d. Multimedia support has been enabled

**44.** CMOS or PRAM stores which of the following? (CompTIA)

a. Date and time

b. CPU and memory size characteristics

c. Floppy and hard disk types

d. All of the above

**45.** The most noticeable feature of the LPX Form Factor Motherboard is that:

a. It is designed specifically for Tower cases

b. It has separate processor and I/O modules

c. The expansion slots are mounted on a bus riser card

d. It is comprised of just the connectors to interconnect the other modules

**46.** Configuration for MCA and EISA communication buses is accomplished through what?

a. Jumpers

b. Software

c. Switches

d. Configuration not needed

**47.** Up until recently, the maximum bus speed in any PC was what?

a. 8.33MHz

b. Same as processor speed

c. 33MHz

d. 66MHz

**48.** The PCI Bus communicates directly to the system processor, or CPU?

a. True

b. False

**49.** A type II PCMCIA card is usually a what?

  a. Modem

  b. Hard drive

  c. Memory

  d. I/O

**50.** The USB (Universal Serial Bus) can connect up to _____ devices.

  a. 64

  b. 8

  c. 127

  d. 21

**51.** Extended memory runs _____ than expanded memory.

  a. slower

  b. at the same speed as expanded

  c. faster

  d. either slower or faster, depending on the software

**52.** Which of the following is not a hard drive interface?

  a. SCSI

  b. ST-506

  c. IDE

  d. PCI

**53.** SCSI is a what?

  a. Disk Drive Interface

  b. Controller

  c. Systems Level Interface

  d. Gateway

**54.** The step pulse signal help position the _____ on a floppy drive.

  a. media

  b. spindle motor

  c. head select

  d. read/write heads

**55.** A SCSI-1 adapter can handle up to _____devices.

   a. 7

   b. 6

   c. 14

   d. 8

**56.** When doing a disassembly of a video monitor, what must be discharged?

   a. Anode lead

   b. High voltage supply

   c. Cathode Ray Tube (CRT)

   d. Power supply circuit

# Answers to sample questions

| | | |
|---|---|---|
| 1. D | 20. A,B,C,D | 39. A |
| 2. D | 21. D | 40. C |
| 3. C | 22. A | 41 B |
| 4. B | 23. C | 42. C |
| 5. C | 24. B | 43. C |
| 6. D | 25. B | 44. D |
| 7. A | 26. A,B,C,D | 45. C |
| 8. B | 27. C | 46. B |
| 9. A | 28. A | 47. D |
| 10. C | 29. B | 48. False |
| 11. A | 30. A,C | 49. A |
| 12. D | 31. B | 50. C |
| 13. A | 32. A,B,C,D | 51. C |
| 14. B | 33. B | 52. D |
| 15. B | 34. C | 53. C |
| 16. C | 35. B | 54. D |
| 17. D | 36. B | 55. D |
| 18. B | 37. D | 56. C |
| 19. A,B,C,D | 38. A,C,D | |

CHAPTER **5**

# The Microsoft DOS/Windows Exam

The specific skills and knowledge that the Microsoft Windows/DOS specialty exam tests are listed below. Each skill or knowledge is then covered in the preparatory materials that follow. We have also presented additional topics where we felt these would be helpful. If upon reviewing a section of this or the other study guide chapters, you feel a need for more information, please refer to Appendices C and D for recommended sources of further reading and training.

The questions in the Windows/DOS specialty exam cover a candidate's knowledge of Windows Version 3.1, DOS Version 6.x, and Windows 95.

Sample test questions (and answers) appear at the end of the chapter to help you prepare for the Microsoft Windows/DOS specialty exam.

The Microsoft Windows/DOS specialty exam tests your ability to do the following:

# Domain 1.0 Function, Structure Operation, and File Management

Identify the operating system's functions, structure, and major system files.

Content may include the following:

Functions of DOS, Windows 3.x, and Windows 95

Major components of DOS, Windows 3.x, and Windows 95

Contrasts between Windows 3.x and Windows 95

Major system files, what they are, where they are located, how they are used, and what they contain.

DOS
  AUTOEXEC.BAT
  CONFIG.SYS
  IO.SYS
  ANSI.SYS
  MSDOS.SYS
  EMM386.EXE
  HIMEM.SYS
  COMMAND.COM

Windows 3.x
  WIN.INI
  SYSTEM.INI
  USER.EXE
  GDI.EXE
  WIN.COM
  PROGRAM.INI
  PROGMAN.EXE
  KRNLXXX.EXE

Windows 95
  IO.SYS
  MSDOS.SYS

COMMAND.COM

REGEDIT.EXE

SYSTEM.DAT

ISER.DAT

Identify ways to navigate the operating system and how to get to needed technical information

Identify basic concepts and procedures for creating, viewing and managing files and directories, including procedures for changing file attributes and the ramifications of changes.

Identify the procedures for basic disk management.

# Domain 2.0 Memory Management

Differentiate between types of memory

Conventional

Extended/Upper

High Memory

Expanded Memory

Virtual Memory

Identify typical memory conflict problems and how to optimize memory use.

# Domain 3.0 Installation, Configuration, and Upgrading

Identify the procedures for installing DOS, Windows 3.x, and Window 95, and for bringing the software to a basic operational level.

Identify the steps to perform an operating system upgrade.

Identify the basic system boot sequences and alternative ways to boot the system software, including the steps to create an emergency boot disk with utilities installed.

Identify the procedures for loading/adding device drivers and the necessary software for certain devices.

Identify the procedures for changing options, configuring, and using the Windows printing system.

Identify the procedures for installing and launching typical Windows and non-Windows applications.

# Domain 4.0 Diagnosing and Troubleshooting

Recognize and interpret the meaning of common error codes and startup messages from the boot sequence, and identify steps to correct problems.

Recognize Windows-specific printing problems and identify the procedures for correcting them.

Recognize common problems and determine how to resolve them.

Identify concepts relating to viruses and virus types, their dangers, their symptoms, sources of viruses, how they infect, how to protect against them, and how to identify and remove them.

# Domain 5.0 Networks

Identify the networking capabilities of DOS and Windows, including procedures for connecting to the network.

Identify concepts and capabilities relating to the Internet and basic procedures for setting up a system for Internet access.

# Preparing for the Exam

In today's IBM-compatible marketplace, there are three major operating environments that service technicians may face during any service call: MS-DOS version 6.0 or higher, Windows version 3.1, and Windows 95. This chapter examines all three of these operating environments.

When servicing computer systems, you need to understand the workings of the operating system(s) that the microcomputer is running. At the same time, you need to understand memory-resident software, and the problems it can cause if not managed properly. Finally, you need to be able to distinguish between hardware- and software-related errors.

Before even beginning to examine the Windows/DOS environment, let's look at the different levels of software code and the order in which they are loaded by the microcomputer at time of power-up. That order is:

- Read-only memory, including basic input/output system (ROM BIOS)
- Disk operating system (DOS)
- Windows environment
- Application software: word processing, databases, spreadsheets, etc.

Each of the four areas must be loaded and must perform its specific function before the next, in order to complete the total computer environment.

**NOTE:** *Because Windows 95 is an operating system, there is no need for MS-DOS to be loaded.*

The various levels of software constantly interact during normal machine operations. For example, when a key on the keyboard is pressed, an interrupt is generated. In order to handle this interrupt, the processor must be directed toward an interrupt routine, usually located in ROM, which tells it how to process the key that has been pressed.

When power is first applied to the machine, many hardware functions activate. Clocks start running, system resets occur, and typically the microprocessor will access a default address. This default address is the address that the microprocessor always goes to at power-up, and is usually located at the high end of the first one megabyte (MB) boundary of random access memory (RAM), which is reserved for ROM. It is by design that the microprocessor always fires up to the same address. Doing this guarantees that it accesses the proper code every time. In the order of hierarchy, ROM is the first level of software or code for the PC to execute. Without ROM, the machine would do nothing but draw power and get warm.

In the early stages of power-up, during the execution of ROM code, the machine is initialized, power-on self-tests (POSTs) are run, and the process of "booting" begins. At the time of booting, the DOS environment is loaded into memory to begin execution.

Once the system environment is established, the POSTs are run to ensure that there is enough system integrity to boot the operating system software. These tests check the central processing unit (CPU), ROM, RAM, interrupt, disk, and other circuits necessary to basic system operation.

Note that the POST diagnostics only test the basic circuits of a computer system. If more detailed testing is required, a set of disk-based diagnostics can be used for diagnosing more serious problems. Once all POSTs are complete, the system is prepared to access the primary boot device, which is typically the system hard disk drive, and the loading of the operating system can occur. The portion of the ROM that contains the code for booting the system is referred to as the bootstrap loader.

We have outlined the basics of the power-on routines that most microcomputer systems go through in order to boot the operating systems. After the boot process, the system is capable of loading the Windows environment and then the applications programs.

Remember that Windows 95 is its own operating environment, so you will not find a collection of files that you can look at and identify as the MS-DOS files. Some of the features of Windows 95 have appeared in other Microsoft products, such as Windows NT and Windows for Workgroups. Windows 95 includes the old features and adds new features to provide a full 32-bit protected mode environment for all Windows applications.

If you are used to working in the previous Windows environments, you will see a dramatic change in the on-screen appearance of the operating system under Windows 95. In addition to changes in screen appearance, other significant changes are:

■ Device-independent color (many devices might have their own device-specific BIOS, but they all conform to Plug-and-Play rules.)

■ Disk and file system support, including format and file utilities

■ Plug-and-play configuration

■ Network support for more networks and greater capability

■ Mobile computing support for laptop and wireless communication devices

The goal of Windows 95 was to make computing easy. This has required hardware manufacturers and software developers to agree on standards so that their products present a similar interface to the user when the user accesses them using Windows 95.

# Configuring Hardware Components and Setup Procedures

A typical hardware environment today consists of the following:

- Pentium or Pentium II microprocessor (166 MHz or greater)
- Twenty-four megabytes or more of RAM
- Large capacity hard drive (2GB or more)
- Fax modems
- SVGA video board and monitor
- CD-ROM
- Sound card with speakers
- 3.5" floppy disk drive

Unlike the systems of a few years ago, many of today's PCs come with all the operating environment software already loaded on the hard drive. This usually includes DOS, Windows, and many applications. Today, customers take their computers out of the box, turn on the power, and start putting them to use.

Many vendors either include copies of the software programs on compact disks, or else provide automatically invoked backup procedures to allow the user to make an initial backup of all pre-loaded software on the system. In addition, many customers get their company software image loaded on the system by their reseller. This way, when a user receives their system, they are ready for business.

Many of the hardware components listed here are needed because of the requirements placed on the system hardware by the operating and applications software environments. Larger amounts of hard disk space are increasingly needed to run applications packages, many of which require anywhere from 15MB or more, just for the initial installation.

Today, all that is needed when installing and setting up new software environments is access to a floppy or CD-ROM drive to run the software's installation program. Not only will the installation program copy all the necessary files, it will also update or modify operating systems files for you. The only thing left for the user to do is to make a backup copy of any new programs that have been added.

# Initializing Media and Backing Up Data

In order for a hard drive to accept information, the hard drive must be partitioned. This is accomplished through a transient command file usually called FDISK. This file is executed by typing FDISK at the DOS prompt and pressing the ENTER key on the keyboard. Note that some manufacturers may have a different name for this file. One manufacturer used to call its partitioning file PREP.

Hard drives also need to be defined to the ROM BIOS. This is usually done in what is referred to as the setup menu. The system needs to be aware of the size of the hard drive in total tracks (cylinders), the number of read/write heads, and whether or not "pre-compensation" and reduced write current are being used.

Precompensation is an analysis by the drive controller of the stream of data bits that is to be written to the hard drive. By altering the timing by which data bits are written to the hard drive, pre-compensation guarantees that magnetic interference between data bits does not cause any read errors.

Reduced write current is the drive logic that reduces the amount of electrical current to the write heads as the heads move to the inside tracks. Because the data bits are more closely spaced around the inside tracks, the electrical current must be reduced as the head moves into that area in order to avoid interference between data bits.

When you purchase a hard drive, the documentation generally specifies the type of drive it is. This drive type number (usually in two digits), when entered into the setup menu, defines all the necessary parameters of the drive to the system. Most setup menus today have a feature called auto-detect, which will automatically analyze the drive and update the setup menu with the pertinent information.

In the original IBM ATs and compatibles, many of these drive types were pre-defined in the ROM BIOS. For drives whose types are not listed, the ROM usually offers a user-defined choice. When that choice is selected, you can manually enter all the various parameters of the drive, including number of heads, number of tracks, etc.

Under DOS, to format a hard disk and copy the system files to it, a basic command such as FORMAT C:/S will suffice. This command instructs the system to format the C drive, and upon completion of that function, to transfer the necessary system files (IO.SYS, MSDOS.SYS, and COMMAND.COM) from the bootable floppy to the hard drive.

Before we discuss the IO.SYS, MSDOS.SYS, and COMMAND.COM files, let's consider file space allocation. DOS allocates space for a file on demand, on a first-come, first-served basis. It does not reserve space in advance. File space is allocated one cluster at a time, as needed. These clusters are arranged to minimize head movement of the disk drive, whether it's the floppy drive or hard drive.

There are many ways that DOS uses clusters. It may use first available or next available. In first available, DOS scans the file allocation table (FAT), uses the first available cluster, and moves on from there. With the next available option, DOS begins where the last write took place and finds the first available cluster from that point.

## Major System Files of DOS

The IO.SYS is a hidden file on a bootable disk that interacts with the devices on the system and the ROM BIOS. A hidden file has system attributes and is not available for viewing or modifying without specialty utilities. The IO.SYS file is usually modified by the manufacturer to match itself with the vendor's particular ROM BIOS.

As mentioned earlier, the ROM BIOS contains all the system's bootstrap codes, power-on self-tests (POSTs), and other software code that is critical to system start-up. That is why it is important to be careful when upgrading DOS from one vendor to another. If you are running IBM DOS and upgrade it with another manufacturer's version, the two may not be compatible.

For a disk to be bootable, the IO.SYS must be listed as the first file in the disk directory and occupy at least the first cluster. The attributes assigned to this file are hidden, system, and read only. It is recommended that you never alter or change the attributes because this can cause many unrecoverable-type problems. This file is usually transferred to a disk during a FORMAT operation or a SYS command, thus making the disk bootable.

MSDOS.SYS, commonly referred to as the core of DOS, contains the disk-handling programs. The MSDOS.SYS file must be the second entry in a root directory and has the same attributes as the IO.SYS.

The COMMAND.COM is the DOS user's interface. Commands available through this file are categorized as resident commands. Resident commands are available whenever the DOS prompt is present. Some resident commands are DIR (runs a file directory of the currently active drive), ERASE, COPY, and MD (make directory).

Transient commands are often called utilities. They are not resident in memory, and the instructions necessary to execute the command must be on disk. Most DOS commands are transient because if all were memory-resident, they would overtax system memory.

## Configuration Tools and Commands in DOS

After the system loads MSDOS.SYS, IO.SYS, and COMMAND.COM, it locates the CONFIG.SYS file, if one is present. CONFIG.SYS is a text file that contains commands to configure your computer's hardware components so that DOS and software application programs can use them. This file must be in the root directory of the system disk. See Figure 5-1 for a sample of a typical CONFIG.SYS file.

Here's what each of the elements in the typical CONFIG.SYS file does:

Device is used to load an installable device driver. A device driver is a list of software instructions that instruct the computer about how to deal with a particular hardware component.

Devicehigh loads an installable device driver into the upper memory area of RAM. The DOS command specifies whether DOS will use high memory and upper memory blocks. (High memory is extended memory—typically memory above the 1MB boundary.)

Files specifies how many files can be open at a time.

Stacks specifies how much memory to reserve for processing hardware interrupts. For every system interrupt that occurs, it is necessary to access the ROM BIOS for an interrupt routine, which instructs the system how to process the interrupt.

Another file that is executed at system start-up is the AUTOEXEC.BAT file. This file contains many DOS commands that execute automatically. These can include prompt commands, path commands, and other DOS statements. See Figure 5-2 for a typical AUTOEXEC.BAT file.

Here is what each of the elements in the typical AUTOEXEC.BAT file does:

The ECHO OFF command directs DOS not to display the commands in the AUTOEXEC.BAT file as they run. It is usually the first command in an AUTOEXEC.BAT file.

**Figure 5-1**
CONFIG.SYS file.

```
DEVICE=C:\DOS\HIMEM.SYS
DEVICE=C\DOS\EMM386.EXE NOEMS X=D000-D8FF
DEVICEHIGH=C:\DOS\SETVER.EXE
DOS=HIGH,UMB
FILES=30
STACKS=9,256
```

**Figure 5-2**
A typical
AUTOEXEC.BAT file.

```
@ECHO OFF
C:\DOS\SMARTDRV.EXE C
PROMPT=$p$g
PATH C:\WINWORD;C:\DOS;C:WINDOWS;
C:\CARDWARE
SET TEMP=C:\DOS
SET MOUSE=C:\MOUSE
LOADHIGH C:\MOUSE\MOUSE
LOADHIGH DOSKEY
CD \WINDOWS
C:\DOS\SHARE.EXE
WIN
CD \
```

The SMARTDrive program, which is part of the later DOS versions, decreases the time your computer spends reading data from your hard disk. The program accomplishes this by reserving an area in extended memory, in which it stores information that it reads from the hard drive. Storing some information in extended memory increases the speed of access because memory access is faster than hard drive access.

The prompt command (PROMPT=$p$g) defines the system prompt, which DOS normally displays as the current drive letter; followed by a greater-than sign, such as C>. If you change the system prompt, you can include any character that DOS can display; plus such items of system information as the time, date, current drive, current directory, and so on. In the command line at the start of the paragraph, the $p says to indicate the current directory of the current drive, and the $g says to end it with the greater-than > sign.

A PATH statement tells DOS where to search for a command file that is not in the directory being currently used. This command path becomes part of the DOS environment, so it is available to every program that DOS carries out during a work session on your computer.

The SET TEMP command creates a directory named TEMP that is used to store temporary files that the system may create during normal operations. Many programs, including DOS, use this command when storing temporary files.

The LOADHIGH command loads a program into higher memory.

The CD command (e.g., CD\WINDOWS) changes the current directory to another. In the example, the CD\WINDOWS command changes the system to the WINDOWS directory.

The WIN command is the command to load Windows (Windows 3.x only). It calls on the WIN.EXE file. If your system automatically comes up in Windows, the WIN command is more than likely a part of your AUTOEXEC.BAT file.

It is important to keep in mind that an incorrect statement or setting in either the CONFIG.SYS or the AUTOEXEC.BAT files can cause the system to fail or operate incorrectly.

If changes are required to the CONFIG.SYS or AUTOEXEC.BAT files, you can use the EDIT command to make them. EDIT is a line-editor program that allows you to examine the current state of these files and, if necessary, add or remove the command lines. We recommend that if you edit these files, you make a backup copy of them first. This way, if something goes wrong, you can at least get back to where you started. Save the file as CONFIG.OLD or AUTOEXEC.OLD. By using the OLD extension, you can distinguish between the copy on disk and the original file stored on the drive.

# Windows 3.x

Windows is a graphical user interface (GUI) that allows you to switch between multiple applications and transfer information between them.

In Windows, the computer screen is called the desktop, and it displays all your work in rectangular areas called windows. Each window displays a certain application, such as word-processing documents or an electronic spreadsheet. These can be arranged on your desktop just as you arrange things on your real desk.

Windows also comes with some useful accessory programs such as an appointment calendar, a calculator, and a notepad, to name a few. It also provides on-line help menus that give quick and concise how-to information. It is easy to understand why Windows has gained popularity.

## Hardware Components used with Windows and Setup Procedures

Although Windows 3.x can run in many different hardware environments, here are some of its minimum requirements:

■ MS-DOS version 3.1 or later

■ A personal computer with an Intel 486 or higher microprocessor

■ Greater than 2MB of memory (2 is usually considered absolute minimum and 4, 8, and 16 are becoming more standard)

- A hard disk drive greater than 100MB (many Windows applications require 8-12MB of free space)
- At least one floppy drive
- A video monitor supported by Windows (VGA or SVGA recommended)
- A printer that is supported by Windows (laser recommended)
- A mouse supported by Windows
- A Hayes-compatible modem for use with the Windows communication software

When installing Windows 3.x, start at the DOS prompt by typing the word "setup" and hitting the ENTER key. The setup program guides you through the installation by first evaluating the existing hardware environment, then copying the essential Windows files onto the hard disk. Along the way, it will ask you to verify critical information and make changes as needed. The information requested during setup includes:

- The directory where you want to store Windows
- The type of computer you are using
- The type of video display
- The type of mouse or pointing device, if any
- The keyboard type (101 or 102, with extended functions, etc.) and language layout (English, Spanish, etc.)
- The type of network, if any
- The type of printer, and which I/O port is being used for it
- Applications on hard disk that you want to run with Windows

After the preliminary installation, Setup loads the Windows 3.x software, installs the remaining files, and offers some options. Setup can run later at any time, just as with any other Windows application. This allows you to review or change previous settings if you wish. You may want to review settings when the customer is experiencing a failure to print, for example. The failure may be caused by the end user selecting the wrong printing device in Setup.

When Windows 3.x first starts, the Program Manager application is open on your desktop. The Program Manager is central to Windows, and allows you to organize your other applications into groups and to start using them. There are basic elements and skills you need to know when working in Windows.

## Major System Files of Windows/Windows Configuration Tools and Commands

Windows 3.x uses initialization files that contain information that defines your software and hardware needs to Windows. Windows for Workgroups and Windows-based applications can use the information stored in initialization files to make their configurations meet your system's hardware needs, and your preferences for the look and feel of the operating environment.

There are two standard Windows initialization files:

▪ WIN.INI, which primarily contains settings that Windows maintains to customize your Windows environment according to your preference for such things as color, "wallpaper," sounds, etc.

▪ SYSTEM.INI, which primarily contains settings that customize Windows to meet your system's hardware needs for such things as I/O devices, memory, video, etc.

There are two ways to change the WIN.INI settings:

▪ You can use the Control Panel to change most settings. This is the safest and recommended way because there is no need to open and edit the WIN.INI file, where it is easier to make mistakes.

▪ You can use a text editor, such as Notepad, to edit the WIN.INI file directly. This method is used to change settings that you cannot change through the Control Panel. Anytime the WIN.INI file is changed, you must restart Windows for the changes to take effect.

As with DOS and other operating systems, when you work with Windows, you'll need some knowledge of its general operation. It is beyond the scope of this book to teach you Windows; however, we do provide a Windows Basic Skills checklist identifying the areas you need to know in the service/repair environment. For additional reading and training on Windows, refer to Appendices C and D in the back of this book.

## Windows Basic Skills Checklist

In order to be considered proficient in Windows, you need a working knowledge of some basic skills. This is critical in a repair scenario, so that you can navigate through the operating environment. As you review the following checklist, compare it with what you already know of the Windows operating environment.

- Types of Windows
  - Application
  - Document

- Parts of a window
  - Control-menu box
  - Window corner
  - Workspace
  - Selection cursor
  - Mouse pointer
  - Title bar
  - Window title
  - Window border
  - Menu bar
  - Scroll bars, horizontal and vertical
  - Maximize and Minimum buttons
  - Icons
  - Application icons
  - Document icons
  - Program item icons

- Working with menus
  - Selecting and canceling
  - Choosing menu commands
  - Using control menus

- Working with dialog boxes
  - Moving dialog boxes
  - Choosing options
  - Closing dialog boxes

- Working with windows
  - Moving windows
  - Changing the size of a window
  - Closing a window

- Working with applications
  - Running two or more applications
  - Switching between applications
  - Arranging application windows

- Working with documents
  - Opening and saving documents/files
  - Switching and arranging document windows
  - Working with text
  - Using on-line Help functions
  - Starting Help
  - Using Help
  - Finding information in Help

- Control Panel
  - Desktop options
  - Installing and configuring printers
  - Connection to network printers
  - Removing an installed printer
  - Configuring communication ports

- CONFIG.SYS file command lines
  - HIMEM.SYS (extended memory manager)
  - SMARTDrive (disk caching program)
  - RAMDrive (to set up a RAM disk)
  - EMM386.SYS (expanded memory emulator)

# Windows 95

The Microsoft Windows 95 operating system is the successor to Windows version 3.1 and Windows for Workgroups version 3.11. Windows 95 was designed to provide network administrators and systems support professionals with a variety of tools and capabilities to better manage the PC environment and to help reduce support costs. Windows 95 also brought new features and an improved user interface to enhance productivity.

New 32-bit printing, graphics, and other subsystems speed up operations for common tasks, such as file saving and/or copying. Networking is also faster in Windows 95 because the 32-bit networking components provide speed improvements. Win95 is as fast or faster than Windows 3.1. Also, as RAM is added, a system running Windows 95 will become comparatively faster, as measured by industry standard benchmarks.

# New Features in Windows 95

- Improved Interface: Windows 95 introduced a new user interface, making the PC easier and more efficient for users, regardless of expertise level. A Start button and taskbar are featured. You can click on the Start button to open programs, find documents, and access system tools. The taskbar easily allows you to switch between programs.

- Increased system security and control: Windows 95 supports pass-through, server-based security for NetWare and Windows NT networks. This includes validated logon, and user-level security. In addition, Win95 provides security for tasks such as Dial-Up networking, supporting encrypted dial-in passwords and callback options.

- System policies: These allow you to centrally define and control user access to the network and desktop functionality.

- Windows Explorer: In Windows 3.x, this was referred to as File Manager. Explorer allows you to browse and manage files, drives, and network connections.

- Long filenames: In the past, any time you saved a new file, you were limited to an eight (8) character length for the filename. Win95 supports long filenames to make files easier to organize and locate.

- Plug and Play hardware compatibility: When a hardware card is newly installed in your computer and it meets the specifications for Plug and Play, Win95 will recognize it and set up the configuration automatically. On the other hand, if you remove an interface card, Win95 will ask you if you wish to uninstall it.

- Enhanced game and multimedia support: Win95 will allow you to enjoy faster video capabilities, better support for MS-DOS based games, and increased performance for video and sound files.

- 32-bit preemptive multitasking: When using 32-bit applications, users do not need to wait for completion of a particular task before they can begin work on another task. For example, you can begin the download of a large file, and then switch to working on a document or spreadsheet while the file downloads in the background

- Customer setup scripts: Win95 supports the scripting of installation processes for predetermined settings and responses to be automatically read from a single file, thus reducing most installation times.

- New tutorial and Help features: Win95 is designed to make it easier for users to obtain information on specific tasks by making Help streamlined and task-oriented.

## Ease of Installation and Configuration on Existing Windows 3.1 Installations

An easy installation requires no more than swapping diskettes or installing from a CD-ROM. Windows 95 can use the configuration information from the previous Windows installation for the new setup. Instead of the lengthy INI files that many of us are familiar with from earlier versions of Windows, Windows 95 uses the Registry. Entries in the Registry are available to application programs through APIs (application programming interfaces). Applications can add to and retrieve their private configuration settings by using Registry access APIs. The Registry should never be edited by the user because serious problems could arise.

Some of the major features in Windows 95 are as follows:

- It presents its own interface to support electronic mail.

- Filenames are no longer limited to the standard 8 characters.

- File viewers allow you to examine a formatted file without having access to the application that created it. For example, it allows you to view a file created with DBase 2, even if you don't have that application loaded.

- Support for Pen systems; for example, those used in the mobile marketplace on systems such as Apple Newton.

- Better support for MS-DOS applications. Even though it is not an MS-DOS environment, Windows 95 performs well with applications written specifically for DOS.

- Easier system administration and reconfiguration procedures.

Every aspect of the existing system was analyzed to improve ease of installation and upgrading. You should not be confused when adding any new device to the Windows 95 environment.

# Installing and Upgrading

## Upgrade Potential and Component Compatibility

As you add new components to the system, such as more RAM, or a different video board or monitor, you will be required to make changes to some of the files. This ensures that the system has all the information needed to work with the total hardware environment, and that the system is optimized for maximum performance. The greatest hardware environment, if not configured properly, will run slowly.

But before beginning any upgrade or installation, it is important to review both the current and the proposed hardware and/or software environment. Is it just a hardware installation, just a software installation, or both? If you are not sure what is to be done, you cannot know if you have everything necessary for successful completion. You need to know at the start if all the elements that must work together after the upgrade or installation are software-compatible, as well as physically and electrically compatible.

For example, it may seem like a good idea to upgrade your VGA video board to an SVGA card. But will the current video display support the new card or will that have to be upgraded also? Do you have enough available hard drive space for the new software package you plan to add? Do you have enough RAM to support the new environment you're creating?

All too often, technicians return to a system two or three times before they have all these questions answered. It's better to answer them all at the start. We also recommend that you don't rely on customers to tell you what they need. If they ask you to install more memory, you might want to ask why. Make sure that adding memory will really give the customer the benefit he or she wants. Too often customers add memory and expect great improvements in performance, only to be disappointed by the results.

## Common Drivers: Function and Configuration

Each of the computer's hardware components is called a device and has characteristics that can be customized by using commands in the

CONFIG.SYS file. For example, you could change the language designation of the keyboard from English to French or Spanish.

MS-DOS uses a program called a device driver to control every device. There are device drivers for your keyboard, hard disk, floppy disk, and I/O ports. Because these device drivers are built-in, you do not have to do anything special to use them.

Some common drivers are:

- ANSI.SYS
- DISPLAY.SYS
- DRIVER.SYS
- EMM386.EXE
- HIMEM.SYS
- RAMDRIVE.SYS

ANSI.SYS supports American National Standards Institute (ANSI) terminal emulation.

DISPLAY.SYS supports high-speed page switching for monitors.

DRIVER.SYS allocates a portion of memory to be used or designated as a logical device.

EMM386.EXE simulates expanded memory and provides access to the upper memory area on a computer that has an 80386 or higher processor with extended memory.

HIMEM.SYS manages the use of extended memory on a computer with an 80286 or higher processor and extended memory.

RAMDRIVE.SYS simulates a hard disk drive by creating a virtual disk drive in the system's RAM.

## Methods for Upgrading DOS

The easiest way to perform any upgrade of MS-DOS is to use the automatic installation and upgrade utility that is built into DOS. By swapping disks as instructed by the utility, you replace the existing version files with the new version.

Another process that could be performed when upgrading is the repartitioning of the hard drive. The hard drive can be partitioned to represent many different logical "devices" (drives). Partitioning dates back to the early days of PCs, when MS-DOS had the capability to recognize a maximum of 32MB for any given logical drive or partition. A 50MB drive might have been partitioned into two sections, and DOS would see those partitions as drive C and drive D.

A disk may still need to be partitioned today—not to divide it into multiple devices, but, as mentioned earlier, to make the hard drive as a whole capable of accepting information.

In today's software environment there is rarely a need to partition the hard drive unless you are configuring a hard drive that has never been partitioned before for the first time.

However, if you do repartition any hard drive that has been partitioned before and has data on it, it is important to first back up all data on the drive to avoid losing it.

# Windows Installation

Methods for installing and upgrading Windows:

To install Windows for the very first time, place the Windows installation disk #1 in floppy drive A.

At the A> prompt, type SETUP and press ENTER.

You will be asked if you want to perform an Express Setup or a Custom Setup. Unless you are experienced with the Custom Setup, choose Express Setup.

Setup checks the configuration of your system, then asks you on which directory of the hard drive you want Windows installed. The default is C:\WINDOWS, but you can select any directory you wish.

Setup begins copying files to the hard disk, and prompts you along the way to insert the next installation disk until all files have been loaded. During this process, the Windows installation program brings up screens that explain the various features and benefits of the Windows environment that you're installing, and gives you a chance to register your software.

At the end of the installation, you will be prompted to choose a printer type. If you do not choose one, Windows will not set up any printer driver for you. A new printer driver can always be selected later.

After selecting your printer, Windows begins searching your hard drive for all application programs, and sets up DOS PATH statements and an icon for each one that it can identify. (Clicking on that icon thereafter will prompt the system to locate and activate that program.) For those applications that the system cannot identify, Windows asks you to assign a name to each one for which it builds a DOS PATH statement and icon.

The last thing Windows asks is whether you want to run a short tutorial on Windows. You can always go back later and run the tutorial at a later session.

When you install Windows for the first time, the first part of the Setup program runs in MS-DOS. Setup switches into the Windows mode and presents you with a Windows interface, offering point-and-click options.

If Setup stops, or locks up while in the MS-DOS mode, it may be because it couldn't identify some system hardware, and therefore didn't know what to do with it. To solve this problem, type SETUP/I at the DOS prompt. This will skip hardware detection and run Custom Setup.

In the system information screen, be sure to select descriptions that match the hardware on your system: for example, VGA video, 486 processor, and 500MB hard drive.

One feature of Windows that allows for easy installation of application programs is its standardization of many common commands, such as SETUP. To install any program designed to run with Windows, from the Program Manager select FILE, and then RUN, and then type A:\SETUP. From that point on, you will be instructed when to change disks or enter information.

The preceding description of the Windows installation is the same for all versions. However, when you install Windows for Workgroups, you are also prompted to supply information about the network you have installed.

**WINDOWS 95 INSTALLATION AND UPGRADE**   Windows 95 can be installed over a previous Windows 3.1 version or a previous MSDOS environment.

# Upgrading a Previous Version of Windows

1. Insert Setup Disk 1 in a floppy drive, or insert your Windows CD-ROM into the CD drive.

2. In File Manager or Program Manager, click FILE, and then click RUN.

3. Type the drive letter, followed by the command: A:\SETUP

4. Follow all instructions through the entire setup process.

# Setting Up Windows 95 from MS-DOS

1. Insert Setup disk 1 in a floppy drive or your Windows CD-ROM is a ROM drive.

2. At the command prompt, type the drive letter, followed by a colon, and a backslash, and the word setup: [C:\] A:\SETUP.

3. Press ENTER, and then follow the instructions on your screen.

During the installation and setup of Windows 95, you will be given four choices of setup options:

▓ Typical—Sets up the most commonly used Windows components.

▓ Portable—Sets up features that are most useful for a portable computing environment while conserving disk space.

▓ Compact—Sets up only the basic files you need to run Windows 95 (this is used if you have limited disk drive space).

▓ Custom—Enables you to choose exactly which components to install.

# Starting Windows 95

After the installation, and rebooting your system, you may be prompted to log on to Windows (if you are attached to a network, you are prompted to log on to your network). If you do not wish to use a password to log on to Windows 95, do not type anything in the password box, and click OK.

## Start Button and Taskbar

As shown in Figure 5-3, the Start button and Taskbar are located at the bottom of the screen when you start Windows 95 for the first time. When you click on the Start button, you will see a menu that has everything you need to begin using Windows 95. Here is an overview of some of the commands:

**Figure 5-3**
The Windows
Taskbar.

- Programs displays a list of programs that are installed on your computer.

- Documents displays a list of documents that have been opened previously.

- Settings displays a list of system components and allows you to change their settings.

- Find enables you to find a folder, file, shared computer, or mail message.

- Help starts the Help feature; and gives you access to Help Contents, Index, or other tabs that will give you information on how to do specific tasks.

- Run allows you to start a program or open a folder when you type a MS-DOS command.

- Shut Down shuts down or restarts your computer, depending on your selection.

In your Taskbar, you may notice a couple of extra buttons such as Infrared and PC eject. These buttons are exclusive to a laptop environment and allow you to utilize infrared communications, or eject the laptop from a docking station.

*NOTE:   Many of us as field service engineers have acted in the role of technical support more than once. How many times in the past have you thought to yourself that the individual you are helping should just "read the manual?" I bring this up because of the previous mention of the Help button. Windows 95 contains a very thorough index of information for almost anything that you wish to accomplish, and it is at your fingertips (see Figure 5-4). One of the best lessons that can be taught to any user is how to utilize the Help Index for locating the information they need. By taking a few minutes and stepping them through the to the answer you may have just given will show them how to locate the answer themselves, thus saving time.*

## Control Panel

To access the Control Panel, click the Start button, point to Settings, and then point and click on Control Panel (see Figure 5-5).

**NOTE:**  *The icons that appear in Control Panel vary, depending on the hardware and software installed on your system.*

**Figure 5-4**
Windows Help.

**Figure 5-5**
Control Panel.

There are many settings you can change by using the Control Panel. These settings include screen colors, hardware and software settings, and setup or change of network settings. Although the Control Panel incorporates most of the components used to effect setup, configuration, and control of a particular area of Windows, there are other ways to access the same function.

The best example of this is printer control. Printers can be accessed through the Control Panel, through its own button in Settings, and through a specialized button in the Microsoft Office environment. Either method of access will get you to the same window.

## Effecting Display Changes

The Display Properties window allows you to configure display drivers/resolutions, change color palettes, customize font size, invoke a screen saver, and choose a background screen. You can also use the settings in Screen Saver to take advantage of Energy Star Monitor support if your hardware supports this feature (see Figure 5-6).

*CAUTION:* *Some monitors can be physically damaged by incorrect display settings. Always review any documentation that comes with a new monitor prior to making any changes.*

**Figure 5-6**
Display Properties
window.

# Adding/Removing New Hardware or Reconfiguring Existing Hardware

**PLUG-AND-PLAY SUPPORT**  "Plug-and-play" is a standard that allows for easy installation, easy reconfiguration, and quick on-the-fly configuration changes for any peripheral device that meets the standard. In order for this standard to be successful, it must have the cooperation of the operating system suppliers, system manufacturers, BIOS developers, and device vendors. By working together, these industry players are contributing common user interfaces; along with common device drivers, installation procedures, and other features helpful to the user.

To fully understand how Plug and Play is implemented in Windows 95, it is important to understand the various elements of the subsystem: the hardware tree, INF files, events, Configuration Manager, and Registry.

The hardware tree is the database of information that describes the current system configuration. It is built by the Configuration Manager and stored in memory.

INF files are a collection of disk files that contain information about particular types of devices. For example, SCSI.INF contains information about every known SCSI device. When a new SCSI device is installed, a new .INF file is created, specific to that new device.

Events are a set of application programming interfaces (APIs) that are used to signal changes in the system's current configuration.

The Configuration Manager is the central component that supports the Plug-and-Play capability. It builds into the Registry the database of information that describes the machine's configuration, and notifies device drivers of their assigned resources.

The Registry is a database maintained by Windows 95 that provides a unified database for storing system and software application configuration data in a hierarchical format. Because the Registry contains all settings required to configure memory, hardware peripherals, and Windows-95 supplied network components, you may find that it is no longer necessary to configure settings in startup configuration and initialization (INI) files. The Registry is similar to the INI files used in Windows 3.x, with each key in the Registry similar to a bracketed heading in an INI file. The following benefits are provided by the Registry:

■ A single source provides data for identifying and configuring hardware applications, device drivers, and operating system control parameters.

■ Users and administrators can configure computer options by using standard Control Panel tools, reducing the likelihood of syntax-type errors in configuration information.

■ A set of network-independent functions can be used to set and query configuration information, allowing system administrators to examine configuration data on remote networked computers.

■ The operating system automatically backs up the last good configuration used to start the computer system.

Each time Windows 95 successfully starts, the operating system backs up the Registry by copying the current SYSTEM.DAT and USER.DAT files to SYSTEM.DA0 and USER.DA0, respectively. If Windows 95 fails to start, the backed-up Registry from the last successful startup can be copied over to the current Registry.

To run the Registry editor, click the Start button, click the Run button, and type REGEDIT (see Figure 5-7).

The screen that appears after you click on OK is shown in Figure 5-8.

**Figure 5-7**
Running the Registry editor.

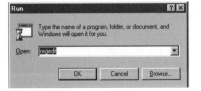

**Figure 5-8**
The Registry Editor window.

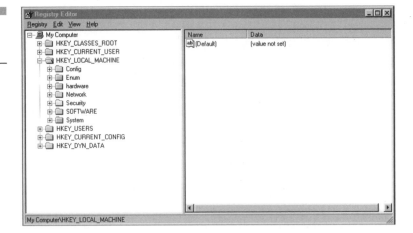

A Registry editor can be used to view or modify a Registry on a local computer or another computer over a network. The network administrator can restrict users from being able to use the Registry Editor by setting a system policy named Disable Registry Editing Tools.

## Device Management

When adding new devices to your computer system under Windows 95, there are Plug-and-Play-compliant devices and legacy devices. Plug-and-play (PnP) devices are those that meet the PnP standard, along with the system they are being installed into. Legacy devices are those that are not PnP-compatible, but can still can be used when installed in a different manner.

When you install a new device, you should first rely on Windows 95 to detect and configure it. For PnP devices, this means inserting the device into the computer. For legacy devices, this means running the Add New Hardware Wizard. After the device is installed, if it is PnP, Windows 95 notifies you that it has identified a new card. If it cannot detect a driver to use, it will request that you insert a disk that contains a driver for the device.

To install a legacy device, you must go into the Control Panel and double-click on the Add New Hardware option. In the Add New Hardware Wizard, click on Next, and then click on the option named Automatically Detect Installed Hardware (see Figure 5-9).

Continue to follow the instructions on the screen to install drivers and to configure the device driver. As we mentioned earlier, if Windows 95 does not have a driver for the device, you can install the driver from a disk by using the Add New Hardware Wizard.

**Figure 5-9**
The Add New
Hardware Wizard.

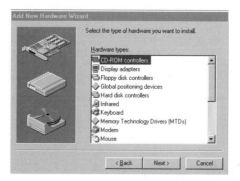

Certain circumstances may require users to change resource settings after they have been configured. This might happen if you cannot configure one device without conflicting with another. Usually, a message will appear to explain what is happening and provide some direction on what to do. The best resource for resolving any conflicts that might occur is the Hardware Conflict Troubleshooting Aid in the Windows 95 online Help (see Figure 5-10).

When you must manually change a device's configuration, use Device Manager. To access Device Manager, double-click on the System option in the Control Panel and select the Device Manager tab (see Figure 5-11). In Device Manager, double-click on the related device type, double-click on your current device to display its properties, and click on the driver tab. This dialog box will then show you the driver files and current settings for that device.

In Device Manager, you can print reports about the system settings, including those on the following:

■ System summary

■ Selected class or device

■ All devices and system summary

The system summary report will give you general system information, including IRQ usage, I/O port usage, memory usage summary, and DMA channel usage summary.

**Figure 5-10**
Using Help to resolve a hardware conflict.

**Figure 5-11**
The Device Manager tab of the System Properties window.

There are many details contained in Windows 95. Please review the online Help section to see the extent of the topics that are available. Looking at some of these on a system will be very beneficial in advancing your education with Windows 95.

# Diagnosing Software Problems

This section is concerned primarily with diagnosing software problems. For more materials on diagnosing hardware problems, see Chapter 4's diagnosing section.

## System Boot Sequences: Approaches to Diagnosing

Earlier in the chapter, we looked at the hierarchy of the system software, from the ROM BIOS to the application programs, and examined the three main files necessary to make a disk bootable (IO.SYS, MSDOS.SYS, and COMMAND.COM). This information is important to the topic of diagnosing. You need to know how systems operate to successfully diagnose problems.

Problems in the microcomputer environment occur in four areas:

- Hardware
- Software
- Environment
- Operator error

You should know how to distinguish between software and hardware errors. The quickest, most efficient way is to have disk-based diagnostics for identifying hardware problems and a copy of DOS with you. Remember to use your own software—the customer's AUTOEXEC.BAT and CONFIG.SYS files may be defective.

Here's a true story that illustrates the helpfulness of bringing your own software with you to the customer site. A customer began to get error messages saying "insufficient memory" when he attempted to run a word processor. The first step the technician took was to run some memory disk-based diagnostics. From his initial conversation with the user, he knew that the memory errors occurred during the loading of that one word processor program; however, he still wanted to be sure of memory integrity.

After a complete test of the memory circuits revealed no errors, the technician loaded a copy of DOS from his floppy disks. With that loaded, he logged over to the hard drive directory that contained the word processor, and executed the command file to load that program. The word processor loaded without fail and executed flawlessly.

At this point, the technician examined the CONFIG.SYS and AUTOEXEC.BAT files. The CONFIG.SYS file was in order, but the AUTOEXEC.BAT file had an unusually large number of memory-resident programs. The customer had received some public domain pop-up programs and wanted them all. The programs took up so much memory that not enough was left when the customer attempted to run the word processor, hence the "insufficient memory" error messages. By having his own software, the technician saved time in isolating the cause of the problem.

If you do not have your own copy of DOS, you can rename the user's AUTOEXEC.BAT and CONFIG.SYS files temporarily, so that they don't execute upon start-up. (Those files are not needed for booting up.) If the system works without those files, but not with them, it's a good sign that they are causing the problem.

These techniques apply to all areas of the operating environment. If a port does not print or receive data, copies of your own software could assist in finding this out. For example, suppose you boot up in the customer's software environment, and the system does not print; when you boot up with your own software, the system does print. Most likely, files in the customer's system have been improperly configured or damaged. But be careful not to modify anything within the customer's operating system environment until you are sure it is the solution to the problem.

The software you should have with you include disk-based diagnostics, an operating environment (such as MS-DOS or Windows), a simple application program familiar to you, and a current virus-scan application. (You do not want to be accused of transferring viruses to your customer's equipment.)

It is generally a good idea to carry more than one copy of any disk-based diagnostic because, at times, a copy might become corrupted. If a floppy disk drive corrupts your disk, you should have another available.

The methods that are required to solve and repair software problems are very simple and straightforward. First, determine whether the problem is hardware- or software-related. As with any problem, you need to consider all the aspects of the software and hardware that are involved. For example, let us assume that a customer is having difficulty printing from a word processor. First look at all the areas that could possibly cause the problem, as follows:

- Serial and/or parallel port
- Software application
- Cabling
- Printer
- Power
- Operator error

**QUESTIONS TO ASK ABOUT CUSTOMER PROBLEMS**  Some questions you might ask the operator in the previous example:

- Does the error occur throughout all applications or with one particular application?
- Is the error intermittent or consistent?
- What error messages, if any, were displayed?
- Can the operator re-create the error?
- Can you continue after the error, or is the machine locked up?
- Is the printer plugged in and loaded with paper?
- Is the Windows Print Manager configured properly?

■ Is all cabling in order?

■ Does the printer successfully perform its self-test?

Questions like these will either quickly identify the cause of the problem or send you on to run diagnostics on the system. Take each challenge step by step.

Many software-related errors are caused by configuration errors. People inadvertently modify or change a setting without realizing it. When investigating any problem, leave no stone unturned. You will, however, face some situations that escape explanation.

Correcting the problem generally requires you to have access to the master diskettes or a current backup for the system. This is necessary to obtain specific device drivers. Always refer to the software documentation, if available.

## Common DOS Failures

A failure means that during execution, the desired action or results were not accomplished for some reason. A failure could be caused by corruption of the operating system (which is software code), by a hardware failure, or by an external influence (magnetic fields, heat, etc.). The failure might even be caused by operator error.

Today, because of graphic-user interface environments like Windows, we meet fewer problems caused by operator error than we did in the days of working from the DOS prompt. For example, today's "Bad command or file name" error message usually means that the file is not on the disk drive, nor in the directory that the command line specified it would be in.

Some common error messages include:

■ Bad command or file name. This message comes up because DOS could not locate the file. In some cases, the problem may be an input error by the operator.

■ Error reading drive. There are a host of messages describing the system's inability to read a diskette or hard drive. The error may stem from anything involved with the read operation. Possibilities include a corrupted disk, an unformatted disk drive, no diskette in the drive, or software errors. The system may be having problems reading only a single file, but gives a message saying that it is unable to read the drive that the file is on.

■ Not enough memory. A message of this nature indicates that the system attempted to load a file or program but had insufficient memory available to do so. This message is common today because many programs require far more memory than in the past. Users also sometimes overload their systems with memory-resident programs, leaving insufficient memory to run application programs.

- Unable to load device driver. This message indicates that the system attempted to load a device driver, but the device could not be found. This message could apply to drivers for any device, such as the mouse, memory driver, or network card. Questions to ask yourself include: Was the device attached? Has the device failed? Has the correct driver been selected for loading the device?

Regardless of the problems you encounter, it is important to know what the computer was attempting to do at the time of error. Common sense will help you from there. If you were attempting to read a disk, don't go looking for errors in the AUTOEXEC.BAT file.

## Common Windows 3.x Failures

There are a number of errors that can be encountered in the Windows environment. Even simple installations can run into glitches. Remember that if your installation falters, it could be because the system does not recognize the hardware. Type SETUP/I at the DOS prompt to skip hardware detection and run Custom Setup.

If you have completed Setup and Windows will not start, one of the following may be the cause:

- The wrong hardware may have been specified for the system during a custom setup.

- The computer may not be running on the required microprocessor (at least a 386SX microprocessor) or it may not have enough memory to support your version of Windows (Windows 3.1, Windows for Workgroups 3.11, or Windows NT).

- The computer system may be running memory-resident (terminal stay resident) programs that are incompatible with Windows and could not be detected during setup. To check this possibility, create a "clean boot" floppy disk that contains only the files necessary to start the computer and Windows. Boot this "clean copy" from the floppy drive. If Windows starts, the system is probably running memory-resident programs that are incompatible with Windows.

■ If you are using Windows for Workgroups and using a network
  card, be sure that all network connections are intact.

If, after checking all of these, Windows still will not start, try the following:

■ If this is Windows for Workgroups and a network is involved, start
  Windows by typing WIN/N at the DOS prompt to start Windows
  without starting the network. If this command is successful in
  starting Windows, contact the network administrator to
  investigate problems on the network.

■ Start Windows by typing WIN/B at the DOS prompt. This creates
  a file, BOOTLOG.TXT, which records system messages generated
  during system start-up. By using the MS-DOS TYPE command,
  you can view this file to see where in the start-up process
  Windows failed. In MS-DOS versions 5.0 or later, use the EDIT
  command instead of TYPE.

■ In the Windows for Workgroups environment, use the
  EMMExclude option when you start Windows, by typing WIN/D:X
  at the DOS prompt. This option excludes the network interface
  card from areas that Windows searches for unused address space.
  (Typically, this is the area A000-FFFF.) The search can cause
  conflicts with adapters that use this area.

## Diagnosing Windows 95 Problems

As with hardware diagnosis you need to analyze symptoms, determine if
there are any common issues, isolate the error conditions, and use any
and all technical resources available.

Many times, performance issues and intermittent system errors can be
resolved by using the system tools provided with Windows 95. Often, problems can be avoided simply by using the maintenance utilities like Scan-
Disk and Disk Defragmenter. ScanDisk will check for any disk corruption
and lost memory allocation units, while Defrag will optimize the use of
the disk space and perform a "quick tune-up." To access these utilities,
click on the Start button, click on Programs, click on Accessories, and then
click on System Tools (see Figure 5-12).

A computer system and its components are not maintenance-free.
Please review all the system tools that are available, and use them to ensure that your system is running at peak performance at all times.

**Figure 5-12**
Accessing
maintenance utilities.

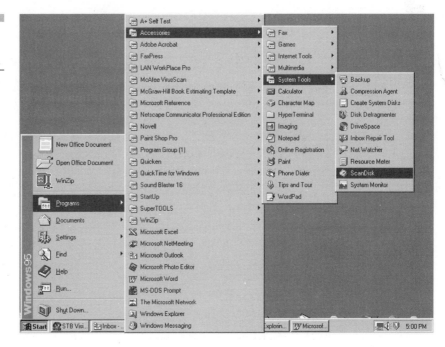

Some of the questions you need to ask yourself when diagnosing troubles are:

- Has the system or configuration ever worked?
- Can the error be reproduced or is it random?
- Is the error specific to an application or configuration?
- What hardware and firmware are involved?
- Does the error occur with Safe Mode?

**SAFE MODE** If Windows 95 fails to start normally, it will usually display a Startup menu with Safe Mode being one of the choices. In addition, Safe Mode will be invoked automatically if system startup has failed or if the Registry is corrupted. When Windows 95 starts in Safe Mode, only the mouse, keyboard, and standard VGA drivers are loaded. This makes it easier to isolate and resolve error conditions caused by Windows drivers.

The Startup menu can contain three to four Safe Mode options, depending on whether the computer system is compressed, or part of a network. Each Safe Mode option will disable a portion of the startup process for further problem isolation.

**USING A STARTUP DISK** A Startup disk can be created during the initial Windows 95 installation or afterward in the Control Panel, by clicking on the Add/Remove Program icon (see Figure 5-13). This disk, which can load the operating system, displays an MS-DOS command prompt, along with additional utilities for troubleshooting.

**NOTE:** *It is recommended that a startup disk be created and a copy maintained each time a configuration is changed on a system. This might be your only chance for recovery should a major catastrophic error occur. All that is needed is a 1.2M floppy disk and a few moments in front of the system.*

There are many areas that can cause failures. Check the following when you diagnose problems:

- Conflicts at system startup
- Device configuration(s)
- Free disk space
- Disk corruption (ScanDisk)

## Windows 95 Networking

The Windows 95 operating system includes networking support with many improvements over earlier versions of Windows. For supported net-

**Figure 5-13**
Creating a Startup disk.

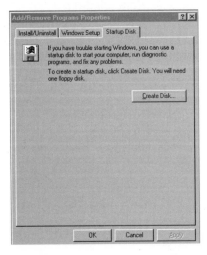

works other than Microsoft networking, the computer system must already have the networking software from another vendor installed. It is beyond the scope of this book to introduce every aspect of networking with Windows 95; that would be a book in itself. However, we will introduce you to enough material so that when working around networked systems, you will be confident in resolving your system issues.

Some of the benefits and network features in Windows 95 are:

■ Networking components, using no conventional memory

■ Quick and easy graphic configuration

■ Automatic setup of Windows 95 on network workstations

■ Connections to multiple networks on a computer system (limited by networking software)

■ Plug-and-play support

■ Unified logon, login script processing, and resource browsing

■ Automatic reconnection for lost server connections

■ Dial-up networking for remote access

If the real-mode network is running when you start Windows 95 Setup, the appropriate network client is installed automatically. This is recommended for installing networking support. When Setup detects existing components, it will install the supporting software and move the configuration settings to the Registry, wherever possible.

**NETWORK CONFIGURATION**   To display the Network option in the Control Panel, right-click the Network Neighborhood icon on the desktop, and then click Properties on the menu (see Figure 5-14).

In the Network option, you can set properties for:

■ Configuration of network clients, adapters, protocols, and services

■ Identification of computer on the network

■ Access control, to specify security for other users

To install networking components, click on the Configuration tab, and then click on Add (see Figure 5-15).

Client—Installs the client software for the types of networks that the computer is connected to.

Adapter—Installs the drivers for the network adapters in the computer. It is recommended, however, that you use the Add Hardware option in the Control Panel.

**Figure 5-14**
The Network option
of the Control Panel.

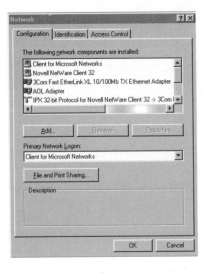

**Figure 5-15**
The Select Network
Component Type
dialog box.

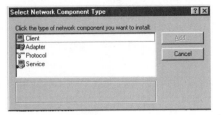

Protocol—Installs the network protocol and sets any related options. (More on this later.)

Service—Installs peer-file and printer-sharing services; and other services including backup agents or additional print services.

**NOTE:** *Some components require that you shut down the system and restart it after installation.*

To specify a computer name, workgroup, and description, click on the Identification tab in the Network Window (see Figure 5-16).

You will then have to type the values for the following:

■ Computer Name—Must be unique, up to 15 characters, with no spaces.

■ Workgroup—Does not need to be unique.

**Figure 5-16**
The Identification
tab.

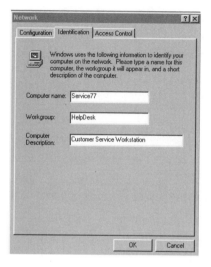

■ Computer Description—This information is displayed as a
comment next to the computer name when users are browsing the
network.

**NETWORK PROTOCOLS—WINDOWS 95** Every networked computer must
have a network adapter driver, which controls the network adapter. Each
network adapter driver is configured to run with a certain type of network
adapter. The networked computer must also have one or more protocol
drivers, also referred to as transport protocols.

For two computers to communicate on a network, they must use identical protocols. The protocol driver works between the upper-level network
software and the network adapter to package data to be transmitted onto
the network. The protocols that are included with Windows 95 are discussed in the following sections.

**Microsoft IPX/SPX-Compatible Protocol**: This protocol is compatible
with the Novell NetWare Internet Packet Exchange/Sequential Packet
Exchange (IPX/SPX). Windows 95 includes 32-bit, protected and real-
mode support for this protocol.

**Microsoft TCP/IP** (Transmission Control Protocol/Internet Protocol):
Windows 95 includes only protected mode support for the TCP/IP protocol, and includes some of the following benefits:

■ Support for Internet connectivity and Point-to-Point Protocol used
for asynchronous communication

- Connectivity across interconnected networks with different operating systems

- Support for automatic TCP/IP configuration, using Windows NT Dynamic Host Configuration Protocol (DHCP) servers

- Support for the NetBIOS interface, commonly referred to as NetBIOS over TCP/IP

If you cannot use DHCP for automatic configuration, the TCP/IP configuration must be done manually. The required values needed are as follows:

- IP address and subnet mask for each adapter card

- IP address for the default gateway (IP routers)

- Whether the computer will use Domain Name System (DNS) and the IP addresses of the DNS servers

- WINS server addresses, if WINS servers are available

For more information on manual configuration, refer to the on-line help available in the Network option in the Control Panel.

**Microsoft NetBEUI:** This protocol is compatible with existing networks that use the NetBIOS extended interface, including Windows for Workgroups peer networks, Windows NT Server, and LAN Manager. Windows 95 provides both protected mode and real-mode support for this protocol.

All three protocols are Plug-and-Play-compliant, so they can be loaded and unloaded automatically. If a network adapter is removed from the computer system, the protocols are unloaded automatically. If there are any dependent applications, notification will result.

## Replacing Hardware

If, after diagnosing the problem, you learn that the cause was hardware-related, you will be faced with having to choose and swap a module. When removing any module, always adhere to ESD standards and practices. Failure to follow these practices may result in either immediate component failure or deterioration and, later, premature failure of the component.

Once you have handled the hardware issues, you can correct software errors by changing configuration settings, including a wrong choice of device driver, or by reloading the software. If there is a current backup of the system, you may also need to reload it.

## Solving Software Problems

Eliminate the obvious. If your printer is not functioning, you can safely assume that your video drivers are not the cause of the problem.

Experience the error. Can you re-create the error and see what happens when the error occurs?

Ask questions. Is the problem application-specific, or could it be related to either your DOS or Windows environments? Ask questions!

Fix it. Replace that driver, reload that application, edit the CONFIG. SYS file, or do whatever else it takes to bring this system back on line.

Take it step by step and you will not miss.

# Sample Test Questions

What follows are sample test questions and answers for the Microsoft Windows/DOS specialty exam. Each sample test question in this chapter comes from one of the same three sources as the test questions at the end of Chapter 4 (Self Test Software, CompTIA, or the authors), and all credits are similarly given.

1. Is it necessary to have WINA20.386 in the root directory to run Windows 3.1 in the enhanced mode? (Self Test Software)

   a. No, it may be removed.

   b. No, it may be moved to another directory.

   c. Yes, WINA20.386 must be in the root directory.

   d. Yes, WINA20.386 is required in any subdirectory.

2. After replacing a hard drive, you try to format it and get a message that says "Invalid media type." What should you do? (Self Test Software)

   a. Run the diagnostics.

   b. Run FDISK.

   c. Run MEDIA.COM.

   d. RUN CHKDSK.

**3.** For a hard drive to boot Microsoft MS-DOS, which of the following files must be present? Choose all that apply. (Self Test Software)

a. IO.SYS

b. MSDOS.SYS

c. COMMAND.COM

d. CONFIG.SYS

**4.** The DOS command FORMAT A:/S does which of the following? Choose all that apply. (Self Test Software)

a. Formats the diskette in the A: drive.

b. Makes the diskette in the A: drive bootable.

c. Creates a subdirectory on the diskette in the A: drive.

d. Saves existing files on the diskette in the A: drive.

**5.** Which of the following files is used to customize the Windows environment? (Self Test Software)

a. WIN.INI

b. SYSTEM.INI

c. SETUP.INI

d. CONFIG.SYS

**6.** Which of the following files is used to load a memory manager? (Self Test Software)

a. AUTOEXEC.BAT

b. CONFIG.SYS

c. COMMAND.COM

d. MSDOS.SYS

**7.** Which of the following commands would NOT be found in the AUTOEXEC.BAT file? (Self Test Software)

a. Path=C:\

b. Echo off

c. Device=HIMEM.SYS

d. Prompt $p$g

**8.** The Windows command SETUP/I will do what? (Self Test Software)

a. Search for incompatible software.

b. Ignore automatic hardware detection.

c. Begin administrative setup.

d. Display information about setup.

**9.** Which of the following commands are found in the CONFIG.SYS file? Choose all that apply. (Self Test Software)

a. Echo on.

b. Buffers.

c. Break.

d. Device.

**10.** What is the FIRST step when installing a new DOS upgrade? (Self Test Software)

a. Delete the COMMAND.COM file.

b. Back up the existing operating system and data.

c. Reformat the currently formatted hard drive.

d. Copy the previous version of the operating system to a subdirectory called OLD_DOS.

**11.** Which of the following is the correct procedure to install a Windows program? (Self Test Software)

a. Type RUN from the DOS prompt, then enter the install program name.

b. Click on File, then Star, and then enter the install program name.

c. Click on File, then Run, and then enter the program name.

d. None of the above.

**12.** When you begin to diagnose a computer problem, what is the best way to differentiate between a hardware and software problem? (CompTIA)

a. Upgrade the operating system.

b. Format drive C: and reload software.

c. Replace the system board.

d. Boot from a "clean boot" diskette.

**13.** How much memory does DOS real mode require? (Self Test Software)

a. 640K.

b. 1024K.

c. 2048K.

d. 4096K.

**14.** To make a program launch automatically immediately after Windows initializes, do which of the following? Choose all that apply. (CompTIA)

a. Add its name to the AUTO= line in the WIN.INI file.

b. Add its icon to the STARTUP program group.

c. Add its name to the RUN= line in the WIN.INI file.

d. Add its icon to the AUTOEXE program group.

e. Add its name to the LOAD= line in the WIN.INI file.

**15.** Which of the following interprets the input entered at the DOS prompt? (Self Test Software)

a. COMMAND.COM

b. IBMBIO.COM

c. IBMDOS.COM

d. CONFIG.SYS

**16.** How many bytes are usually stored on a hard drive sector running DOS? (Self Test Software)

a. 512

b. 1024

c. 512K

d. 1024K

**17.** When adding a second hard drive, who determines the drive letter? (Self Test Software)

a. The end user.

b. The drive manufacturer.

c. DOS.

d. SETUP utility.

**18.** Which function key retrieves the last input from the DOS command prompt? (Self Test Software)

a. F1

b. F2

c. F3

d. F4

**19.** A system will boot from a diskette but not from the hard drive. Which of the following procedures should you do? Choose all that apply. (Self Test Software)

a. Verify that the two hidden files are present.

b. Verify that COMMAND.COM is present.

c. Replace the hard drive.

d. Format the hard drive.

**20.** Which file contains the commands that configure a computer's hardware components? (CompTIA)

a. CONFIG.SYS

b. DOSSHELL.EXE

c. SETVER.EXE

d. COMMAND.COM

**21.** Which of the following is an incorrect entry for the CONFIG.SYS file? (Self Test Software)

a. DEVICE=ANSI.SYS

b. DEVICE=HIMEM.SYS

c. DEVICE=MOUSE.COM

d. DEVICE=EMM386.EXE

**22.** Which of the following file extensions are executable from the DOS command prompt? Choose all that apply. (Self Test Software)

a. .BAT

b. .EXE

c. .SYS

d. .COM

**23.** Which of the following statements describes the DOS=HIGH?
Choose all that apply. (Self Test Software)

a. Loads the DOS kernel between the addresses 1024 and 1088.

b. Provides additional conventional memory.

c. Loads the DOS kernel in HMA.

d. Frees up extended memory.

**24.** In which of the following is KEYBOARD.SYS found? (Self Test
Software)

a. CONFIG.SYS

b. AUTOEXEC.BAT

c. INSTALL.BAT

d. SETUP.EXE

**25.** When having difficulties booting Windows 95, what tools/utilities
should be used? Choose all that apply. (Authors)

a. Boot system in Safe Mode

b. Use a Win95 Startup diskette

c. Manually step through the loading of the AUTOEXEC.BAT
files

d. Reinstall the operating system

**26.** You are attempting to run a DOS application in Windows 95 and
get the error message "Illegal Operations Error." This would
indicate which of the following? (CompTIA)

a. The DOS application is not compatible with Windows 95.

b. The application attempted to run in Full-Screen Mode instead
of Windows mode.

c. The DOS application attempted to access memory reserved for
another function.

d. Windows 95 detected a virus in the executable file.

**27.** Which protocol does the Internet use? (CompTIA)

a. DLC

b. TCP/IP

c. NetBEUI

d. IPX/SPX

**28.** What is the special mode for starting Windows 95 with simple default settings? (CompTIA)

a. Safe

b. Normal

c. Virtual

d. Enhanced

**29.** A Windows 95 Startup diskette can only be made during the initial installation of the operating system to the computer? (Authors)

a. True

b. False

**30.** Plug and Play first became available with what Operating System? (CompTIA)

a. MS-DOS

b. PC-DOS

c. Windows 3.1

d. Windows 95

**31.** Which Windows 95 utility can be used to track the performance of key system components? (CompTIA)

a. Resource Meter

b. System Monitor

c. MEMMAKER

d. PCONSOLE

**32.** If a Window contains a question mark button, this means what? (Authors)

a. Online help is available on this specific topic.

b. More information is needed by the operating system.

c. It did not understand your request.

d. An error occurred.

**33.** A Windows 95 Computer can be shut down at any time by just turning off the power switch? (Authors)

a. True

b. False

**34.** A folder in Windows 95 is the same as a(n) _____ in MS-DOS (Authors)

a. Configuration file

b. Directory

c. Executable file

d. System file

**35.** When you delete a file in Windows 95 the file is_____. (Authors)

a. totally erased

b. put in the Recycle Bin

c. held in a separate directory for a period of 5 days

d. only erased in the FAT (File Allocation Table)

**36.** The most efficient method of uncovering printing problems in Windows 95 is to do which of the following? (Authors)

a. Run diagnostics.

b. Place a service call for your system.

c. Utilize the on-line troubleshooter.

d. Reload all associated drivers.

**37.** Which of the following are Network components in Windows 95? Choose all that apply. (Authors)

a. Client

b. Adapter

c. Protocol

d. Service

**38.** Disk-drive maintenance in a Windows 95 environment is accomplished with the following utilities. Choose all that apply. (Authors)

a. System Agent

b. ScanDisk

c. System Monitor

d. Disk Defragmenter

**39.** In Windows 95, if the Registry becomes corrupted, there is a way to restore the previous Registry. (Authors)

a. True

b. False

**40.** If you are having problems with a network in a Windows 95 environment, which of the following should be checked? Choose all that apply. (Authors)

a. Logon setting

b. User and workgroup names

c. Connections to network resources

d. Adapter and protocol configuration

# Answers to the Sample Questions

| | |
|---|---|
| 1. A | 8. B |
| 2. B | 9. B, C, D |
| 3. A, B, C | 10. B |
| 4. A, B | 11. C |
| 5. A | 12. D |
| 6. B | 13. A |
| 7. C | 14. B, C, E |

15. A

16. A

17. C

18. C

19. A, B

20. A

21. C

22. A, B, D

23. A, B, C

24. A

25. A, B, C

26. C

27. B

28. A

29. B

30. D

31. B

32. A

33. B

34. B

35. B

36. C

37. A, B, C, D

38. B, D

39. A

40. A, B, C, D

# APPENDIX A

The following lists of funding and sponsoring partners are valid as of May, 1998.

# Funding Partners

Apple Computer, Inc.

AST Research

Compaq Computer Corporation

Computer Reseller News (CMP Publications, Inc.)

CompuCom Systems, Inc.

CompUSA

Data Train Institute

Digital Equipment Corporation

Entex Information Services

Exide Electronics Group, Inc.

GE Capital Technology Service

Hayes Microcomputer Products, Inc.

Hewlett-Packard Company

IBM Education & Training

IBM PC Company, N.A.

InaCom Corporation

Information Technology Management Institute

Ingram Micro, Inc.

Intel Corporation, Inc.

Intelligent Electronics, Franchise Division, Inc.

Learning Tree

Lotus Development

MicroAge, Inc.

Microsoft Corporation

NCR (formerly AT&T Global Information Systems)

Packard Bell Electronics

*PC Week* (Ziff-Davis Publishing)

Service News

Systems & Support Management

Tandy Services/Computer City

Technology Service Solutions

Toshiba America Information Systems, Inc.

U.S. Robotics, Inc.

VAR Business (CMP Publications, Inc.)

Wave Technologies

Zenith Data Systems/Groupe Bull

# Sponsors

Aerotek-Data Services Group

American Power

Aurora/Century Computer Marketing

Banctec Service Corporation

Chattahoochee Technical Institute

Computer Curriculum Corporation

Computer Dynamics Institute

Epson America, Inc.

Gateway 2000

Graymark International

Heathkit Educational Systems

Lexmark

Marcraft International Corporation

MindWorks Professional Education

OKIDATA

PC Parts Express

Permond Solutions Group, Inc.

Self Test Software

SHL Key Systems

TechForce

Total Seminars

VanStar

Wang Laboratories

Wurts & Associates

# APPENDIX B

There are two important components to this appendix. First, the Core technologies that were identified as key to the service technician position. These tie directly to the A+ certification test. Second, the tasks that over 500 technicians identified as key to the service technician job role. These are what keep you employed. We encourage you to study both. The A+ test questions are designed to test these steps for competency.

# Core Module

## Content Area 1: Configuring

1. Describe the most common field replaceable units and identify examples of their functions and most common failures.
2. Identify and explain the main parts and functions of displays, storage devices, printers, modems, CD-ROMs, and NICs.
3. Show, by example, different connectors, ports, and devices; and define their basic functions.
4. Describe basic testing parameters and be able to identify normal and abnormal operation.
5. Explain the performance of mechanical and electrical connections among various components.
6. Specify the proper tools and procedures used during system setup; including visual inspections, documents, and diagnostics.
7. Define the proper steps to secure a system for transport

## Content Area 2: Installing and Upgrading

1. Define common drivers used by MS-DOS and Macintosh computers.
2. Define the most common peripheral ports, discuss their symbols and connectors, and describe their functions.
3. Identify, adjust, and replace parts of a system board; and define their functions.

4. Identify proper jumper settings.

5. Describe system logic board processor upgrading, and define performance enhancements.

## Content Area 3: Diagnosis

1. Identify proper and professional questioning techniques used during problem determination with a customer.

2. Identify common sensory (visual, auditory, smell, etc.) indicators of a system malfunction.

3. Define the basic functions of a multimeter.

4. Identify possible environmental hazards to a computer system.

5. Define the steps necessary to perform logical troubleshooting.

6. Define the steps necessary to determine a faulty printer, memory problem, faulty monitor, and other faulty external peripherals.

7. Determine whether a personal computer system problem is caused by hardware or software.

## Content Area 4: Repair

1. Identify the correct microcomputer components required to repair a specific problem.

2. Determine the proper conditions and procedures necessary to replace suspected swap-out components and repair the problem.

3. Identify the logical steps in a microcomputer repair process for both hardware and software problems.

4. Define and describe the proper safety procedures related to electricity, microcomputer systems, personnel, ESD, and parts (FRUs).

5. Define the appropriate use of electrical safety, system safety, ESD, and use of the manual when handling FRUs.

6. State the major function of each of the following field replaceable system modules: system logic boards; power supplies and associated fans; memory assemblies; video controller; mass storage devices (including floppy drives, hard drives, optical drives, tape drives, etc.); displays, coprocessors; system ROM; I/O controllers; and communications controller/devices.

## Content Area 5: Preventive Maintenance

1. Identify common preventive maintenance procedures and routines for microcomputer systems (i.e., vacuuming, cleaning display screens, keyboards, and covers).
2. Describe common preventive maintenance routines for dot-matrix and laser printers.

## Content Area 6: Safety

1. Identify the potential risks to equipment when failing to use ESD procedures.
2. Identify the basic ESD protection procedures, tools, and technology.
3. Identify the potential hazards when working with displays, printers, and other equipment.
4. Describe disposal procedures for batteries, cathode ray tube (CRTs), etc., which are in compliance with environmental guidelines.
5. Describe the proper steps to safely discharge a CRT.

# Tasks

Following are the tasks that were identified as key for the service technician position. The A+ test questions are designed to test these steps for competency.

## A. Configuring

1. Identify the major components of the microcomputer and their functions.
2. Identify the major components of the display and their functions.
3. Identify the major components of the storage devices and their functions, including SCSI devices.
4. Identify the major components of the printers and their functions.

5. Identify the major components of a local area network.

6. Identify the components of various operating systems: DOS, System 7, OS/2, and Windows.

7. Describe the system's RAM and ROM functions and capabilities.

8. Follow the general steps for setting up (initializing) the system.

9. Identify external connectors and ports.

10. Test each part to be connected in the system, including the printer.

11. Connect parts of the system, per the specifications.

12. Verify that the system is properly set up.

13. Boot the system from the diskette (all four operating systems).

14. Identify the functions of each operating system component (internal commands, external commands).

15. Initialize, format, and back up the diskette drive and hard disk drive, per the operating system.

16. Disassemble the system for shipping to the customer.

17. Practice sound safety procedures to reduce the risk of ESD.

# B. Installing and Upgrading

1. Install all microcomputer components (CPU, motherboard, floppy drives, video controller, I/O ports, modem, power supply, mass storage devices, memory).

2. Perform complete system checkout upon completion of installation.

3. Connect peripherals (external drive, printer, etc.).

4. Explain to the customer the basic functions of what is installed and what has been done to the system.

5. Inspect all components of the system.

6. Install, set up, and cable the system at the customer site; including setting switches and jumpers; with peripherals, operating system, and communications interface, per the specifications.

7. Connect the system to the network, and verify communications within the network.

8. Use self-diagnosis and other testing techniques/tools to optimize (tune) the system performance.

9. Perform machine moves at the customer site.

10. Practice sound safety procedures and reduce the risk of ESD.

## C. Diagnosis

1. Question customers to determine service request situational details.

2. Use visual and audio indicators of system malfunctions.

3. Identify problems (failures) as the customer sees it; that is, re-create the problems.

4. Determine (hypothesize) the hardware, software, environmental factor, and/or operator as the cause(s) of the problem.

5. Confirm the working elements of the hardware, software, and the system; including following the standard test procedures for microcomputers, displays, storage media, and printers to the FRU level.

6. Identify probable actions to take to correct system failures (including problems with drivers, printer interfaces, printers, async communications, etc.).

7. Determine when to use appropriate diagnostic tools, aids, and test equipment.

8. Utilize the tools, aids, and test equipment appropriately and effectively.

9. Practice sound safety procedures and reduce risk of ESD

10. Overall sequence of tasks: identify the problem; observe behaviors and make a hypothesis re: cause; test the hypothesis; record results; ensure that the problem is repeatable.

## D. Repair

1. Follow modular repair strategy.

2. Follow the steps in the repair process and standard procedures to remove and replace FRUs, repair machine failures, and remove

and replace modules (including cover, main board, power supply, SIMMS, video board, display, drives, chips, etc.) by using appropriate safety and ESD procedures.

3. Repair printer failures, using standard procedures.

4. Verify that the problem is fixed.

5. Explain the function performed by each replaceable service module and each repair.

6. Reassemble, clean, and adjust the system.

7. Prepare for shipping.

8. Solder, as needed, to accomplish high-reliability work.

9. Identify the proper tools, aids, and test equipment for safe and appropriate use.

## E. Upgrading

1. Install a new basic version of the software (operating system and device drivers—not applications) on existing systems.

2. Install new microcomputer components, including ROM and SCSI devices, on existing systems.

3. Install new display components on existing systems.

4. Install new storage media components on existing systems.

5. Install new printer components on existing systems.

6. Practice sound safety procedures and reduce risk of ESD.

7. Maintain a level of awareness of existing and potential customers and/or machine problem situations.

8. Verify system operation.

## F. Interacting with Customers

1. Display a high degree of tact, ethics, and courtesy to promote good customer relations that express professional business attitudes and experience, including:

   ▪ owning the problem

   ▪ knowing when to escalate problems to a higher authority

   ▪ recognizing sales situations

2. Disengage at the completion of the customer interaction, including transferring requests to other professionals, as needed (for example, respond to customer service requests on appropriate equipment).

3. Notify the customer to schedule and explain the status of the repair job.

4. Seek information from customers related to problems leading to the service request.

5. Explain the service procedures, quality standards, and customer service commitment, if requested by the customer.

6. Address customer needs in a timely fashion to minimize disruption of customer operations.

7. Inform the customer of the distinctions between billable activities, warranties, and contracts.

8. Work well under pressure.

## G. Other

### SAFETY

1. Use preventive equipment to reduce the risk of damage from ESD, knowing when/when not and why to do so.

2. Follow and implement standard safety procedures.

3. Recognize how and why to use tools (basic devices and procedures) and test equipment.

### BUSINESS MANAGEMENT (NOT TESTED IN A+)

4. Keep management informed of existing or potential customer or machine problems.

5. Determine whether a given situation is covered by warranty, contract, or time and materials.

6. Report problems and customer dissatisfaction to management.

7. Communicate the most common failures to supervisors.

### PARTS (NOT TESTED IN A+)

8. Plan and order the correct parts, as needed.

9. Submit work orders promptly and accurately.

10. Deliver, load, unload, count, and organize the service center inventory.

## ADMINISTRATION (NOT TESTED IN A+)

11. Complete service paperwork accurately and on time.

12. Maintain organized records and failure analysis data.

## PROFESSIONALISM (NOT TESTED IN A+)

13. Prioritize and schedule the workload on a daily basis to ensure customer satisfaction, making optimum use of time and productivity,

14. Keep abreast of all products by studying manuals, continuing education, and reading bulletins.

## PREVENTIVE MAINTENANCE

15. Implement proactive, preventive maintenance procedures, as required by vendor or environmental conditions; including inspections, testing, cleaning, and adjusting; which minimize disruption to customer operations at time of service call.

# BIBLIOGRAPHY

One of the following lists includes books and films to help you prepare for the A+ exams. This list incorporates the recommendations of dozens of IT trainers, managers, technicians, and consultants, all of whom are intimately familiar with the content of the A+ exams.

The second list includes book titles to help you in your career. These books cover the topics of job networking, resumes and cover letters, interviewing, and job opportunities for computer professionals.

## Books and Films for Exam Preparation

### Computers (General)

Gertler, Nat. *Computers Illustrated*. Carmel, IN: Que Corp., 1994.

White, Ron. *How Computers Work*. Emeryville, CA: Ziff-Davis Publishing, 1992.

### Hardware

Anderson, Douglas T. The Hard Disk Technical Guide (Micro House Technical Series). Micro House, 1997.

Aspinwall, Jim and Mike Todd. *Troubleshooting Your PC* (3rd Edition), 1996.

Asser, Stuart M., et al. *Microcomputer Servicing : Practical Systems and Troubleshooting*, 1997.

—— *Microcomputer Theory and Servicing*, 1996.

Awwad, Mike Mutasem. *The Personal Computer: Operating, Troubleshooting & Upgrading*, 1997

Barbarello, James J. J. *PC Hardware Projects: A Complete Guide to Building Practical Addons to Your Computer,* Vol 1., 1997.

Beeson, Dan L. *Assembling and Repairing Personal Computers*, 1996.

Bigelow, Stephen J. *Troubleshooting, Maintaining, & Repairing PCs*. 2nd ed. (Book and CD.) New York: McGraw-Hill, 1999.

—— *Bigelow's Build Your Own PC Pocket Guide*, 1998.

—— *Bigelow's Computer Repair Toolkit.* Paperback, 1997.

—— *Bigelow's PC Technician's Troubleshooting Pocket Reference.* 1997.

—— *PC Hardware Fat Faqs: Troubleshooting, Upgrading, Maintaining, and Repairing*, 1997.

—— *The Tab Electronics Technician's On-Line Resource Reference*, 1996.

—— *Troubleshooting, Maintaining, & Repairing Personal Computers: A Technical Guide / Book and Disk*, 1995.

—— *Troubleshooting & Repairing Computer Printers* (Tab Electronics Technician Library), 1996.

—— *Troubleshooting and Repairing Computer Monitors*, 1996.

—— *Troubleshooting and Repairing PC Drives and Memory Systems* (Troubleshooting & Repair Series), 1998.

—— *Troubleshooting and Repairing PC Drives and Memory Systems* (Tab Electronics Technician Library), 1997.

Boyce, Jim, et al. *Upgrading PCs Illustrated,* 1997.

Chubb, Bruce A. *Build Your Own Universal Computer Interface,* 1997.

Desposito, Joseph, et al. *Computer Monitor Troubleshooting & Repair,* 1997.

Dwiggins, Boyce H. and Edward F. Mahoney. *Automotive Electricity and Electronics: Concepts and Applications,* 1996.

Fulton, Jennifer and Joe Kraynak. *The Complete Idiot's Guide to Upgrading Your PC,* 1996.

Halderman, James D. *Diagnosis and Troubleshooting of Automotive Electrical, Electronic, and Computer Systems*, 1996.

Harris, Michael. *Build, Upgrade, Repair Your Own Computer: Get Exactly What You Need and Save Money,* 1998.

Harris, Natalie F. (Editor) and Nils Conrad Persson (Editor). *Es&t Presents Computer Troubleshooting and Repair,* 1997.

Heath, Steve. *The PC and Mac Handbook: Systems, Upgrades and Troubleshooting*, 1996.

Hordeski, Michael. *Personal Computer Interfaces*, 1995.

Hordeski, Michael F. *Setting Up and Troubleshooting Windows PCs*, 1997.

—— *Troubleshooting and Repairing PCs: Beyond the Basics* (Tab Electronics Technician Library), 1997.

—— *Troubleshooting and Repairing PCs: Beyond the Basics* (Tab Electronics Technician Library, 1997.

Jamsa, Kris A. *Rescued by Upgrading Your PC*, 1996.

Johnson, Dave and Todd Stauffer. *Upgrading & Repairing Your PC Answers, Certified Tech Support* (Busy People Series).

Kanter, Elliott S. *Opportunities in Computer Maintenance Careers* (Vgm Opportunities), 1995.

Karney, James. *Upgrade & Maintain Your PC*, Paperback, 1996.

Keller, Peter A. *Electronic Display Measurement: Concepts, Techniques, and Instrumentation* (Wiley/Sid Series in Display Technology), 1997.

Lee, Arnie. *Building Your Own PC : Buying and Assembling with Confidence,* 1996.

Lewallen, Dale. *PC Magazine Guide to Upgrading PCs*, Sally, 1996.

MacDonald, L. W. (Contributor*)*, et al. *Display Systems: Design and Applications* (Wiley Sid Series in Display Technology), 1997.

Margolis, Art and Abraham Pallas. *Troubleshooting and Repairing Personal Computers* (Glencoe Tech Series), 1994.

Miller, Mark A. *Lan Troubleshooting Handbook: The Definitive Guide to Installing and Maintaining Arcnet, Token Ring, Ethernet, Starlan, and Fddi Networks*, 1993.

Minasi, Mark. *The Complete PC Upgrade and Maintenance Guide*. 7th ed. (Book and CD.) Alameda, CA: Sybex, 1996.

—— *The Complete PC Upgrade and Maintenance Guide*, 1997.

Morgantini, Dean F. (Editor), et al. *Chilton's Engine Code Manual* (Total Service Series), 1996.

Mueller, Scott. *Upgrading & Repairing PCs*. 6th ed. (Book and CD.) Carmel, IN: Que Corp., 1996.

—— *Upgrading and Repairing PCs* (8th Ed), Carmel, IN: Que Corp., 1997.

Norton, Peter. *Outside The IBM PC and PS/2: Access to New Technology*. Englewood Cliffs, NJ: Brady, 1992.

Norton, Peter and Michael Desmond. *Peter Norton's Upgrading and Repairing PCs,* 1997.

*PC Guide for Upgrading and Fixing Your Computer: The Easiest Way to Learn to Upgrade & Fix Your Computer: Step-By-Step Learning Guide* (Book and Video), 1995.

*PC Upgrade and Repair Bible.* Barry Press, 1997.

*PC Upgrade and Repair Bible: Professional Edition* (1st ed). Barry Press, 1998.

Pilgrim, Aubrey. *Build Your Own Multimedia PC*, 1996.

―――― Pilgrim, Aubrey. *Build Your Own Pentium Pro Processor PC* (Save a Bundle Series), 1996

―――― *Upgrade and Repair Your PC* (Save a Bundle Series), 1997.

Poor, Alfred E. *The Underground Guide to Troubleshooting PC Hardware: Slightly Askew Advice on Maintaining, Repairing, and Upgrading Your PC* (Underground Guide series), 1996.

Preston, John. *Upgrading & Repairing PCs*, 1997.

Rathbone, Andy. *Upgrading & Fixing PCs for Dummies* (For Dummies), 1997.

Robertson, Ian. *Build Your Own Multimedia PC : A Complete Guide to Renovating and Constructing Personal Computers* (Save a Bundle Series), Sinclair, 1997.

―――― *Easy-PC Handbook: Pcb Layout and Circuit Design*, Sinclair, 1995.

Rohrbough, Linda and Michael F. Hordeski. *Start Your Own Computer Repair Business / Book and Disk* (Entrepreneurial PC Series), 1995.

Rood, Stephen C. and Steven D. Domenikos. *Computer Hardware Maintenance: An Is / It Manager's Guide* (Datamation Professional Series), 1996.

Rosch, Winn L. *The Winn L. Rosch Hardware Bible.* Englewood Cliffs, NJ: Brady, 1994.

Rosch, Winn L. *Winn L. Rosch Hardware Bible: Premier Edition*, 1997.

Rosenthal, Morris. *The Hand-Me-Down PC: Upgrading and Repairing Personal*, 1997.

Schueller, Ulrich, et al. *Upgrading and Maintaining Your PC*, 1997.

Schueller, Ulrich, et al. *Upgrading and Maintaining Your PC*, 1997.

Theakston, Ian. *Netware Lans: Performance and Troubleshooting* (Data Communications and Networks Series), 1995.

Tooley, Michael. *Newnes PC Troubleshooting Pocket Book*, 1994.

*Upgrading & Repairing PCs.* Que Education, et al., 1997.

*Upgrading & Repairing PCs Workbook: Instructor's Manual,* Que Education, et al., 1997

Wilkins, Mark, et al. *Bulletproofing NetWare: Solving the 175 Most Common Problems Before they Happen Bulletproofing*, 1997.

Zacker, Craig, et al. *Upgrading and Repairing Networks*, 1996.

# DOS

Albrecht, Robert and Michael Plura. *Stepping Up to OS/2 Warp/the Fastest Path from DOS and Windows to Warp*, 1995.

Arick, Martin R. *Unix for DOS Users*, 1995.

Brown, Margaret. *Learning DOS/Book and Disk/Includes Practice Disk 6.1 and 6.2.* 1993.

Campbell, Mary V. and David R. Campbell. *Understanding DOS 6/Book and Disk,* Published 1993.

*CBIOS for IBM PS/2 Computers and Compatibles: The Complete Guide to ROM-Based SystemSoftware for DOS* (Phoenix Technical Reference Series.)

Curtin, Dennis P. *Microcomputers and DOS: A Short Course* (Computer Applications Software), 1993.

Ericksen, Linda and John Preston. *Works for DOS Smartstart*, 1997.

Freese, Peter. *Ms-DOS: 3.3 to 5.0*, 1993.

Fulton, Jennifer. *10 Minute Guide to Ms-DOS 6.2*, 1994.

—— *The Complete Idiot's Guide to DOS*, 1994.

Glossbrenner, Alfred. *DOS 6: An Intermediate/Advanced Guide to Everything You Need to Know About Ms-DOS 6*, 1993.

Gookin, Dan. *DOS for Dummies: Windows 95 Edition*. San Mateo, CA: IDG Books Worldwide, 1996.

—— *DOS for Dummies: Windows 95 Edition* (For Dummies), 1996.

—— *More DOS for Dummies* (For Dummies), Indianapolis, IN: 1994.

Harvey, Greg. *DOS for Dummies Command Reference*. San Mateo, CA: IDG Books Worldwide, 1993.

—— *DOS for Dummies Quick Reference*. San Mateo, CA: IDG Books Worldwide, 1993.

—— *DOS for Dummies Quick Reference* (3rd Ed.), 1998.

Heller, Lisa. *Stacker for OS/2 and DOS: An Illustrated Tutorial*, 1994.

Howard, Kathleen. *All You Need to Know About MS-DOS* (Ptp Need to Know, Book 102), 1994.

Jamsa, Kris A. *DOS: The Complete Reference / Covers All Versions, Including DOS 6*, 1993.

—— *DOS: The Pocket Reference*, 1993.

Knowlton, Joseph, et al. *Getting Started With DOS 6* (Wiley's Getting Started Series), 1995.

Langevin, Leo J. *Advanced VSE System Programming Techniques* (Qed IBM Mainframe Series), 1993.

Ledesma, Ron. *PC Hardware Configuration Guide: For DOS and Solaris*, 1994.

Lindenmeyer, Leonard R. and Anne Arundel. *The DOS Operating System Featuring DOS 5*, 1994.

Lowe, Doug. *The Only DOS Book You'll Ever Need / Covers All Versions Through 6.0*, 1993.

Menefee, Craig, et al. *Byte's DOS Programmer's Cookbook*, 1994.

Minasi, Mark, et al. *Inside Ms-DOS 6.22,* 1994.

Morrison, Connie, et al. *Microsoft Word 5.5 / DOS* (Easy Reference Guide), 1993.

Murphy, Jerry. *Getting Started With DOS 5.0 / Book and Disk* (Wiley PC Companion), 1993.

Nelson, Kay Yarborough and Kay Nelson. *The Little DOS 6 Book*, 1993.

Neuman, Sally. *Ms-DOS 6.2 Quick Reference* (Que Quick Reference), 1993.

Norton, Peter. *Peter Norton's Complete Guide to DOS 6.22*, 1994.

Nye, Christopher, et al. *DOS 6: Visual Quickstart Guide*, 1993.

*Office Power With Wordperfect 6 and DOS, Paperback,* 1994.

Podanoffsky, Michael. *Dissecting DOS / Book and Disk*, 1994.

Pronk, Ron and Keith Weiskamp. *DOS 6 Insider*. Coriolis Group Book (The Wiley Insider), 1993.

Pugh, Kenneth. *Unix for the Ms-DOS User*, 1994.

Reader, Michele and John Preston. *Ms-DOS First Run*, 1997.

Rosner, Lisa. *Quick Success: DOS 6.2*, 1995.

Routledge, Gerald R., et al. *Using DOS*, 1995.

Schwartz, Karl. *Microsoft DOS 6* (Quick Reference Guide), 1993.

Schwartz, Karl, et al. *Ms-DOS: Versions 6 and 6.22* (Quick Reference Guide), 1994.

Shelly, Gary B., et al. *Learning to Use Microcomputer Applications: dBASE 5 for DOS* (Series), 1995.

——— *Learning to Use Microcomputer Applications: DOS 6 and Microsoft Windows 3.1. Introductory Concepts and Techniques / Book and Disk.,* 1994.

Siegel, Kevin A. *Introduction to the PC & Windows 95 Vol 1.* Spiral-bound, 1996.

Siyan, Karanjit S. *CNE Training Guide: Netware 4.1 Administration* (Cne Training Guide), 1995.

Southworth, Rod B. *PC-DOS / MS-DOS Simplified*, 1993.

——— *DOS 6.2 Simplified*, 1994.

Stiles, Diana and Winston Nathaniel Martin. *Microsoft MS-DOS Step by Step* (covers versions 6.0 and 6.2). Redmond, WA: Microsoft Press, 1993.

Thomas, Robert M. and Robert Thomas. *DOS 6.2 Instant Reference*, 1993.

Underdahl, Brian. *Novell DOS 7: Memory Management, Multi-Tasking, Networking, and Data Protection,* 1994.

Villani, Pat. *The FreeDOS Kernel*, 1996.

Weber, Jeff. *DOS in a Day*, 1994.

Weixel, Suzanne. *MS-DOS 6 Quickstart / The Step-By-Step Approach.* Carmel, IN: Que Corp., 1993.

Wempen, Faithe and Robert Mullen. *One Minute Reference: Ms-DOS 6.2*, 1993.

Wyatt, Allen L., W. Edward Tiley, and Jon Paisley. *Using MS-DOS 6.2.* Carmel, IN: Que Corp., 1993.

Wyatt, Allen L., et al. *Using Ms-DOS 6.2*, 1993.

# Windows

Bierer, Doug. *Inside NetWare 4.1*, 1995.

Blakely, Jim. *Windows NT Server 4.0 Exam Guide: Microsoft Certified System Engineer Productivity Point International*, 1997.

Gookin, Dan. *DOS for Dummies: Windows 95 Edition* (For Dummies).

Heywood, Drew. *Inside NetWare 3.12.* (Book and CD-ROM.), 1995.

Nagar, Rajeev. *Windows NT File System Internals: A Developer's Guide,* 1997.

Pearce, Eric. *Windows NT in a Nutshell: A Desktop Quick Reference for System Administrators*, 1997.

Poniatowski, Marty. *Windows NT and HP-UX System Administrator's 'How-To' Book*, 1997.

Rajagopal, Raj. *Windows NT, Unix, Netware Migration and Coexistence: A Professional's Guide*, 1998.

Rice, Jim. *HP-UX User's Guide*. Onword Press Development Team, 1995.

Siegel, Kevin A. *Introduction to the PC & Windows 95,* Vol. 1, Spiral-bound, 1996.

Solomon, David A. and Debra J. Wasserman. *Windows NT for OpenVMS Professionals,* 1996.

———— *Inside Windows NT: The Official Guide to the Architecture and Internals of Microsoft's Premier Operating System*, 1998.

## Networking

Cohen, Alan M. *A Guide to Networking,* 2nd edition. Danvers, MA: Boyd and Fraser, 1995.

Derfler, Frank J. and Les Freed. *How Networks Work*. Emeryville, CA: Ziff-Davis Press, 1993.

Novell, Inc. *Netware System Interface Technical Overview*. Reading, MA: Addison Wesley Computer, 1990.

————. *Novell's Quick Access Guide to Netware 3.11 Networks*. Alameda, CA: Sybex, 1992.

————. *Novell's Quick Access Guide to Netware 3.12 Networks*. Alameda, CA: Sybex, 1993.

————. Novell's Quick Access Guide to Netware 4.0 Networks. Alameda, CA: Sybex, 1993.

## Microsoft Windows

Christian, Kaare and Pamela Drury Wattenmaker. *How Windows Work*. Emeryville, CA: Ziff-Davis Press, 1994.

Microsoft Corporation. *Microsoft Windows NT Resource Kit* (book and disks). Redmond, WA: Microsoft Press, 1993.

————. *Microsoft Windows 3.1 Resource Kit* (book and disks). Redmond, WA: Microsoft Press, 1994.

Rathbone, Andy. *Windows for Dummies*. San Mateo, CA: IDG Books Worldwide, 1993.

## Macintosh Computers

Datatech Institute, 429 Getty Avenue, Clifton, New Jersey 07015 (Phone: 201-478-5400, extension 2301-for the video department) offers a variety of courses worldwide and also two videos on Macintosh computers: *Troubleshooting the Mac*, and *Advanced Troubleshooting for the Mac.*

Bigelow, Stephen J. *Maintain and Repair Your Notebook, Palmtop, or Pen Computer*, 1993.

Goodman, Danny, and Richard Saul Wurman. *Danny Goodman's Macintosh Handbook*. New York: Bantam Electronic Publishers, 1992.

Heath, Steve. *The PC and Mac Handbook: Systems, Upgrades and Troubleshooting*, 1996.

MacIntosh, Dan Crabb. *MacWeek Upgrading and Repairing Your Mac*, 1995.

Naiman, Arthur, Nancy E. Dunn, and Susan McCallister. *The Macintosh Bible,* 4th edition. Berkeley, CA: A Goldstein and Blair Book from Peachpit Press, 1992.

Pogue, David. *Macs for Dummies*. San Mateo, CA: IDG Books Worldwide, 1994.

Rietmann, Kearney, and Frank Higgins. *Upgrading & Fixing Macs for Dummies*. San Mateo, CA: IDG Books Worldwide, 1994.

———. *Upgrading & Fixing Macs for Dummies (For Dummies),* 1996.

Rizzo, John, and K. Daniel Clark. *How Macs Work*. Emeryville, CA: Ziff-Davis Press, 1993.

Vandersluis, Kurt, and Amr Eissa. *Troubleshooting Macintosh Networks: A Comprehensive Guide to Troubleshooting and Debugging Macintosh Networks (book and disk)*. San Mateo, CA: M&T Books, 1993.

## Customer Interaction Skills

Aguilar, Leslie and Linda Stokes. *Multicultural Customer Service: Providing Outstanding Service Across Cultures* (Business Skills Express), 1995.

Becker, Dennis and Paula Borkum Becker. *Customer Service and the Telephone* (Business Skills Express), 1994.

Davidow, William H., and Bro Uttal. *Total Customer Service: The Ultimate Weapon*. New York: Harper Collins, 1990.

Davis, Edwin G. *Customer Relations for Technicians*. Mission Hills, CA: Glencoe/Macmillan McGraw-Hill, 1991.

Glanz, Barbara A. *Building Customer Loyalty: How You Can Help Keep Customers Returning* (Business Skills), 1994.

*How to Handle Tough Customers: Five 20-Minute Self-Study Sessions That Build the Skills You Need to Succeed* (Dartnell High-Performance Skill Builder), 1997.

MacNeill, Debra J. *Customer Service Excellence* (Business Skills Express), 1993.

Sewell, Carl, and Paul B. Brown. *Customers for Life: How To Turn That One-Time Buyer Into A Lifetime Customer*. New York: Pocketbooks, 1992.

Lucas, Robert W. *Customer Service: Skills and Concepts for Business*, 1996.

## Certification

Drake Prometric. *The Complete Guide to Certification for Computing Professionals*. New York: McGraw-Hill, 1995.

# Books for Career Development

*101 Great Resumes*. Career Press (Editor), 1995.

Allen, Jeffrey G. *The Resume Makeover*, 1995.

Beatty, Richard H. *175 High-Impact Resumes*, 1996.

Bloch, Deborah Perlmutter. *How to Have a Winning Job Interview*. Lincolnwood, IL: VGM Career Horizons, 1991.

Bone, Jan. *Opportunities in CAD/CAM Careers*. Lincolnwood, IL: VGM Career Horizons, 1993.

Ettinger, Blanche. *Opportunities in Customer Service Careers*. Lincolnwood, IL: VGM Career Horizons, 1992.

Faux, Marian. *The Complete Resume Guide*, 1995.

Foxman, Loretta D. and Walter L. Polsky (eds.), *Resumes That Work: How to Sell Yourself on Paper,* 1992.

Fry, Ronald W. *Your First Resume,* 4th edition. Franklin Lakes, NJ: Career Press Inc., 1995.

Jackson, Tom. *The Perfect Resume.* New York: Doubleday, 1990.

———. *Guerrilla Tactics in the New Job Market.* New York: Bantam Books, 1993.

———. *Tom Jackson's Interview Express.* Westminster, MD: Times Books, 1993.

———. *Tom Jackson's Power Letter Express.* Westminster, MD: Times Books, 1995.

Kaplan, Robbie Miller. *101 Resumes for Sure-Hire Results.,* 1994.

———. *Resume Shortcuts: How to Quickly Communicate Your Qualifications With Powerful Words and Phrases,* 1997.

———. *Sure-Hire Cover Letters,* 1994.

Krannich, Ronald L., et al. *201 Dynamite Job Search Letters,* 1997.

Lott, Catherine S, and Oscar C. Lott. *How to Land a Better Job,* 3rd edition. Lincolnwood, IL: VGM Career Horizons, 1994.

Makos, Marc L. *Resumes for the Smart Job Search  The Ultimate Guide to Writing Resumes in the 90s,* 1993.

Marcus, John J. *The Resume Doctor: How to Transform a Troublesome Work History into a Winning Resume,* 1996.

Marler, Patty and Jan Bailey Mattia. *Cover Letters Made Easy,* 1995.

Martin, Eric R. and Karyn E. Langhorne. *How to Write Successful Cover Letters,* 1994.

Medley, H. Anthony. *Sweaty Palms: The Neglected Art of Being Interviewed.* Berkeley, CA: Ten Speed Press, 1992.

Miller, Maryann. *Your Best Foot Forward : Winning Strategies for the Job Interview* (Life Skills Library), 1994.

Moore, David J. *Job Search for the Technical Professional.* New York: Wiley and Sons, 1991.

Noble, David F. *Collection of Quality Resumes by Professional Resume Writers,* 1996.

Provenzano, Steven. *Slam Dunk Resumes...That Score Every Time!* 1994.

*Resumes for Computer Careers* (Vgm Professional Resumes Series). Vgm Career Horizons (Editor), 1996.

*Resumes for Ex-Military Personnel* (Vgm's Professional Resumes Series). Vgm Career Horizons (Editor), 1995.

*Resumes for High School Graduates* (Professional Resumes Series). The Editors of Vgm Horizons, 1992.

*Resumes for High-Tech Careers* (Vgm Professional Resumes Series).Vgm Career Horizons (Editor), 1997.

*Resumes for Midcareer Job Changes* (Vgm Professional Resumes Series). Editors of Vgm Career Horizons, 1993.

*Resumes; Real Sample Resumes and Proven Advice from Successful Job Hunters and Career Counselors.* Business Employme National, 1994.

Rosenberg, Arthur D. and David V. Hizer. *The Resume Handbook: How to Write Outstanding Resumes and Cover Letters for Every Situation* (3rd Ed.), 1996.

Stoodley, Martha. *Information Interviewing: What it is and How to Use it in Your Career.* Garret Park, MD: Garret Park Press, 1990.

VGM. *Resumes for High Tech Careers.* Lincolnwood, IL: VGM Career Horizons, 1991.

Wendleton, Kate. *Through the Brick Wall.* New York: Five O'Clock Books, 1994.

Yate, Martin. *Cover Letters That Knock 'Em Dead.* Holbrook, MA: Bob Adams, Inc., 1995.

———. *Resumes That Knock 'Em Dead.* Holbrook, MA. Bob Adams, Inc., 1995.

———. *Knock 'Em Dead, 1996: The Ultimate Job Seeker's Handbook,* 9th edition. Holbrook, MA. Bob Adams, Inc., 1996.

## Other Resources

3COM Web site

Acronyme Alley Web site

Duracell USA, Berkshire Coporate Park, Bethel, CT 06801

Hayes Web site

Intel Web site

*Microsoft Windows 95 Resource Kit,* Microsoft Press, 1995. ISBN 1-55615-678-2

Minasi, Mark. *The Complete PC Upgrade and Maintenance Guide—* Fourth Edition. Sybex.

# Index

Note: boldface numbers indicate illustrations.